POLITICAL ECONOMY

POLITICAL ECONOMY

A Marxist Textbook

by

JOHN EATON

INTERNATIONAL PUBLISHERS
NEW YORK

CONTENTS

Of the works cited in the text, the following have been published in the United States by International Publishers:

Dobb, Maurice. *Soviet Economic Development Since 1917*, 1948; new revised edition, 1966.

—*Studies in the Development of Capitalism*, new edition, 1964.

Eaton, John. *Socialism in the Nuclear Age*, 1962.

Engels, Frederick. *The Origin of the Family, Private Property and the State*, 1942.

—*Socialism: Utopian and Scientific*, 1935.

Marx, Karl. *Capital*, Vol. I, edited by Dona Torr, 1947. (Page references in the text, designated by "A," are to this edition.)

—*Critique of the Gotha Programme*, 1938.

—"Preface to the *Critique of Political Economy*," in *Reader in Marxist Philosophy*, Howard Selsam and Harry Martel, eds., 1963.

—*Value, Price and Profit*, 1935.

—*Wage-Labour and Capital*, 1933.

Marx, Karl and Engels, Frederick. *Selected Correspondence, 1846-1895*, 1942.

Lenin, V. I. *Imperialism: The Last Stage of Capitalism*, 1939.

INTRODUCTION

There are considerable differences between this present book and many contemporary text books on economics. The differences begin with differences in definition of the subject matter of economics. Much of current university teaching presents economics as the theory of how men choose between scarce goods that have alternative uses. For example, Cairncross (*Introduction to Economics* 1960, page 14) bases himself on the following definition: "Economics is a social science studying how people attempt to accommodate scarcity to their wants and how these attempts interact through exchange." This approach, it is to be noted, focuses attention more on exchange than on production and more or less excludes the study of economic relations between classes and also the process of development in the economy considered as a whole.

The political economy here presented deals in the main with capitalism as a system of production. It is not directly concerned with the technical side of production but with the relations between men in the process of production and exchange. The process of production—the labour process—is the process by which labour converts the material supplied by nature into wealth, the process of changing nature to serve the needs of man. "It is the everlasting, nature-imposed condition of human existence", writes Marx, "and therefore, is independent of every social phase of that existence, or, rather, is common to every such phase." (*Capital*, Vol. I, LW p. 184, A pp. 163-4).*

Ever since the dawn of history men have carried on production not individually but together with other men. In the earliest times of savagery men hunted in bands and there was a rough division of tasks between men and women. Today the co-operation of many people is involved in the production of the com-

* References to *Capital* are to the English edition published by F.L.P.H. Moscow and Lawrence and Wishart, London, vol. 1, 1954; vol. 2, 1957; vol. 3, 1959 (LW); to the Allen and Unwin edition of vol. 1, edited by Dona Torr, 1938 (A); and to the Kerr edition of vols. 2 and 3, 1909 (K).

monest objects. One needs, for example, only to consider how many workers in what widely divided parts of the world have contributed to the production and distribution of the commonplace objects such as pencils, knives, chairs, lubricating oils, nails and so forth.

For many thousands of years primitive men lived together in classless communities; the societies which emerged from this "primitive communism" have been class societies in which the basic class divisions have been between those who own the land or other things (such as buildings or plant) needed for production and those who are compelled to produce for others—exploiters and exploited. This was the character of the ancient slave societies and, after them, of feudalism, and today of capitalism.

Capitalism is a system of social production within which there are exploiters and exploited—the capitalist and the workers. For the working class exploitation is the starting point in the study of political economy. The need and desire to study social science, to study how human society is organised and how its organisation changes and can be changed, develops out of this experience of exploitation, as a part of the struggle against exploitation. For the capitalists, of course, their starting point is how to maintain their wealth and dominant position, and it is from this standpoint that the problems of economics are approached by them.

The standpoint of this book is that of Marxism and scientific socialism. The starting point for Marx in the development of his ideas was the most advanced philosophical, economic and political thought of nineteenth-century Europe. This he developed on the basis of concrete, scientific study of human society and capitalist society in particular. As a world outlook the strikingly new feature of Marxism is that it looks to no authority other than the world itself and applies to all aspects of reality an approach similar to that of the natural sciences.

The study of change is central to Marxist political economy. It is, says Lenin, "the science dealing with the development of historical systems of social production." Marx made it his aim to find out how capitalism came into being, how and why it changes, how and why it decays. His object was to discover "the economic law of motion of modern society" (*Marx, Capital* Vol. I, LW p. 10, A p. xix).

The differences between bourgeois and Marxist schools of economics are only in part differences in interpretation and explanation of actual processes; they are also differences in angle of approach and choice of subject matter. It is as well, for this reason, to be clear that the standpoint of this book in its approach to political economy is that of the interests of the working class. Generally the focusing point of its analysis is the relationship between broad economic classes and in this respect it follows basically in the tradition of "classical economics". "The produce of the earth—all that is derived from its surface by the united application of labour, machinery and capital," writes David Ricardo in the Preface to his *Principles of Political Economy*, "is divided among three classes of the community; namely, the proprietor of the land, the owner of the stock or capital necessary for its cultivation, and the labourers by whose industry it is cultivated. But in different stages of society, the proportions of the whole produce of the earth which will be allotted to each of these classes, under the names of rent, profit, and wages, will be essentially different. . . . To determine the laws which regulate this distribution, is the principal problem in political economy." (vol. I, page 5, Cambridge University Press edition 1951, ed. Piero Sraffa.)

The aim of this book is to present a reasonably brief but scientifically accurate picture of the economic processes of capitalism. Marx attached the highest importance to scientific accuracy and objectivity; but he and his close friend and collaborator Engels, the originators of the world outlook of Marxism, were not only great intellectuals, they were also fighters for the cause for which their humanity and vision led them to fight. Marx was the enemy of capitalism because he was the enemy of poverty and oppression. In 1867 he wrote as he finished the first volume of *Capital*: "I had to use every moment in which I was capable of work in order that I might finish the task to which I had sacrificed my health, my happiness in life and my family . . . if one chose to be an ox one could, of course, turn one's back on the agonies of mankind and look after one's own skin. But I should really have regarded myself as *unpractical* if I had pegged out without completely finishing my book at least in manuscript."

CHAPTER I

THE PLACE OF CAPITALISM IN HUMAN HISTORY

Primitive Communism

A million or more years ago there was beginning to appear upon the earth a new kind of ape, an ape that used his forepaws more freely than the other apes. Indeed, his forepaws were no longer paws but hands in which he grasped sticks and stones which served him as crude tools. This was a development of tremendous importance. It is the making of tools and the activity of production, shaping nature to serve man's needs and purposes, that distinguishes man from other animals. Thus the "man-like" ape came to move about not on four feet but erect on his hind legs, and developed a larger brain than his monkey cousins. He became man—the "tool-making animal".

The history of man proper covers a span of about forty thousand years. For the first seven-eighths of this period he lived in savage communities. His first tools were the spear and the hunting trap that he used against his prey. With fire he warmed himself and cooked his food. His implements were made of sticks and stones, and by "flaking" flints he made points for his spears and instruments with which to prepare his food and make his clothes from the skins of the beasts he slew. Such vegetable foods as he ate he picked wild as they grew. In the course of time, the instruments of hunting were improved; the bow and arrow, the fishing net, and the canoe and paddle were invented. Man learned how to make artificial dwellings to replace the caves and rocks that had in earlier times given him shelter. These savage communities hunted in bands and shared in common the spoils of the chase. The only division of labour was that between the sexes, the men hunting and making their weapons, the women controlling the home, gathering and preparing the food, making clothes and so forth. Such in briefest outline was "primitive communism" in its early stages and the first beginnings of the process of adapting nature to human needs—the "production process" undertaken by human beings living together and working together. At work or hunting men communicated by signs combined with noises out of which grew the complexities of spoken language and the various means of communication indispensable to working together. There was no exploitation of man by man but the material conditions of life were poor and the fruits of men's labour barely sufficed to provide the means with which to continue life.

For some forty thousand years mankind continued to live in this state of primitive savagery. However, in the course of time, some tribes of men (the first of these, it is believed, dwelt in Asia) developed new means of getting their living which were destined to cause great changes in the manner of man's life and the relations of men to one another. Instead of killing the beasts they hunted, they captured them and kept them alive. Thus they had food in reserve to eat when they wanted it and were the less dependent on the day-to-day fortunes of the chase. They learned also to grow food that they and their beasts needed instead of gathering it where it grew wild. With the capture of animals came also breeding to suit the needs of man.

In this way primitive agriculture began to develop and with it man's way of life changed. As men began to see themselves apart from the natural surroundings they now strove to change and master, views of the world began to find expression for each tribal community in "totemic religions" (tribal or clan rituals associated with animals or plants). The "supernatural" religions did not appear until later when class society began to emerge and the authority of the rulers representing propertied classes came to find reflection in the religious picture of a divine authority and divine hierarchy.

In places some differentiation began to develop between the tribes; in particular that between the backward tribes without herds whose main form of production was hunting and the pastoral peoples or "farmers". The latter no longer moved from season to season into new hunting grounds but lived in more settled farming communities which moved only in search of new and more fertile land. These pastoral peoples could regularly produce a surplus above their immediate needs and in their cattle they had a form of property in which their wealth could be accumulated. Surpluses could be exchanged with other communities and some division of labour developed between the pastoral peoples and the backward tribes. This provided a basis for regular exchange.

This stage of society in which communities of men began to sow seed and rear cattle on the land they shared in common prevailed for some two and a half thousand years (5500 B.C. to 2000 B.C.).

In this more settled farming existence communities of men tended to become larger. Man began to calculate the seasons of the year more carefully so that he might the better control his crops. In the valleys of the Nile, the Indus, and the Euphrates, the value of the flood waters as a means of increasing the fertility of the soil was learned, and growing communities in these areas began to work together to control the waters by means of irrigation. From this came great increases in the supply of food, but it involved more organisation of human effort. More metals were discovered and the ways of working them were learned. The art of alloying metals was discovered. New crafts were developed, such as wheel-made pottery, wheeled vehicles, sailing vessels, the making of bricks, and the plough with metal coulter. These advances were possible only as the result of greater specialisation; they made manifest a further great division of labour as between agriculture and handicrafts. This was of decisive importance; it resulted in more and more being *produced especially for exchange*, that is, *commodity production*. "The advent of private property in herds of cattle and articles of luxury led", writes Engels, "to exchange between individuals, to the transformation of products into *commodities*. Here lies the root of the entire revolution that followed. When the producers no longer directly consumed their product but let it go out of their hands in the course of exchange, they lost control over it. . . . The possibility arose that the product might be turned against the producers, used as a means of exploiting and oppressing them" (*Origin of the Family*, Chapter V).

When in earlier times primitive tribes went to war they sometimes killed and ate their captives, but could in no other way gain advantage from them. Enslave them or exploit them they could not since in those times a man could produce no more than the bare sufficiency to maintain his own existence. No surplus was produced and so there was no possibility of exploitation. Now, however, things had changed. Man produced with his new tools, his new crafts, and his new methods of farming more than his day-to-day needs; a surplus was produced and commodity-exchange was developing. Under these changed circumstances captives in war could be used to produce wealth for their captors.

Men were made slaves. They became commodities entering into exchange. They were fed and cared for as a farmer cares for his cattle. They received the bare necessities of life; but they produced more than they received. All that they produced belonged to their owners, who were richer by the difference between what their slaves produced and what they gave them in food and clothing.

Commodity-exchange and the new forms of property that came with it led also to the enslavement of men within the tribe; it provided, too, the basis for the development of class divisions within the society of "free men"; ruling castes and their officials exacting tribute from the peasant producers and craftsmen; usurers and debtors; rich and poor. A class of merchants also began to appear for the first time, "a class of parasites . . . who . . . skim the cream off production at home and abroad, rapidly amass enormous wealth and corresponding social influence" (Engels *Origin of the Family*, Chapter IX).

For primitive man property had had little significance. Personal rights in weapons, vessels, bracelets, and like objects were recognised in primitive communism, but hunting grounds were held in common and food enjoyed in common. With the development of agriculture, though the land was still deemed the common property of the tribe, its private tenure began to develop. In early times the practice arose by which families would be annually allotted plots for their own use, while pasture land was still used in common. The fiction that the land belonged to the tribe was fostered long after this had ceased in practice to be so, and when communal ownership had in fact turned into its opposite.

Primitive communist society had no internal antagonisms and its social organisation was controlled by no coercive power other than public opinion. "It was destroyed by the division of labour and by its results, the division of society into classes. Its place was taken by the *State*. . . . The State . . . is the admission that . . . society. . . is cleft into irreconcilable antagonisms which it is powerless to dispel. . . . A power . . . became necessary for the purpose of moderating this conflict . . . and this power, arising out of society, but placing itself over it, and increasingly alienating itself from it, is the State" (Engels, *Origin of the Family*, Chapter IX).

Civilisation and Slave Society

Civilisation, which is "that stage of society in which division of labour, the resulting exchange between individuals, and the production of commodities which combines the two, reach their fullest development and revolutionise the whole of hitherto existing society" (Engels, *Origin of the Family*, Chapter IX), first appeared on the banks of the Nile and the Euphrates (and probably at about the same time in India and China also). Later there arose the great slave civilisation of Greece which in its turn succumbed to the Roman Empire, which in the first two centuries A.D. was master of the whole civilised world apart from China and the Far East. With the development of class society and new forms of property there developed the instruments of government by which the exploiting classes maintained themselves in power; the armies and police forces, the courts of justice, officials and tax-collectors, the whole apparatus of force and administrative control which protected the wealth and enforced the privileges of the dominant class. There appeared also new religions and new gods, gods who were "like men writ large", gods of power who ruled in heaven like the emperors who ruled on earth.

The great antagonism of the ancient world was that between the slave-owners and the slaves who were the source of their wealth; but the importance of the antagonisms amongst the many classes of "freemen" must not be overlooked. For example, in Rome there were from earliest times conflicts between the privileged patricians and the under-privileged plebeians. In later times new conflicts developed within Roman society between the wealthy landowners, merchants, and tax-gatherers on the one hand and the impoverished farmers and the city mob, the *proletarii*, on the other.

At the base of the social pyramid, however, stood the slave workers. The slave worked dully and grudgingly with the fear of his master's lash as his only incentive. His lot (if we except the more favoured household slave) was one of poverty and squalor; in one respect, however, he was more fortunate than the "free" worker in capitalist society—he had the security of belonging to his master who, to preserve the value of his own property, had to continue to provide his slave with the necessities of life.

The Break-up of the Ancient World

The potentates of the ancient world did not look to improved methods of production as a source of increased wealth, but to conquest of new territories from which the supply of slaves was increased and from which taxes and dues were extracted. The wealthy slave-owners and the privileged officials who reaped the fruits of their victories constituted only a small fraction of the population of the imperial power. In the Roman Empire, for example, the "free" peasantry profited nothing by the great victories of Roman arms. On the contrary, they were ruined by compulsory service in the army and in consequence were often driven by debt from their farm lands, which fell into the hands of the large proprietors and became part of the great estates worked by slave labour. In the towns the use of slave-labour tended more and more to oust the free craftsman from his livelihood. In this way great masses of the "free" population became impoverished and without means of earning a living. New conquests provided only temporary relief; though they enriched the narrow caste of officials, tax-gatherers, and merchants who followed in the wake of the Roman armies and even though they provided a means from which a "dole" could be paid to the impoverished masses of the metropolis, they also sowed throughout the provinces of the Roman Empire the seeds of the same decay that was destroying Rome itself. The dull and grudging labour of the slave hordes that conquest provided could barely suffice to sustain the vast edifice of Roman rule; and, moreover, the spread of slave labour also spread ruin and destruction amongst the craftsmen and peasants despite the greater productivity of their free labour.

The Roman Empire was shaken by periodical slave revolts; it was threatened ever by the revolt of subject peoples; embracing, as it did, a debt-ridden peasantry, a property-less city mob, wealthy merchants and usurers, great landowners and privileged officials and nobles, it was ceaselessly torn by strife between these several classes.

Feudalism (See also Chapters IV and VII)

Rotten already with internal decay, the powerful and highly civilised Roman Empire was finally destroyed by the invasions of the northern barbarians. In the disintegration of the ancient world serfdom (see below), of a sort developed on the great estates, replaced slave-exploiting agriculture and crafts. Moreover, the tribal society of the invading Teutons was itself in course of change; a warrior aristocracy was gaining domination and forms of serfdom were developing also *within* the tribal society. In the course of a prolonged period of time new productive forces developed—improved methods of working iron, the iron plough, the loom, and improved methods of farming—and corresponding to these new forces of production a new type of society, feudal society. This new society was in the main agricultural, and in the countryside the labour of the slave was replaced by that of the serf.

The serf stood half-way between the slave and the free man. His lord did not have over him the power of life and death; but neither was the serf free to do as he willed or go as he willed. From the land that he cultivated he provided the means of his own subsistence; but he also had to work for his lord—so many days for himself, so many for his lord. He "possessed" land in the sense that he had "his own piece of land" from which to get his living, but he had to stay on the estate where he lived; he was "tied to the land". If the estate passed to other hands the serf passed with it to the new lord. In so far as he worked for himself, he reaped the fruits of his own labour and had an incentive to increase production, which the slave did not have. His labour was therefore more productive and efficient. His main means of production—the land—he did not, however, "possess", in the sense that his feudal lord could dispose of it together with the serf "attached" thereto. But the implements which he used to work the land were his own (as much at least as the serf's own person was his own).

Such was the main form of exploitation in feudal society. The fact and the extent of exploitation was open for all to see; every serf knew how many days' (or how much) work he did for himself and how many (or how much) for his master. Exploitation, though not disguised, was justified and defended as a part of a divine order of things expounded to the people by the Church (which itself drew great wealth from feudal land holdings). The Church taught the virtues of subservience and depicted a heavenly hierarchy governing the universe in much the same way as the feudal system dominated the lives of men on earth. Nevertheless, revolts by the serfs against the power of the feudal lords were frequent and developed at times into widespread rebellion, as witness Wat Tyler's revolt in England in 1381, the Hussite wars in Bohemia in the fifteenth century, and the Peasant War in Germany in the sixteenth century.

Production on the feudal estates was in the main self-sufficient, that is to say, food was grown, clothes were made, and so on, by those who lived on the estates *to meet the needs of the local population*. Production was mostly for use, not for sale. However, part of the surplus would be sold by the nobles to buy luxuries for themselves. In the course of time, trade and transport developed, and the appetite of the nobles for luxuries and wealth in the form of money increased.

Trade gave an impetus to new crafts, new knowledge about the working of metals, new specialisation and division of labour, in short, to new forces of production which were developing. The power of the towns was growing. Great wealth was being accumulated by individual merchants. However, ultimately the growth of trade was to lead to the disintegration of feudal society. The struggle of classes was intensified and this further accentuated the economic decay of feudalism. The whole structure of feudal society —the feudal production relations of lord and serf on the land, and in the towns the guild system with all its restrictive regulations— acted as a fetter obstructing the new forces of production which were developing within disintegrating feudalism. Feudal society was being challenged by a new social system that was struggling to be born out of the old, a new social system in which a new ruling class and new forces of production, already growing within the womb of the old society, would be freed to expand and develop. That new social system was *capitalism*. (The origin of capitalism out of feudalism is more fully treated in Chapter III.)

Production and Social Relations

It may be seen from the brief sketch which has been given that forms of society differ not only in that different methods of production are used, but also in that the relations between men and between classes, men's *social relations*, are different. "These social relations", writes Marx, "into which the producers enter with one another, the conditions under which they exchange their activities* and participate in the whole act of production, will naturally vary according to the character of the means of production. . . . Thus the social relations within which individuals produce, the social relations of production, change, are trans-

---

* We shall see later that exchange of products only occurs in some forms of society; exchange of *activities*, i.e., division of labour, occurs in every form of society.

formed, with the change and development of the material means of production, the forces of production. The production relations in their totality constitute what are called the social relations, society, and indeed a society at a definite historical stage of development, a society with a special distinctive character. Ancient society, feudal society, bourgeois society are such totalities of production relations, each of which at the same time denotes a special stage of development in the history of mankind." (Marx, *Wage-Labour and Capital*).

Past forms of society linger on into the present. Traces of some primitive communistic societies and of slave society lingered on within feudalism, and traces of feudalism and earlier forms of society linger within capitalism. Moreover, old forms of society continue to exist side by side with the new; today there are in different parts of the world savage and primitive communistic societies, feudal societies, capitalist societies, socialist societies, and societies in transition to socialism.

However, despite the continuing "sediment of history" and the myriad variations between actually existing communities, the broad stages of development referred to by Marx (viz. Asiatic society, ancient society, feudal society, and bourgeois society) are identifiable. The causal and determining factor in these profound social changes through which human history passes is change in the forces of production, that is, the instruments of production and the skills and techniques of the people who use them. Economic processes underlie all other social processes. This fundamental relationship is very tersely summarised by Marx in the Preface to his *Critique of Political Economy*, where he writes:

"The general conclusion at which I arrived and which, once reached, continued to serve as the leading thread in my studies, may be briefly summed up as follows: In the social production which men carry on they enter into definite relations that are indispensable and independent of their will; these relations of production correspond to a definite stage of development of their material powers of production. The sum total of these relations of production constitutes the economic structure of society—the real foundation, on which rise legal and political superstructures and to which correspond definite forms of social consciousness. . . . At a certain stage of their development, the material forces of production in society come in conflict with the existing relations of production, or—what is but a legal expression for the same thing—with the property relations within which they have been at work before. From forms of development of the forces of production these relations turn into their fetters. Then comes the period of social revolution. With the change of the economic foundation the entire immense superstructure is more or less rapidly transformed."

This view of history (though Marxism is often caricatured as saying this) should not be interpreted as meaning that economic factors determine everything. "According to the materialist conception of history," wrote Engels to Bloch (September 21, 1890), "the *ultimately* determining element in history is the production and reproduction of real life. More than this neither Marx nor I have ever asserted. Hence if somebody twists this into saying that the economic element is the *only* determining one, he transforms that proposition into a meaningless, abstract, senseless phrase. . . . We make our history ourselves, but, in the first place, under very definite assumptions and conditions. Among these the economic ones are ultimately decisive. But the political ones, etc., and indeed even the traditions which haunt human minds also play a part, although not the decisive one."

TABLE LISTING SOME IMPORTANT INVENTIONS
Period of Primitive Communism:
Food gathering began to change to farming somewhat before 5000 B.C.
Ancient Slave Societies:
The first dynastic civilisations date from about 3000 B.C. Slave civilisations dominated until the "decline and fall" of the Roman Empire during the first millennium A.D.
Feudal society predominated from the latter half of the first millennium A.D. into the middle of the second millennium A.D.
Thereafter *capitalism* predominated until the emergence of the socialist economic and political systems in the twentieth century.
The following brief table of inventions signposts the development of man's productive forces and the social development that has gone with them in European civilisation.

Some important inventions:	*Date*
New Stone Age begins	1500-1200 B.C.
Agriculture	7000-6000 B.C.
Hoe, sickle, pottery, spindle, loom.	5550-4250 B.C.

Some important inventions:	*Date*
Smelting and casting of copper.	4250-3750 B.C.
Wheeled vehicles, plough, harness, sail, potter's wheel, balance.	3750-3250 B.C.
Bronze, bellows, developed tools for many handicrafts.	3250-2750 B.C.
Spoked wheels.	1800 B.C.
Smelting and effective use of *iron*.	1400-1100 B.C.
Many improved and more specialised tools for handicrafts and farming— pulley, sheep shears. [Draw loom, China.]	700-450 B.C.
Screw of Archimedes, cranes, heavy plough, nail-making anvil, wire-drawing blocks, more general use of animal power.	250-100 B.C.
Carpenter's plane, watermill, screw press, shears with block and tackle. [Chinese harness.]	100-0 B.C.
Overshot water-wheel. [Block printing and stirrups in China, A.D. 550-650]	about A.D. 475
Modern saddle harness in Europe. Horseshoe. Modern draft harness. [Persian windmill, A.D. 950] [Moveable type, China, A.D. 1041]	A.D. 850-950
European windmill, woodcuts for letters, water-power for fulling, crushing, sawing, and tilt-hammer. Magnetic compass. Completed evolution of harness; generalised use of animal-power.	A.D. 1050-1225
Mechanical clock, modern plough, modern rudder, block printing in Europe, lathe, wire-drawing machine, cast iron.	A.D. 1225-1400
Spring-clock, railways at mines, knitting machine, pendulum clock (1641).	A.D. 1500-1650
Newcomen engine (1712), smelting with coke, flying shuttle (1733), carding-machine (1748), chrono-	A.D. 1650 and after

meter (1766), spinning jenny (1768), Crompton's mule (1779), Watt's rotative engine (1781), balloon (1783), Maudslay's improved lathe (1794), Stephenson's first locomotive (1814), water turbine (1827), electric bell (1831), telegraph (1837), turret lathe (1845), Bessemer steel (1856), steam turbine (1884), etc., etc.

(Inventions shown in brackets [   ] were outside the stream of develop ment of European civilisation)

CHAPTER II

COMMODITY PRODUCTION

Three main features give capitalism its essential character. These are as follows:

(1) Wealth is concentrated in the hands of a few people (the *capitalist class*) who own the means of production, that is, raw materials, factories, machines, etc., as well as wealth in money form.

(2) Wide masses of the people have no means of getting a living except by selling their power to work for wages (this class of propertyless workers Marx calls the *proletariat*).

(3) Virtually all production is not for the personal use of the producers, but for exchange, for sale on the market. Goods produced for exchange are termed *commodities*. Under capitalism, *commodity production* prevails.

These features of capitalism did not suddenly appear from nowhere; they developed within pre-capitalist society over a long period of time. Chapter III will deal with the coming into being of the two main antagonistic classes within capitalist society, the capitalist class and the proletariat. Here we deal with the development of commodity production, which had its origin within primitive communist society and accelerated its disintegration, which hastened social change in the ancient world and in its turn played no small part in the disintegration of feudal society. Where commodity production prevailed, man lost control of it and was placed at the mercy of economic forces that function independently of human purpose and will—like natural forces. It will be remembered that Engels said that in the first transformation of products into commodities lay the root of the entire revolution that followed. *Capitalism is the culminating stage in the rule of the commodity.*

Simple Commodity Production

Production of goods for exchange stands in contrast to production for use, e.g. by the tribe, household, or estate producing them. As has been explained, goods produced for exchange are called *commodities*, and commodity production arises from the division of labour and both fosters and is fostered by the division of society into classes. For many centuries commodity production existed alongside "production for use", which remained the main source of supply, and was supplemented only to a minor degree by the exchange of commodities. A substantial part of the commodities entering into exchange consisted of products produced by slave labour belonging to the slave owners, but from the earliest times, right up to modern times, independent "peasant" producers and craftsmen have played an important part in the production of goods for exchange, though the methods of production, relations to other types of production, and the relative importance of the independent producers have varied very much at different times and at different places. The production and exchange of goods by small independent producers who own their means of production is called *simple commodity production*.

The Commodity—"*The Seed of Capitalism*"

"The wealth", writes Marx, in the opening words of *Capital*, "of those societies in which the capitalist mode of production prevails, presents itself as an 'immense accumulation of commodities', its unit being a single commodity. Our investigation must therefore begin with the analysis of a commodity" (*Capital*, Vol. I, LW p. 35, A p. 1).

Use-Values

In order that goods may be exchanged, they must be useful to somebody; they must satisfy human wants. A thing which cannot be used for any purpose, obviously cannot be exchanged for a useful article. This characteristic of usefulness, that is, satisfaction of human wants, is called *use-value*. A commodity, therefore, must have *use-value*.

It is important to be clear what the expression "human wants" means in this definition of use-value. Men need food, shelter, clothing, protection, and clearly the goods by means of which these needs are satisfied have use-value; but from the earliest stages of his history, man has felt a need for art, ornament, entertainment, ceremonies and rites, drugs and stimulants, and so forth. The material goods used in the satisfaction of such wants have use-value (in the sense we here use the term) every bit as much as the goods that satisfy physical wants. "The nature of such wants, whether, for instance, they spring from the stomach or from fancy, makes no difference." (*Capital*, Vol. I, LW p. 35, A p. 1.) Likewise, wool, wood, shears, tools, and other implements and materials used in production have use-value. Clearly the needs and the wants of man defined in this broad way vary very greatly for different countries, times, and classes. With the whys and wherefores of these variations we are not here concerned; all that matters now for us is that to become a commodity a thing must satisfy some human want.

Commodities are Products of Labour

Use-value, however, is not in itself enough to make a thing a commodity. The air which we breathe, fresh water from a spring, the rays of the sun, all satisfy human wants, but they are not commodities. Commodities are goods *produced* for exchange.

Produced here means produced by the expenditure of human labour. All the goods that are bought and sold on the market are (with a few exceptions "that prove the rule", such as land—see Chapter VII on "Value of Land") the products of labour. The fur of an animal is the product of the hunter in so far as he must trap the animal and prepare the skin; metals are the products of the miner who mines, and of the craftsman who refines the metal. In speaking of production, therefore, political economy refers to the expenditure of human labour on material existing in nature. Man transforms the "products of nature" to serve his human needs; and "in this work of changing the form he is constantly helped by natural forces. We see, then, that labour is not the only source of material wealth. . . . As William Petty* puts it, 'labour is its father and the earth its mother'." (Marx, *Capital*, Vol. I, LW p. 43, A p. 10.)

* Britain can, with proper pride, claim to have given birth to the science of political economy, which grew to full maturity with Marx. Sir William Petty (1623-87) was described by Marx and others as the founder of modern political economy. Adam Smith (1723-90) may be said to have transformed economic thought into a science; in the *Wealth of Nations* he gives a systematic exposition of his economic theories, which were refined and enriched by the penetrating thought of David Ricardo (1772-1823). In the works of these three great capitalist economists—the "classics" of economic theory—emphasis is laid on labour as the source of wealth, and for them the analysis of the productive activities of labour forms the foundation of their studies of the economic system as a whole.

The fact that commodities are the products of labour, how labour is expended and how the fruits of labour are distributed, are matters of central importance in economic science. Its originators (unlike most academic economists today) put productive labour at the centre of their analysis. This, for example, is how Adam Smith opens his *Wealth of Nations*: "The annual labour of every nation is the fund which originally supplies it with all necessaries and conveniences of life."

Exchange-Values

Commodities are goods, possessing use-value, produced by human labour, and for *exchange*.

In exchange, commodities have certain "quantitative relations"; for example, hunters who in early times traded furs for iron or cloth would expect to receive certain definite quantities of iron or cloth in return for a given quantity of furs; ten sealskins might be exchangeable for 5 lb. of iron or 30 yards of cloth. Commodities, therefore, have a value which is quite distinct and different from their use-value; they have value in exchange, or *exchange-value*. Use-value depends on the qualities and properties of a commodity; for example, to serve as the shaft of a spear, wood must have certain qualities—it must have strength to stand up to shocks without fracturing, and be shaped long and thin so that it can be easily held and thrown. In order to be exchangeable, commodities must satisfy a human need, possess use-value, but the value that they have in exchange is of quite a different kind from use-value.

Whereas use-value is qualitative (that is, depends on the qualities, shape, size, etc., of the commodity), exchange-value is *quantitative*. Use-value cannot (as is explained below) be quantitatively measured, since use-value depends on the satisfaction of the subjective wants of individual men. But exchange-value is altogether different from use-value. A product which may remain identical in use, may at one time command one value in exchange and at another time another value.

Exchange-Value Determined by Labour

In terms of what are commodities measurable?

Things to be measurable must have some common quality in terms of which they can be measured. Commodities have in common the quality of being use values and also of being products of labour. Bourgeois economic theory, turning the emphasis of

25

its analysis away from labour, has looked for its fundamental explanation of value in terms of usefulness or *utility*, despite the obvious difficulty of finding measurable units or standards for a subjective aspect such as this; that is, *utility* is based on one individual's attitude and desires and does not provide a common objective standard by which the values of commodities generally can be compared.

The fact that commodities are all *products of labour* is a common quality, however, that is objectively measurable. As such they embody some specific part of the sum total of social labour that has gone to the production of the mass of commodities entering into exchange. They are equal or unequal in so far as they represent equal or unequal parts of the total product, in so far as they embody a smaller or greater share of the sum total of labour time expended in production.

The value of commodities is determined by the labour-time socially required for their production. This is the objective basis of exchange value. The fact that commodities have value in terms of which they may be equated does not, of course, mean that actual exchanges are necessarily equal, that like values always exchange for like; but it does mean that to speak of equality in exchange—or inequality—has a definite meaning. For example, suppose that a hunter normally expects to catch and prepare the skins of ten seals in fourteen days and a weaver takes the same period of time to prepare and weave his wool into 30 yards of cloth (it is assumed he also spends some time in tending the sheep from which his wool is shorn), then there is a quantitative equality between the labour-time taken to produce ten sealskins and 30 yards of cloth. In this way commodities can be measured one against the other in terms of the labour-time required to produce them.

In fact, just this tended to happen for many centuries when peasants and artisans bartered their products against each other.

Exchange-value, it will be seen from what has been said above, expresses a relationship between men; it expresses the amount of labour-time expended in production. It reflects also, as will be seen from the following paragraphs, the effectiveness of the productive labour expended.

Socially Necessary Labour

"Some people might think that if the value of a commodity is determined by the quantity of labour spent on it, the more idle and unskilful the labourer, the more valuable would his commodity be, because more time would be required in its production." (Marx, *Capital*, Vol. I, LW p. 39, A p. 5.)

This evidently cannot be so. An artisan who does not master his craft, or who works with obsolete, inefficient tools, or with less speed and energy than is usual, may demand more in exchange, but he will not get more, if the buyer can get what he wants from some one else; in short, he is in competition with other producers.

In commodity exchange what counts, therefore, is not the time that a particular producer may have taken to make the commodity which he offers, but the time it normally takes—the average time. It is the time it takes men in general that matters. Just as the sloth and inefficiency of one particular craftsman would have redounded to his disadvantage in that, though his commodities took longer to produce, he got no more for them in exchange, so the craftsman whose skill and technique was in advance of the others, would, in exchange, reap the advantage. Marx describes this average time as the "*socially necessary labour time* . . . required to produce an article under the normal conditions of production and with the average degree of skill and intensity prevalent at the time." (*Capital*, Vol. I, LW p. 39, A p. 6.)

From what has been said it will be seen that, as new and better methods of production are introduced and become general, the average socially necessary labour-time (and therefore value also) for each commodity falls.

Bourgeois Theories of Value

Marxist economic theory was built on the scientific foundations laid by the great capitalist economists of the late eighteenth and early nineteenth centuries, Adam Smith and Ricardo, for whom the labour theory of value was the keystone of economic science. However, the development of the labour theory of value in the course of the nineteenth century enabled Marx to show the nature of capitalist exploitation and that capitalism itself was doomed to extinction. The defence of capitalism called, therefore, for an attack upon the labour theory of value. Bourgeois theory was quick to sense this and from about 1830 has been in quest of an economic theory that rejected the labour theory of value.

Bourgeois theory attempted to argue that value is determined by demand and supply. Demand and supply certainly play a part in determining short-term rises and falls in prices but a fundamental explanation of exchange-value in terms of demand and supply is not possible. Supply is not fixed; if, for example, demand increases, supplies in due time will be increased. What, it must be asked, determines supply? The answer given is—costs of production. That is, bourgeois theory, setting out to explain prices, discovers that these depend upon the prices of goods used in production. Prices depend upon prices; the argument runs in a circle.

Bourgeois theory sought some way out of this circle and looked for something *other than labour* which might determine value. Inevitably they had to turn to use-value. Marxists, of course, emphasise that exchange does not take place unless the goods to be exchanged are wanted by some one; a commodity, we say, to be a commodity must have use-value, but the value of commodities in exchange cannot be determined by use-value. Use-value is subjective, that is, it expresses wants felt in men's minds. Different men have different wants at different times and these wants cannot be measured against one another. A definite amount of "being wanted" cannot become embodied in commodities and cannot be measured. Men's wants cannot exist outside their own minds; they are *subjective*. Despite these shortcomings, heroic efforts have been made by bourgeois economists, particularly from 1870 on, to explain value in exchange in terms of use-value, or, to use their word, utility. Their theories are described as subjective utility theories, of which the most commonly met version is known as the theory of marginal utility which maintains that value is determined by the utility not of all goods but of goods "on the margin" which divides the goods that are sold from those that are left unsold. We need not here explain these various theories in detail and it will suffice to say that none of them escapes difficulties. The attempts that have been made to overcome these difficulties have absorbed a high proportion of the theoretical output of bourgeois economists, but no satisfactory conclusion has been reached. The inadequacy of all variations of the subjective value theories is now quite generally recognised and a number of theoreticians prefer to try to do without a theory of value altogether. This leads to a purely empirical approach in which various forms of value theory come to be tacitly assumed in an eclectic manner that causes confusion and deprives economic science of structural unity. By contrast, the labour theory of value provides a more solid framework for economic analysis. Its *raison d'être* is the simple fact that productive activity, that is, human labour engaged on changing man's natural surroundings to serve human needs, is the condition underlying the existence of all and any economic systems. The problem in studying the capitalist system in particular is to relate this basic condition of all economic activity to the particular circumstances of an economy in which virtually all production is for sale (commodity production). The guiding thread in doing this is provided by the labour theory of value which, despite outstanding theoretical problems affecting its refinement and precision of expression (see, for example, page 95) has held its own against all alternative theories of exchange value.

How the Law of Value Works: Supply and Demand

Marx formulates *the law of value* as follows: "The magnitude of the value of any article is the amount of labour socially necessary, or the labour-time socially necessary, for its production." (Marx, *Capital*, Vol. I, LW p. 39, A p. 6.)

In saying that value in exchange is determined by socially necessary labour-time, it is not suggested that in all exchanges the labour-time embodied in the commodities exchanged has always been exactly equivalent. Suppose, for example, a community had many blacksmiths and few weavers; the blacksmiths would not be able to dispose of their products easily since supply would exceed demand and they would, therefore, be compelled to take in return products that embodied a smaller amount of labour-time. For the weaver, the position would be reversed. Clearly, the blacksmith's life would be harder. He would have to work more intensively and longer to get as much as others who worked less. Under these circumstances, who would have cared to be a blacksmith? This occupation would be deserted in favour of others and thus matters would have righted themselves again. In this way, as a result of competition and the workings of supply and demand, commodities would tend again to be exchanged according to their values—the law of value would assert itself and deviations from the exchange of equal values would tend to be eliminated.

Thus as exchange became more general, the law of value operated in such a way as to shape the distribution of labour, since inequalities in exchange which result from excesses of supply in relation to demand, or vice versa, tend to be corrected by the expansion or contraction of different branches of production.

Value Appears in Exchange

It has been shown in the preceding paragraph how deviations in value tend to be corrected, and how the law of value asserts itself. Thus, the value of commodities becomes apparent in exchange, and in men's minds the value of a commodity is seen not in terms of so many labour hours, but in terms of the commodities for which it can be exchanged. At first, no doubt, trade was arbitrary, but as trade became regular, exchanges settled down to a regular basis, that is, they tended to be based on the labour-time needed to produce the articles exchanged.

In very early times, few goods would enter into exchange; for example, a cattle-raising community might exchange only its surplus cattle. The value of the cattle would be seen in terms of the goods which they would fetch in exchange, such as: one ox equals 5 lb. of iron. As exchange developed, more goods would enter into exchange, and it would become established that an ox would fetch 5 lb. of iron or 10 yards of cloth or four hides or 30 bushels of corn, and so on. The farmers raising cattle would measure the value of their cattle in terms of certain quantities of the use-values (cloth, iron, corn, etc.) for which cattle could be exchanged. Clearly, if an ox would fetch 5 lb. of iron *or* 10 yards of cloth, 5 lb. of iron equals in exchange-value 10 yards of cloth.

As exchange developed still further and more and more commodities entered into exchange, the equating of each commodity with a sizeable list of commodities became an unwieldy and unnecessary process.* Instead, there emerged a new way of looking at the rates at which commodities exchanged with other commodities. Those who had goods to exchange began to measure the exchange-values of their products in terms of one and the same commodity; for example, the weaver would know that

---

* That primitive communities had, in fact, to assess the value of commodities in terms of many others is illustrated by the following passage from Homer's *Iliad*, Book 7, line 472: "Then the long-haired Achæans supplied themselves with wine, some paying in bronze, some with tawny iron, some with hides, some with cattle, and some with slaves."

10 yards of cloth was worth one ox, the farmer that 90 bushels of corn were worth three oxen, and so on. In fact, cattle were, in very early times, frequently used in this way as a measure of value; commodities were, it might be said, priced in terms of oxen.

Money: A Generally Exchangeable Commodity

Goods were not only *valued* in terms of a particular commodity; goods also tended to be *exchanged for* a particular commodity which could and would be readily taken in exchange by other people.

Barter is a very primitive form of commodity exchange, which is restricted in scope and limited in opportunity; a farmer would need to sell the produce of his land as and when he could, and although his ultimate aim might be to buy cloth or iron, he would often do well to exchange his corn or fruit for oxen, with the object of exchanging the oxen for cloth or iron when a favourable opportunity presented itself. In fact, intermediary transactions of this kind tended to occur in the transitional stage from barter to new forms of exchange; in early Greece (about 1000 B.C.) cattle were fairly generally taken in exchange (as well as being used as a measure of the value of other commodities). A commodity which was used in this way acted as a temporary store of exchange values and bridged the gap between the sale of the surplus product and the purchase of the commodity required for its use-value (such as cloth to wear, grain to eat).

In this way, as commodity exchange developed, the form of exchange advanced from simple barter.* The universally exchangeable commodity that acts as the "go-between" in sale and purchase, and as measure of value, is termed *the money commodity*, or, simply, *money*.

Why Precious Metals Came Into Use As Money

Cattle, of course, are not a very practical kind of money. In a transitional stage they could function as such after a fashion, but as trade developed they had, together with other commodities, such as furs, which were so used in certain parts of the world, to give way in favour of a more adequate money commodity.

* In our times we have seen how under certain circumstances when official money backed by the State loses its value, an ordinary commodity generally accepted in exchange assumes the money function as measure of value and as means of circulation. In this way cigarettes replaced money in Germany when paper money was depreciated and discredited by uncontrolled inflation.

Phoenicians, Greeks, Egyptians, and others, many hundreds of years before Christ, had already developed a considerable commerce across the seas. For such traders, transportation of cattle as a means of exchange was out of the question, and trade could not have developed without a more convenient form of money. Further, whilst a herd of cattle may be divided into heads of sheep or oxen, division beyond that is impossible; cattle, moreover, have to be fed and cared for, etc. The ideal money commodity to serve as a measure of value and means of circulation must be one that is easily transportable, imperishable, and perfectly divisible.

Metals, and especially the precious metals, silver and gold, had these properties which favoured their use as money. To produce a small weight of gold much labour-time is necessary; a small piece of gold embodies, therefore, a large exchange-value and yet is easy to handle, carry, and store. Gold is divisible without detriment; therefore the exchange-value embodied in a piece of gold can be directly and simply measured in terms of its weight. Indeed, gold, for reasons given in the next paragraph, is admirably suited to the role it has had to play as the commodity that represents the exchange-value of other commodities.

Abstract and Concrete Labour

When men work, they are doing two things simultaneously: first, they are working at a definite craft or trade (as carpenters producing chairs or tables, weavers producing cloth); secondly, they are forming part of a social labour force whose collective activity in production supplies the community with all its "necessaries and conveniences of life". As carpenters or weavers, men are doing a specific kind of work (*concrete labour*) producing particular use values (tables or cloth); but, as part of the labour force of society as a whole, their labour needs to be considered as labour in general,* without reference to its particular characteristics or purpose, as *abstract labour*.

In the process of exchange the values of different products or different kinds of work have to be compared with one another. They can only be compared in so far as they are the same. Therefore the value (exchange-value) of what a group of men produces is greater or smaller according as their labour con-

* In the English language the words "*work*" and "*labour*" draw this distinction.

stitutes a greater or smaller part of "social labour", that is, the effort of all productive workers looked at as one undifferentiated whole. In creating exchange-value, it is not the specific type of work (*concrete labour*) that counts, but the fact that labour in general (*abstract labour*) is expended in doing this work. The term *abstract labour* describes what is the same—"the common element"—in all productive labour. It is so called because there has been *abstracted* or set aside from each man's work its specific characteristic (carpentry or machining or metal working), which as such plays no part in the creation of exchange values, and consideration is given only to what is the same, the fact that it is labour in general. As gold and silver coins can be in different forms (e.g. a round or square piece) and different amounts (one ounce or one pound) so labour can take different forms (carpentry or weaving) and vary in amount (one day or one hour); but as in gold so in labour, there is always the common element in the different forms which makes comparison possible.

As gold or silver came more and more to be used as a medium of exchange, it became a matter of great importance to the trader to know for sure the exact weight and quality of the gold or silver received in exchange for goods. The verification of weight and testing of quality would be troublesome and sometimes difficult. To save trouble and risk, pieces of metal of standard weight and quality were stamped and so guaranteed by public authority. This was the origin of *coinage* which dates back to the early Iron Age, to the eighth century B.C. (see *What Happened in History*, Gordon Childe, Pelican edition, p. 23 and p. 171). It is not, as is sometimes thought, the image of a king or some other magic that gives gold a definite value. It is the labour-time necessary to produce it, which enables it to measure the value of other commodities and serve as a means of exchange.*

Skilled and Unskilled Labour

Gold varies in composition or degree of refinement (12 carat, 18 carat, etc.) but so, too, labour varies in degree of skill. Here

---

* It is sometimes argued that gold is valuable because it is scarce, and it is suggested that this, and not the labour theory, is the true explanation of its value. This argument is fallacious. There is no *absolute* scarcity of gold; in the earth's crust there are considerable quantities of gold, but it requires a vast amount of human labour-time to locate, mine, and refine this gold. So to say that gold is scarce means little more than that it requires much labour-time to win.

again gold admirably mirrors the nature of the "substance that creates value in exchange", that is, abstract labour; as pieces of gold of differing fineness are equated (2 oz. of 18 carat gold = 3 oz. of 12 carat gold), so more skilled labour is in the process of exchange equated with less skilled. "Skilled labour counts only as simple labour intensified, or rather, as multiplied simple labour, a given quantity of skilled being considered equal to a greater quantity of simple labour. . . . The different proportions in which different sorts of labour are reduced to unskilled labour as their standard, are established by a social process that goes on behind the backs of the producers, and consequently appears to be fixed by custom." (Marx, *Capital*, Vol. I, LW p. 44, A pp. 11–12.)

Marx points out, however, that the bulk of the labour force in capitalist society is composed of unskilled workers expending their time on routine operations. He comments that the reduction of different kinds of labour to uniform, homogeneous, simple labour which is qualitatively the same appears to be no more than an abstraction, but he adds, "it is an abstraction that takes place daily in the social process of production . . . [it] virtually exists in the average labour which an average individual of a given society can perform—a certain productive expenditure of human muscles, nerves, brain, etc. It is unskilled labour to which the average individual can be put and which he has to perform in one way or another. . . . Unskilled labour constitutes the bulk of all labour performed in capitalist society." (*Critique of Political Economy*, Ch. 1.)

The Money Commodity as a Mirror of Value

So one may say that the money commodity is one that mirrors an essential economic reality underlying a commodity-exchange economy—namely, the social labour process that constitutes man's productive activity, the common element of labour in all productive activity despite the varous forms it takes and the different specific purposes it serves. A process of natural selection established with the powerful force of historical tradition certain commodities, precious metals and gold in particular, as money commodities. This force gives them a special position even today when the evolution of centralised banking and financial institutions has created other means of performing the original economic functions of the precious metals.

It is well to note also that good as gold was as a mirror, as a sort of "analogue computer" whose behaviour was like or "analogous" to that of the underlying economic reality, it was still only a mirror and not the reality itself. Being separate from and something other than the reality itself, it could always come about—and often this was the case as with all mirrors—that the reflection distorted the reality.

Price and Value

The value of a commodity expressed in money is its *price;* originally this was the amount of gold which embodied an equal amount of socially necessary labour.

"Price," says Marx, "is the money name of the labour realised in a commodity. . . . Magnitude of value expresses a relation of social production, it expresses the connection that necessarily exists between a certain article and the portion of the total labour-time of society required to produce it. As soon as the magnitude of value is converted into price, the above necessary relation takes the shape of a more or less accidental exchange ratio between a single commodity and another, the money commodity. But this exchange ratio may express either the real magnitude of that commodity's value or the quantity of gold deviating from that value, for which, according to circumstances, it may be parted with. The possibility, therefore, of quantitative incongruity between price and the magnitude of value or the deviation of the former from the latter, is inherent in the price form itself. This is no defect but, on the contrary, admirably adapts the price form to a mode of production whose inherent laws impose themselves only as the mean of apparently lawless irregularities that compensate one another." (*Capital*, Vol. I, LW pp. 101-2, A pp. 74-5.) Good or bad harvests, changed requirements due to substitution (e.g. shortage of metals causing increased demand for earthenware utensils or, vice versa, ample supplies of earthenware cutting out demand for metal utensils), the opening up of communications with new sources of supply, changes in purchasing power available to different classes of the community, and many other such occurrences cause prices to swing up or down, deviating temporarily from values.

In modern capitalism prices generally tend to rise above value in boom and fall below in slump. Government measures such as taxes, tariffs and controls, national institutions and administra-

POLITICAL ECONOMY

tions, monopoly pricing policies and many other powerful and
persisting factors today affect the way and the proportions in
which the national product is distributed. This means that such
measures must influence relative prices considerably. Also in any
fully developed capitalist economy (as mentioned in Chapter VI)
the principle that prices mirror labour time is modified by the
principle that equal capitals tend to earn equal rates of profit.
But as some industries (e.g. power generation) require much and
others (e.g. quarrying and mining) require relatively little
capital per employee, the capital employed is not proportionate
to the labour time embodied in the products. For this reason the
products of some industries tend to be stabilised at prices below
and others at prices above value.

But all these circumstances, which tend to create differences
between actual prices and values in a modern capitalist economy,
do not destroy the underlying force of the law of value as the key
factor governing exchange relationships between commodities
and, consequently, between the human beings who own them,
individually and as classes. All scientific laws have this character
of explaining the principle according to which *underlying* forces
operate, rather than the details of actually occurring events. The
variation of prices from values no more invalidates the labour
theory of value than the variations of water level (due, for example, to winds, changing land formations etc.) invalidate the
lunar theory of tides.

Causes of Price Changes

In the preceding paragraph it has been shown that price
changes occur because

(1) Prices deviate from values.

However, prices also change for other reasons which do not
involve any deviation of prices from values, and, in particular,
because

(2) the *value* of commodities changes (as a result of changed
productivity of labour engaged on the production of commodities),

(3) the *value* of the money commodity changes (as a result of
changed productivity of labour engaged on the production of the
money commodity, normally gold),

(4) the currency is debased, or (in paper currencies) inflated.

If, as a result of improved methods of weaving, for example, the
labour-time required to weave cloth is halved, the value of cloth

36

expressed in money will also be halved (assuming prices are not deviating from values). If, on the other hand, the labour-time required to produce gold falls, then all prices will rise. Such a general rise in prices actually occurred in the sixteenth century when new gold mines were opened by the colonial conquests of the Spaniards, and again at the end of the nineteenth century with the mining of gold in the Transvaal.

Prices are expressed in terms of coins of well-known shape, size, and superscription, such as dollars, sovereigns, doubloons, etc. When, as often happened, the gold or silver from which such coins were minted was alloyed with cheaper metals and the amount of the precious metals in them was reduced,* the value embodied in the coins was, of course, reduced accordingly, but their names remained the same. The coinage was *debased*, each coin embodied a smaller amount of labour-time and prices expressed in terms of these coins rose accordingly. Thus price, without departing from value, may change because the coinage is debased. Similarly, in a country where paper money has replaced gold, inflation of the currency may produce the same result.

The Process of Circulation

When the weaver took his cloth to market, he sold his cloth as a rule not in order to keep the money he received, but to purchase with this money either means of personal consumption or raw materials or tools he needed to continue his work. Money is acting here as a go-between, linking together the sale and the purchase which takes place some time later. This process is symbolised by the formula:

Commodity—Money—Another Commodity (C—M—C).

The sale (C—M) is separate from the purchase (M—C). It is therefore quite possible that the weaver, having sold his cloth, is unable or unwilling to buy the shoes or the grain he intended to purchase. The completion of the transaction sticks; against the sale (C—M) there is no corresponding purchase (M—C). This seemingly commonplace fact warrants careful notice, since in the study of economic crisis in fully developed capitalist society it will prove to be of great importance. However, the "simple commodity producer" of pre-capitalist times, the craftsman or

---

* Note that we are not here referring to *token* coinage (see p. 38) such as the silver or copper coins used in Britain today.

peasant who sold his commodity, would as a rule use the money he received in order to make a purchase. The commodity in circulation would change hands at most only a few times before reaching the final consumer. But while the commodities are bought for use and pass out of circulation, the money goes on circulating from hand to hand.

Money as a Store of Value

The function of money as a store of value is in a certain sense the counterpart of its function as a medium of exchange. In exchange a commodity is given up and its value in money form received in its place (C—M in the formula given above). The money is then paid in purchase of the commodity required (M—C), and so the cycle of exchange of commodities is completed. If, however, the cycle of exchange is not completed, if commodities are sold without corresponding purchases being made, then in return for the commodities sold their owner has not other commodities but their value stored in money form.

Money as Capital

The starting point for the capitalist process of production is the accumulation of values in money form. The process of circulation of capital is very different, indeed the opposite of that in simple commodity production. The capitalist starts with a store of money with which he buys commodities in order to sell again at a profit. The formula is Money—Commodities—More Money, $M—C—M^1$, not C—M—C. In this process (as will be shown in Chapter VIII) the likelihood of a hitch, of purchase not following sale, becomes much greater.

Token Money

The wearing out of money in the course of its service as a means of circulation involves loss of some of the substance of the valuable commodity, money. Therefore, as the exchange of commodities expands, in place of the precious metal itself, a token or symbol comes to be passed from hand to hand. Naturally as the gold coin itself only comes to be generally accepted in so far as reliance has come to be placed on it from long custom and the authority whose superscription it bears, so the token coin or symbol of value only becomes acceptable in so far as its status has been established by custom and the backing of authority.

One of the earliest forms of token money known to history was the sealed purse in ancient Carthage used to symbolise a quantity of gold. In more modern times paper has become the most widely used form of token money. (It may here be pointed out that, when paper money is "inflated", the pieces of paper which represent certain accepted units of currency, such as the pound sterling or the dollar, cease to be worth as much as before the inflation, though they look the same and bear the same name; for example, a pound note which previously bought goods in which say, five hours of labour-time were embodied, now only buys goods embodying, say, three hours of labour-time.) Coins used for small change are also token money, since their value depends on the value they represent rather than on the value of the metals of which they are made; for example, before 1914 a shilling represented one-twentieth of a gold sovereign, and not the value of the silver it contained. Thus in a variety of ways symbols of value come to be used in the place of the money commodity itself in order to perform money's function as a means of exchange.

Commodities may thus enter into exchange in ratios corresponding to the value they embody, even though the symbols which serve as "go-betweens" in the act of exchange themselves have no value.

Money as a Means of Payment

The general use of token money corresponds to a fairly high stage in the development of commodity exchange. A still higher stage gives rise to a separation in time between the act of purchase and the act of payment. For example, goods are purchased against an undertaking to pay at some later date. The "bill of exchange" is such an undertaking, drawn up in legally binding form, which has come into general use in modern commercial transactions. The ordinary bank cheque is another.

As commerce developed there came into being a whole network of financial transactions and financial specialists experienced in how to turn such transactions to profit. In the hands of the financial houses and banks that specialise in such dealings, promises to pay collect alongside of rights of payment, and then in each trader's account debts are cancelled out against credits or vice versa. Thus, commercial payments tend to pass through certain central points, and purchases and sales can be

39

effected without the direct intervention of the money commodity, which now serves rather as a means of repayment "on settlement day" than as a direct intermediary in each individual transaction.

Gold as World Money

As commodity exchange spreads throughout the world, the means of effecting sale and purchase between nations are developed. Here the coin marked and shaped in accordance with currency standards of a national authority no longer has the same significance; here it is the weight of the crude metal, the bullion, that counts. Currencies count only for the gold they can be turned into or the labour-time they command. In this way, gold and silver came to serve as world money. "The more the exchange of commodities between different national spheres of circulation is developed, the more important becomes the function of world money to serve as a *means of payment* for the settlement of international balances." (Marx, *Critique of Political Economy*, II, 3, b.) Gold (supplemented to a certain extent by silver) has continued thus throughout the capitalist era to function as the world money in which settlement is made of outstanding balances from trade and financial transactions between nations; but today even in this field, the importance of gold is diminishing and the extent to which settlements are effected in terms of national currencies is extending.

The Functions of Money

From the foregoing paragraphs it will be seen that money in developed commodity production has a number of functions, which may be briefly summarised as follows:

(1) Measure of value.
(2) Medium of exchange.
(3) Means of payment.
(4) Store of value.

Hoarding

Money can satisfy neither hunger nor thirst, and it is not to enjoy the use-value of the metal that men want money. Once trade has developed on any considerable scale, the usefulness of gold for making utensils or ornaments becomes of purely secondary importance. Hoards of gold are coveted not for the beauty or usefulness of the metal, but because gold is the embodiment of exchange-value, because it is abstract labour incarnate, because it is money. At will it can be turned into any commodity. Gold commands the product of other men's labour—and much else besides.

"Gold! Yellow, glittering, precious gold! . . .
Thus much of this will make black, white; foul fair;
Wrong, right; base, noble; old, young; coward, valiant.
. . . Why this
Will lug your priests and servants from your sides;
Pluck stout men's pillows from below their heads.
This yellow slave
Will knit and break religions; bless the accurs'd;
Make the hoar leprosy adored; place thieves,
And give them title, knee and approbation
With senators on the bench; this is it
That makes the wappen'd widow wed again;
She, whom the spital house and ulcerous sores
Would cast the gorge at, this embalms and spices
To the April day again."
—Shakespeare, *Timon of Athens*, Act IV, Scene III.

A humble craftsman or peasant must use the money that he gets for the sale of his produce to buy the wherewithal to maintain his existence. He can at best save but little against misfortune. But not so the slave-owner or feudal lord. They could, from the surplus wealth which came to them from the labour of slaves or serfs, live in pomp and luxury, and at the same time lay by great stores of precious metals. But neither the potentate of ancient times nor the feudal lord could be charged with miserliness. They got and held the sources of their wealth by force and knew little of the "virtue of abstinence".

The development of trade, however, brought with it a class of men who worshipped money with a greater single-mindedness. These were the merchants. "All along the line of exchange", writes Marx, "hoards of gold and silver of varied extent are accumulated. With the possibility of holding and storing up exchange-value in the shape of a particular commodity, arises also the greed for gold. Along with the extension of circulation, increases the power of money, that absolutely social form of wealth ever ready for use. . . . The desire after hoarding is in its very nature insatiable. In its qualitative aspect or formally considered money has no bounds to its efficacy, i.e., it is the universal representative of material wealth, because it is directly convertible into any other commodity. But at the same time, every actual sum of money is limited in amount and, therefore, as a means of purchasing, has only a limited efficacy. This antagonism between the quantitative limits of money and its qualitative boundlessness, continually acts as a spur to the hoarder in his Sisyphus-like labour of accumulating. It is with him as it is with a conqueror who sees in every new country annexed, only a new boundary." (*Capital*, Vol. I, LW pp. 131–3, A pp. 108–10.)

CHAPTER III

THE ORIGINS OF CAPITALISM

Capitalism today differs fundamentally from all previous economic systems. Production is carried on in large units employing hundreds or thousands of workers. Industry predominates over agricuture. In industry vast and rapid developments have carried the technique of production far away from the homely craftsmanship of feudal times. The application of science to methods of production has had far-reaching consequences. Specialisation and the division of labour, both within and between productive units, has been carried to a very high degree. The whole of the world is linked by commercial and economic ties, and dependence on markets—not merely local markets, but world markets—is constantly invading the self-sufficiency of natural production which still persists. The development of capitalism in Britain, the U.S.A., Germany, and the other leading capitalist countries has brought in its train an unprecedented increase in production, wealth, and population, but it has brought also mass poverty for the workers and exploitation of colonial and subject peoples, devastating economic crises, and wars affecting the whole of the world.

In Chapter II it has been shown how, long before the appearance of capitalism on the scene of history, production for exchange and trade, for the *market*, developed and existed alongside "production for use" in ancient slave society and feudal society. This development of exchange and the market was a necessary pre-condition for the development of capitalism; capitalism could not have developed if commodity exchange had not developed first. Moreover, the growth of trade aided the rise of capitalism by breaking down the old social relationships and creating *new class divisions* both in the villages and in the handicraft guilds in the towns. However, the development of the market by itself was not sufficient to cause the capitalist system of production to develop. In the ancient world trade developed to a considerable extent, but nevertheless it did not give birth to a capitalist system of production. Before capitalist production can become general other conditions, as well as the growth of the market, must first have developed; there must have been new advances in technique making possible new methods of production and there must have emerged two new classes, the *capitalist class* and the *working class* or *proletariat*.

The Capitalist Class

The capitalist class is the class which owns as private property the means of production, the factories, mills, mines, machinery, and raw materials. However, the ownership of the means of production does not in itself distinguish the capitalist class from other exploiting classes. Other exploiting classes have owned the means of production; for example, the slave-owner of the ancient world owned the crude instruments and other means of production with which the slave worked. What else, then, characterises the capitalist class? Is it the possession of large sums of money? It is true that capitalists, in order to be capitalists, need to possess large sums of money, but money fortunes existed long before the advent of capitalism and the possession of large sums of money cannot in itself characterise the capitalist class. The essential characteristic of the capitalist is that he *hires workers* who work for *wages*, producing goods for exchange.

The capitalist class, therefore, is a class of persons possessed of wealth in money form and owning means of production which are set to work by hiring wage-workers. There can, therefore, be no capitalist production unless in addition to the capitalist class there is also a class of wage-workers.

The Working Class or Proletariat

Capitalists will not be able to hire wage-workers unless there are those who need, and also are free, to sell their power to work for wages. If men can get their living by themselves, as do the independent or simple commodity producers using their own labour and their own tools and other means of production (such as the peasant working his own land or the craftsman working for himself), then they do not need to sell their power to work, their *labour-power*. If men are not free to leave their lord's land, being "tied" to the land as is the serf, then they are not able to sell their labour-power. Therefore, that a class of wage-workers might develop, it was necessary that there should be men who were freed from the bondage of serfdom and at the same time "free" from the opportunity of getting a living for themselves as independent producers, as peasants or craftsmen. In short, men torn from the means of production, dispossessed of land, raw materials, and tools, free to sell their labour-power for wages—or starve. This new propertyless, dispossessed class, whose coming into being was a necessary condition for the development of capitalism, Marx termed *the proletariat* after the *proletarii* who constituted the propertyless class of free citizens in ancient Rome.

An understanding of capitalism must begin with an understanding of how there came into being, on the one hand, the *propertied* class owning the means of production—the *capitalist class*; and, on the other hand, the propertyless class, free and yet compelled by necessity to sell its labour-power to the capitalists—the *proletariat.*

Merchant Capital

The earliest form of capital was merchant capital, which existed many hundreds of years before the advent of the capitalist system of production, e.g., in Egypt, Asia Minor, Greece, and Rome. Merchant capital first began to appear in history when commerce between distant lands developed on a substantial scale. From such traffic, the traders of the ancient world became wealthy and powerful, and not infrequently they speeded the growth of their wealth and power by combining commerce with piracy.

With the development of feudal society, trade and commerce again grew. During the eleventh and twelfth centuries there was a great expansion of trade, mainly maritime trade from country to country, which stimulated the growth of rich trading cities such as those of Northern Italy and Flanders, the towns on the Baltic, and, in England, Norwich and London. The Crusades (the first at the end of the eleventh century, the seventh and last in the middle of the thirteenth century) greatly stimulated trade between Europe and the Middle East. The crusaders and the merchants who followed in their wake acquired the riches of the East by the unholy methods of robbery and cheating. Once more trade and violence went hand in hand.

45

Growth of the Market and its Effects

With the opening up of trade with the East demand for the luxuries in which the merchants trafficked—spices, silks, carpets, and so forth—grew apace in the feudal courts and castles. This was one of the ways in which the growth of commerce broke down the self-sufficiency of the feudal estates. What the traders brought, the feudal lords were eager to buy. The surplus produced by the labour of the serfs had therefore to be made to provide them with the means of buying goods that commerce offered. The feudal lords' concern was not only to turn their wealth into money but also to increase the amount of money at their command. Land and men owing allegiance had in the past meant power; now, with the expansion of trade, money was becoming power. The basis for trade was exploitation; it was primarily the surplus product, the fruit of exploitation, that entered into trade. It was therefore a frequent consequence of the growth of trade and commerce that serf labour was more ruthlessly exploited in order that, from the greater surplus thereby appropriated, more products might be sold to yield money revenue.

In the fifteenth and sixteenth centuries, a further impetus was given to the growth of commerce by the discovery of America and the opening of the sea route to India. Once again piracy and plunder went hand in hand with commerce. The expansion of commerce and its ever deeper penetration into feudal society had by now brought about changes that were destined to have far-reaching consequences. "The development of commerce and merchants' capital", writes Marx, "brings forth everywhere the tendency towards production of exchange values, increases its volume, multiplies and monopolises it, develops money into world money. Commerce therefore had everywhere more or less of a dissolving influence on the producing organisations, which it finds at hand and whose different forms are mainly carried on with a view to immediate use. To what extent it brings about a dissolution of the old mode of production, depends on its solidity and internal articulation. And to what this process of dissolution will lead, in other words what new mode of production will take the place of the old, does not depend on commerce, but on the character of the old mode of production itself. In the antique world the effect of commerce and the development of merchants' capital always result in slave economy; or, according to what the next point of departure may be, the result may simply turn out

46

to be the transformation of a patriarchal slave system devoted to the production of direct means of subsistence into a similar system devoted to the production of surplus value. However, in the modern world, it results in the capitalist mode of production. From these facts it follows, that these results were conditioned on quite other circumstances than the mere influence of the development of merchants' capital." (*Capital*, Vol. III, LW pp. 326–7, K pp. 390–1.)

The Internal Decay of Feudalism

Money and commerce acted as a solvent, breaking down the old societies. "Money revenue, as well as services of bondsmen, grew to be a lordly ambition; a market in loans developed, and also a market in land. As one writer, speaking of England, has said: 'the great roads which join London to the seaboard are the arteries along which flow money, the most destructive solvent of seignorial power'." (Maurice Dobb, *Studies in the Development of Capitalism*, p. 38.) The merchant capitalists became a new power in the land; they were able, because of their great wealth, to seek alliance with the greater lords, and, in return for the money they put at their disposal, were given special protection and monopolies in trade. New conflicts and divisions resulted from the growing power of the merchants.

All this "softened up" and weakened the structure of the old society, but the root cause underlying the dissolution of feudalism was the failure, or rather inability, of the feudal mode of production to develop. "Not only", writes Dobb, "did the productivity of labour remain very low in the manorial economy, owing both to the methods in use and the lack of incentive to labour, but the yield of land remained so meagre as to lead some authorities to suggest an actual tendency for the system of cultivation to result in exhaustion of the soil." (*Studies in the Development of Capitalism*, p. 43.)

The feudal structure of society—which in its origin had been a vehicle of progress giving scope for new methods of tilling the soil, new productive possibilities which could not be developed within slave society—itself turned into a fetter on further development of the forces of production. The peasant did nothing to enrich the land which the medieval cropping system exhausted. It was not only poverty that debarred him from manuring his land adequately; he knew also that "any improvement in the soil was but the pretext for some new exaction" and that the

47

lord "being a mere parasite . . . discouraged initiative and dried up all energy at its source by taking from the villein an exorbitant part of the fruits of his work, so that labour was half-sterile." (P. Boissonnade, *Life and Work in Mediaeval Europe* quoted by M. Dobb in *Studies in the Development of Capitalism*, p. 44.)

Thus the growing needs of the feudal ruling class for money and the new exactions and pressure on their subjects to which this led coincided with productive stagnation, which was made the worse by the poverty which their added exactions imposed upon the peasantry.

What the feudal lords could not get by grinding down their subjects they sought by military adventures against rival lords. Consequently "the number of vassals were multiplied . . . in order to strengthen the military resources of the greater lords. This, combined with the natural growth of noble families and an increase in the number of retainers, swelled the size of the parasitic class that had to be supported from the surplus labour of the serf population. Added to this were the effects of war and of brigandage, which could almost be said to be integral parts of the feudal order, and which swelled the expenses of feudal households and of the Crown at the same time as it spread waste and devastation over the land." (M. Dobb, *op. cit.*, p. 45.)

The more the feudal lords strove severally to master their circumstances the deeper was the crisis into which their class as a whole was plunged. The very means by which each strove for survival accelerated the downfall of feudal power in general; and as feudalism grew weaker, the merchants and manufacturers, the men from the towns, grew stronger.

The antagonisms that shaped the course of social development in the era of the decay of feudalism may be thus summarised: (i) The conflict between serf and lord—serf fighting back against the lord, who was ever struggling to exact a bigger surplus product. (ii) Lord warring against lord, each trying to win salvation at the expense of a rival, and, in so doing, sowing a harvest of universal decay. (iii) Feudal power against the merchants and budding capitalists in the towns and on the land. As the struggles proceeded the basis of feudal power was continually narrowing; the old order was less and less able to manœuvre, less and less able to find a way out for itself. Feudalism was struggling on its death-bed, as today moribund capitalism struggles ever more desperately against the rising power of socialism.

In the towns an unceasing fight had been carried on against the domination of the feudal lords, the king, and the church. Trade and commerce sought to free itself from such hampering obligations as military service, consent of the lord to admission of new burgesses, monopoly held by the lord in milling of grain and baking of bread, the tyranny of the king's sheriffs and the "clerk of the king's markets". In this fight the townsmen, reinforced by the wealth of commerce, gained their ends to a very substantial extent, winning self-government and charters that defined the dues to be paid. However, the towns, whilst fighting against the tolls on sales imposed by the feudal lords, themselves imposed numerous tolls and closely controlled the town market with the object of keeping down prices of food and materials consumed in the towns and keeping *up* prices paid for goods sold to outsiders.

In the course of time, the guilds of craftsmen and merchants in the towns, which at the outset had been fraternities of equals, changed their character beyond recognition. The progress from apprentice to journeyman and from journeyman to master was no longer a royal road that most might expect to follow. The masters were able in the course of time to establish themselves as a narrow and restricted class, ruling the affairs of the guilds and the town in their own interests, and using property qualifications to block the advancement of the common journeyman to positions of control. Again, the guilds of merchants separated themselves from the guilds of productive craftsmen, and used their wealth to establish themselves in a dominant position. The regulative control which had once been the proper function of the guilds became instead an exclusive monopoly supported by royal enactment. As allies of the monarchy (which was in great need of allies against the seditious moves of the barons) the monopolistic merchants became a bulwark of the old order and resisted the aspirations of the lesser merchants and of the rising class of capitalists, who were beginning to put their capital into production.

What were the issues which underlay the shifting alignments of class forces, and the religious and moral precepts that inspired the contending parties in the prolonged struggle that culminated in the English revolution of 1640-1688? The root issue was State-power, that is, whether the rising capitalist class or the representatives of the old feudal order controlled legislation, administration, the armed forces, and the legal system. More specifically the capitalists needed control of the State apparatus in order that they might have freedom to buy and sell the land and do with it as they willed (in which they were baulked by the customs and legal provisions of the feudal system). They sought freedom to manufacture whatever they wished, in whatever way they wished, and to sell their products wherever they wished (and in this they were obstructed by the customs and legal provisions under which the guilds and corporations in the towns exercised control of economic activities). They wanted freedom to employ whom they wished as they wished (and in this they were obstructed by the customs and legal provisions under which the serf and peasant was tied to his lord's land and under which the apprentice and journeyman in the town was subject to jurisdiction of the guilds).

"Primitive Accumulation" and the Origin of the Proletariat

Capitalism could not develop until, in addition to the accumulation of wealth in a few hands, there were also men and women *free* to sell their labour-power for wages and at the same time "free" from any other means of getting a living.

The origin of this two-fold condition, which had to exist before capitalism could come into being, has been the subject of more hypocritical rubbish from the pens of the defenders of capitalism than perhaps any other topic. "This primitive accumulation", writes Marx, "plays in Political Economy about the same part as original sin in theology. Adam bit the apple, and thereupon sin fell on the human race. Its origin is supposed to be explained when it is told as an anecdote of the past. In times long gone by there were two sorts of people; one, the diligent, the intelligent, and above all, frugal élite; the other, lazy rascals, spending their substance, and more, in riotous living. The legend of theological sin tells us certainly how man came to be condemned to eat his bread in the sweat of his brow, but the history of economic original sin reveals to us that there are people to whom this is by no means essential. Never mind! Thus it came to pass that the former sort accumulated wealth and the latter sort had at last nothing to sell except their own skins. And from this original sin dates the poverty of the great majority that, despite all its labour, has up to now nothing to sell but itself; and the wealth of the few that increases constantly—although they have long ceased to work. Such widespread childishness is every day preached to us in the defence of property." (*Capital*, Vol. I, LW p. 713, A p. 736.)

Trade, helped by war, brigandage, and cheating, fostered the accumulation of wealth; how did the other condition necessary to the development of capitalism, namely, the existence of a "free" working class, the *proletariat*, come about? In Britain the landless, propertyless, dispossessed classes, the proletariat to be, were formed as a result, in the main, of violent expropriation through the Enclosures, the Reformation, and differentiation amongst the peasantry. (Similar causes operated in the formation of the proletariat elsewhere in Europe.)

In feudal society the peasantry was the main producing class and it was by depriving of land those who had, as serfs or tenant farmers, once lived off their own fields, that the proletariat was primarily formed. This happened in a number of ways: sometimes the peasants, pressed too hard by the greed and cruelty of the landowners, deserted to the woods and to the towns; sometimes the peasants' land was simply taken by force in order that the landlords might turn the land thus appropriated into pasturage for sheep, and so get themselves moneyed wealth from the sale of wool, for which the growing textile industry provided a ready market in the fifteenth and sixteenth centuries. "Forcible usurpation . . .", says Marx, "generally accompanied by the turning of arable into pasture land, begins at the end of the fifteenth and extends into the sixteenth century. But, at that time, the process was carried on by individual acts of violence against which legislation, for a hundred and fifty years, fought in vain. The advance made by the eighteenth century shows itself in this, that the law itself becomes now the instrument of the theft of the people's land". (*Capital*, Vol. I, LW p. 724, A p. 748.) The extent of "legal" enclosures in the eighteenth century may be gauged from the fact that in the reign of George III alone 3,554 Acts of Enclosure were passed appropriating 5½ million acres of land. Extensive enclosures continued into the nineteenth century, 3½ million acres being appropriated between 1801 and 1831.

The process of the formation of the proletariat continued in Britain through five hundred years, from the fourteenth to the nineteenth century. The entry of British capital into East Africa causes what is in essence the same process to be re-enacted in the twentieth century. In Kenya between 1905 and 1941, 4,400,000 acres were expropriated from the natives and given to English settlers, who forthwith began agitating for the administration to provide them with labour to work their estates. This the administration speedily did by restricting the area of native reserves and imposing a poll-tax (1908), to pay which the native could only get the money by leaving his own land to work for a wage. Gestapo methods, including registration at a Central Fingerprint Bureau, were then invoked to enforce these measures. The same ruthlessness and violence has throughout the world and throughout the centuries been used in the creation of conditions suitable to capitalist production, and in particular in the formation of a proletariat "free" to be exploited.

By the end of the sixteenth century the masses of the people in Britain had, in long and bitter struggles, won for most of their number freedom from the more degrading obligations of serfdom. In the countryside, the dominance of the lords of the manors was still firmly maintained; but the bulk of the population were small peasants holding their land as tenants of the great lords. Some, however, had acquired (or retained) full freedom, and owned their own land. Of these a few had become yeoman farmers of substance who aspired to the status of the squires and lesser nobles who were now beginning to farm their lands on capitalist lines, employing wage-workers. At the other end of the scale there were the many peasants who were forced by debt to sell all their property and leave their land to become beggars or wage-labourers.

The effects of the enclosures, impoverishment and exploitation, were supplemented in the sixteenth century by the Reformation, an onslaught on the Church of Rome which brought in its train suppression of the monasteries and the sharing out of the estates of the Church (which had been one of the largest landowners). Thus the Reformation helped to bring into being the new capitalist landowners, who employed but few labourers in sheep-raising, and at the same time swelled the numbers of the landless proletariat.

A glance at the historical facts is sufficient to expose the falsity of the tale that the origin of capital is thrift, abstinence and "thought for the morrow". Marx speaks in these terms of the two-fold process of *primitive accumulation*, by which simple and non-capitalist commodity production turned into capitalist commodity production: "This so-called primitive accumulation is nothing else than the historical process of divorcing the producer from the means of production. . . . The history of this, their expropriation, is written in annals of blood and fire. . . . In the history of primitive accumulation, all revolutions are epoch-making that act as levers for the capitalist class in the course of formation; but above all, those moments when great masses of men are suddenly and forcibly torn from their means of subsistence and hurled as free and 'unattached' proletarians on the labour market. . . . The spoliation of the Church's property, the fraudulent alienation of the State domains, the robbery of the common lands, the usurpation of feudal and clan property, and its transformation into modern private property under circumstances of reckless terrorism, were just so many idyllic methods of primitive accumulation. They conquered the field for capitalist agriculture, made the soil part and parcel of capital, and created for the town industries the necessary supply of a 'free' and outlawed proletariat." (*Capital*, Vol. I, LW pp. 714–15, 732, A pp. 738, 739, and 757.)

Alongside these violent transformations of the agricultural economy of feudalism, means no less violent were used to acquire and "accumulate" money and other forms of wealth that could be turned into capital. "The discovery", writes Marx (*Capital*, Vol. I, LW p. 751, A p. 775), "of gold and silver in America, the extirpation, enslavement, and entombment in mines of the aboriginal population, the beginning of the conquest and looting of the East Indies, the turning of Africa into a warren for the commercial hunting of black-skins, signalised the rosy dawn of the era of capitalist production."

The Development of the Capitalist Mode of Production

Capitalist production at first developed slowly within the feudal society. Its early forms were restricted and encumbered by the old order; once, however, capitalism had won its political and therewith economic freedom, it revealed with startling speed the undreamed-of forces of production that lay hidden in social labour. In the remaining paragraphs of this chapter a brief account will be given of the stages through which the capitalist mode of production changed and developed until it reached its fully mature form in the industrial capitalism of the nineteenth century.

The Putting-Out System

As trade increased the character of the medieval guilds of craftsmen greatly changed. The master who worked with a few apprentices and perhaps one or two journeymen temporarily attached to his household, and belonging to a guild which controlled the quantity and quality of goods produced, was in the fifteenth century in England already becoming a relic of the past. The merchant guilds had attained a position of dominance over the craft guilds, a few wealthy guild-masters were concentrating power in their hands, the journeymen were assuming more the position of exploited wage-labourers, and—most important of all—the pressure of the growing market was breaking down the restrictions and monopolies of the guilds. Merchants and well-to-do craftsmen, in their eagerness for more plentiful and cheaper supplies of goods to sell than they could obtain from the urban guilds, turned their attention to production from new sources.

So developed an almost capitalist form of industry—the *putting-out system*, also known as *domestic industry*, which made its appearance on a considerable scale, particularly in the cloth industry in England, in the fifteenth century. The merchant-employer (almost a capitalist) bought raw material, such as wool, and "put it out" to the smaller craftsmen, the spinners, weavers, carders, fullers, dyers, etc. In order to avoid the guild restrictions of the towns, this work was generally put with workers in the countryside outside the jurisdiction of the towns. The "capitalist" paid the worker for his labour and became the owner of the finished cloth, which he sold at a profit.

In this "in-between" kind of capitalism, the worker often owned his own means of production, and worked at his loom, for example, in his own house; but now he no longer owned all his means of production, since his raw materials belonged to his employer. To this extent he therefore depended on his employer. The worker was in effect forced to borrow the means of carrying on production—at a high rate of interest. Apparently this domestic system of production involved no technical change, but it should be noted that under it the various craftsmen were subordinated to the capitalist whose concern it was to see that the various processes of production were dovetailed together as economically as possible.

"The transition from the feudal mode of production", writes Marx, "takes two roads. The producer becomes a merchant and capitalist, in contradistinction from agricultural natural economy and the guild-encircled handicrafts of medieval town industry. This is the revolutionary way. Or, the merchant takes possession

54

in a direct way of production. While this way serves historically as a mode of transition—instance the English clothier of the seventeenth century, who brings the weavers, although they remain independently at work, under his control, by selling wool to them and buying cloth from them—nevertheless, it cannot by itself do much for the overthrow of the old mode of production, but rather preserves it and uses it as a premise. As soon as manufacture gains sufficient strength, and still more large-scale industry . . . commerce becomes the servant of industrial production", whereas "in former periods . . . merchants' capital [held] the supremacy over industrial capital." (*Capital*, Vol. III, LW pp. 329 and 331, K pp. 393 and 396.)

Co-operation and Manufacture

"When numerous labourers work together side by side, whether in one and the same process, or in different but connected processes, they are said to co-operate or work in co-operation." (*Capital*, Vol. I, LW p. 325, A p. 315.) Long before capitalism, men "co-operated" in production in considerable numbers. Without co-operation neither the Egyptian pyramids nor the Roman roads could have been built; but with the emergence of capitalism, co-operation of many men working alongside one another in production becomes no longer something occasional or exceptional, but, to an increasing extent, normal and regular. Co-operation brings with it a great increase of productive power, overhead costs (per unit of output) are reduced, efficiency is stimulated by the contact of workers with one another in production, joint efforts make possible achievements of an altogether different kind from those within the power of individual workers.

This new productive power becomes general and widespread with the development of capitalism. It is the fruit of the new technical developments and consequently new social conditions which make possible the "working together" in "co-operation" of many workers, but "because the labourer does not develop it [i.e. this new productive power] before his labour belongs to capital, it appears as a power with which capital is endowed by nature—a productive power that is immanent in capital". (*Capital*, Vol. I, LW p. 333, A p. 324.)

This *social* labour-process, this working together of many men (and with it the wide distinction of the capitalist employer, not himself a productive worker, from the wage-earning worker) is a feature that distinguishes the capitalist mode of production from feudal production, characterised by the individual peasant and farmer and by the independent craftsman with a limited number of apprentices working with him.

From the sixteenth to the eighteenth century, prior to the age of modern industry with its use of large-scale powered machinery, the most mature form of capitalist production was what Marx terms *manufacture*, which involved extensive division of labour between many workers who were brought together in one place of work, or factory. Most of the newer industries, such as paper, gunpowder, cannon-making, sugar-refining, etc., which developed in England in the sixteenth century, were—indeed, had to be— undertaken in this way. Manufacture was, however, adopted also in the older industries (where the domestic or putting-out system still lingered for many long years).

The development of manufacture followed two courses: first, craftsmen whose several skills contributed to the production of one article would be assembled together and would so become specialists in their crafts as applied to this particular product. (Marx quotes as an example carriage manufacture, which calls for wheelwrights, upholsterers, locksmiths, and many other artificers, who became no longer experts in upholstery, wheel- making, etc., of all kinds, but only in upholstering carriages, making the wheels of carriages, etc.) Secondly, craftsmen in one trade would be brought together and in the course of time would divide up their process of work so that individual workmen be- came specialists in particular operations. (Adam Smith in *Wealth of Nations*, Book I, Chapter I, quotes pin-making as an example: "One man draws out the wire, another straights it, a third cuts it, a fourth points it, a fifth grinds it at the top for receiving the head; to make the head requires two or three distinct operations; to put it on is a peculiar business; to whiten the pin is another; it is even a trade by itself to put them into the paper; and the important business of making a pin is, in this manner, divided into about eighteen distinct operations." He adds: "Ten persons . . . could make among them upwards of forty-eight thousand pins a day. . . . But if they had all wrought separately and independently and without any of them having been educated to this peculiar business, they certainly could not each of them have made twenty, perhaps not one pin in a day.")

"The collective labourer", writes Marx, "formed by the combination of a number of detail labourers, is the machinery specially characteristic of the manufacturing period." (*Capital,* Vol. I, LW p. 348, A p. 341.)

This far-reaching division of labour and specialisation of functions carries with it a down-grading of labour—all that the worker requires is a highly specialised dexterity; he loses his general skill as a craftsman and his ability for independent work. What once were the products of seasoned craftsmanship, are now the products of "collective labour", of a few skilled and many unskilled workers.

Manufacture adapts not only the worker to specialised work, but also his tools. Implements of all kinds used in the process of production, such as cutting tools, hammers, drills, lathes, etc., are adapted each to a special purpose. "The manufacturing period simplifies, improves, and multiplies the implements of labour by adapting them to the exclusively special functions of each detail labourer. It then creates at the same time one of the material conditions for the existence of machinery which consists of a combination of simple intruments." (Marx, *Capital,* Vol. I, LW pp. 341-2, A p. 333.)

The period of *manufacture,* which dates from the middle of the sixteenth century, ends with the industrial revolution at the end of the eighteenth and the beginning of the nineteenth century. With the industrial revolution, for which *manufacture* paved the way, capitalist production, based on large-scale mechanised industry, reaches the conditions for its full development.

The Productive Forces of Capitalism released by the English Revolution

The advance from manufacture to full-blooded industrial capitalism could not have taken place if the capitalist class had not been able to free itself from the shackles of feudalism. Up to a certain point capitalism was able to develop within the old feudal society, but in order to realise their full potentialities the capitalist class sought to "employ the power of the State, the concentrated and organised force of society, to hasten, hothouse fashion, the process of transformation of the feudal mode of production into the capitalist mode, and to shorten the transformation. Force," writes Marx, "is the midwife of every old society pregnant with a new one," (*Capital,* Vol. I, LW p. 751, A p. 775.)

In Britain the forceful struggle between the old society and the new reached its culmination in the Revolution of 1640. In this struggle the Parliamentary cause had wholehearted support from capitalists connected with industry, particularly in the woollen manufacturing districts such as Gloucestershire, Yorkshire, and East Anglia. The merchant capitalists on the whole supported Parliament, but those who did, did so with many reservations and vacillations; they were the right wing of the Parliamentary forces. The holders of Royal patents giving them monopoly rights in their own industries supported the King, despite the fact that their undertakings were some of the most capitalistically advanced in the country. Their connection with the Court and the monopoly privilege that they enjoyed placed them in the ranks of reaction. The small and medium-sized yeoman farmers were staunch supports of the Revolution, especially in south-eastern and eastern England; however, in the west and north of England, where the feudal tradition was strong, the landholding interests and the gentry fought for the King and were able to enrol in their forces considerable numbers of their tenants and retainers. A contemporary writer sketches the alignment as follows: "A very great part of the knights and gentlemen of England . . . adhered to the King. . . . And most of the tenants of these gentlemen, and also most of the poorest of the people, whom the others call the rabble, did follow the gentry and were for the King. On the Parliament side were (besides themselves) the smaller part (as some thought) of the gentry in most of the counties, and the greater part of the tradesmen and freeholders and the middle sort of men, especially in those corporations and counties which depend on clothing and such manufactures." (Baxter, *Autobiography*, Everyman edition, p. 34.)

The issue was Parliament versus the Absolute Monarchy. Parliament represented the interests of the rising capitalists. The monarchy, which in earlier Tudor times had in certain respects facilitated the development of capitalism, now recognised that the only real threat to the power and privilege of the Court came from the capitalist class. The monarchy became the bulwark of feudal reaction and rallied to its support the feudal lords whose privileges were threatened by the rising capitalist class.

The immediate cause of the outbreak of the Civil War between King and Parliament was the attempt to impose taxes without the consent of Parliament. However, the root issue was who should hold State-power, the rising capitalist class or the old feudal ruling class and those now mustered about the King. The issue was who should control legislation, taxation, administration, the armed forces, and the legal system.

Machinery and Large-scale Industry

"According to the theory of Marx, the term large-scale machine (factory) industry, applies only to a definite and precisely to a higher stage of capitalism in industry. The principal and more important symptom of this stage is the employment of a system of machines in production. The transition from manufacture to the factory marks a complete technical revolution which eliminates the age-old skill of the craftsman and this technical revolution is followed by an extremely sharp change in the social relations in production, by a final rupture between the various groups taking part in production, a complete rupture with tradition, the intensification and expansion of all the gloomy sides of capitalism, and at the same time the mass socialisation of labour by capitalism. Thus large-scale machine industry is the last word of capitalism, the last word of its negative and 'positive' aspects." (Lenin, *Development of Capitalism in Russia*, Chapter VII.)

With the development of capitalism, the market grew, and with the growth of the market the capitalist producer sought always to increase his production of goods with which to supply the market. The ever-expanding market for the capitalists' products, together with the methods of production which developed in the "manufactories" (that is, pre-machine-age factories in which production was at the stage of *manufacture*) provided unusually fertile soil for mechanical inventions. In many lands and in many past ages, craftsmen and scientists had made inventions, but the incentive and appetite for using and stimulating inventions had never been great, since the social conditions were not such that these inventions could give rise to far-reaching and revolutionary changes in productive technique. In eighteenth-century England, conditions were ripe for such changes and a whole series of inventions, destined completely to transform the face of industry, followed in quick succession: the flying shuttle in 1733, the spinning jenny in 1765, the spinning frame worked by water power in 1769, the spinning mule, combining the jenny and the water frame, in 1779, the steam engine in 1782, the power loom in 1785, and finally the automatic mule in 1825.

59

In the period of industrial capitalism the basis for the expansion of the market, in each capitalist country and later in the colonial and economically more backward countries, has always been the destruction of the independent craftsman, through the competition of machine-made goods. Moreover the increasing production of machines itself created new markets. New industries producing machines arose, and these in turn created a new demand for iron and steel, and stimulated the invention of new methods of smelting, more efficient furnaces, and so on.

The great development of industry that occurred in the nineteenth century would not have been possible if it had not been for the invention of a new driving power—steam. However, this new source of power was not the most revolutionary aspect of the new industry; already in times long past water, wind, and cattle had been used to replace human power. In the new machinery—which comprised the motor mechanism, the transmitting mechanism, and the mechanised tool—the really revolutionary feature was the mechanised tool, which replaced the skilful motions of the human hand.

This great revolution in the mode of production, namely large-scale industry developing on the basis of powered machine production, brought far-reaching changes in its train. The productivity of labour, the output per man hour, and the total volume of production were immensely increased. In sixty years (1820-1880) output per man in Britain increased sixfold in spinning and over twelvefold in weaving, as the following figures show:

		Production in 1,000 lb.	No. of workers	Production per worker in lb.
Spinning				
1819-20	..	106,500	111,000	968
1880-82	..	1,329,000	240,000	5,520
Weaving				
1819-20	..	80,620	250,000	322
1880-82	..	993,570	246,000	4,039

With the introduction of this new machinery, an ever wider gulf was fixed between capitalist and worker. The new forms of production called for a vast outlay of capital on machines; unskilled labour more and more replaced skilled; women and children took the place of men. With growing power to produce came growing wealth for the capitalists, and growing degradation and squalor for the working masses. At the same time, the machine production in the "dark satanic mills" spelt ruin for the hand-workers in domestic industry, who were forced into the ever-growing ranks of the proletariat.

Now the implements of production were no longer such as the man who worked them might handle and own for himself. They were giant machines, vast factories, great power stations. Production had become social. Never again could the worker own for himself his means of production; either he must remain subject to the clique of wealthy capitalists who hold in their private control the productive resources of society, or else he must free himself by uniting with all other workers to take into social control and ownership the socialised means of production on which the life of modern society had come to depend.

CHAPTER IV

THE ESSENCE OF CAPITALIST EXPLOITATION

What is Profit?

Capitalists use many subterfuges to pretend that the amounts they take in profits are not great; but the facts show what an enormous total is in reality taken by the propertied class in rent, interest, and profit. In 1947 "incomes from property and enterprise" (as given by Dudley Seers in the *Oxford Bulletin of Statistics*, October 1948), that is, rent, interest from production, profits, and National Debt interest, totalled £3,605 million; in the same year incomes from wages were £3,530 million. There are some twenty million wage-earners, whereas unearned incomes go to about 200,000 wealthy people who own the bulk of the industrial and commercial property.* (Unearned income in fact takes many forms—and many disguises—such as, interest on loans, debentures, preference shares, ordinary shares, etc., undistributed profit, ground-rent, and so forth—see Chapter VI; for the sake of simplicity, however, unearned income will in this present chapter be described by the one general term *profit*.)

In ancient slave society the source of the wealth of the slave-owner was for all to see. What the slave produced, the slave-owner owned. Feudal exploitation was likewise open and

* Private property of all kinds in Britain in 1924-30 (according to the estimate of Daniels and Campion in *The Distribution of National Capital*) totalled about £15,000 million; of this almost 60 per cent was owned by persons (over twenty-five years of age) with fortunes of £10,000 or more, who numbered less than 200,000—less than 1 per cent of the population (over twenty-five). Of some £5,000 million privately owned stocks and shares—which better illustrate ownership of means of production—two-thirds were in 1930 owned by 200,000 individuals and one-third by 10,000 individuals with private fortunes of £100,000 or over. Post-war figures show the same picture. The reduction in big fortunes has been marginal only; for example, Kathleen Langley in the *Bulletin of the Oxford University Institute of Statistics* (December 1950 and February 1951) shows 52 per cent of the capital (which was the total of the individual fortunes of £10,000 or more) was owned by 1.3 per cent of the persons over twenty-five years of age whereas 88 per cent of persons over twenty-five own less than £1,000 each, that is little more than their personal belongings.

without mystery; the serf knew, only too well, for whom he was working and how much. Slave and serf alike could legally be forced to work by their masters. But capitalist exploitation is different. There is no law compelling the worker to work for the capitalist. There is no law or custom saying how much the capitalist is to get and how much the worker. To see the source of capitalist profit it is necessary to study political economy. The worker sells his power to work and the capitalist buys it. The worker stays poor, the capitalist becomes rich and powerful. What is the secret of the capitalist's wealth and the worker's poverty? What is profit and where does it come from?

Profit—the Motive Force of Capitalism

The process of the circulation of capital is represented by the formula M—C—M^1. The capitalist starts with a sum of money (M) which he converts into commodities (C), machinery, raw materials, and labour-power; he then sets the labour-power to work on the raw material, and sells the product for more money than he started with (M^1). This additional money that he gets from the sale of the product is his profit.

It is the capitalist's ceaseless, unremitting aim to make profit and ever more profit. As capitalism develops, so the true type of capitalist develops, the capitalist who with complete single-mindedness seeks to pile up more and more wealth. The driving force behind this singleness of purpose is not satisfaction of personal needs (which, of course, can be as well satisfied by a large as by a very large fortune and therefore reaches a limit) but a necessary condition of the economic system itself, namely competition. Economic theory which neglects this and argues as if the activities of capitalists had no other purpose but the rational satisfaction of wants and tastes, is bound to lack realism. The very conditions of capitalist production and exchange inevitably create an insatiable appetite for more capital and, therefore, for more profit. Failure to seize an opportunity of making profit is to reduce competitive strength *vis-à-vis* other capitals and is a step towards elimination from the race between capitals. To take and again to take opportunities of increasing capital resources is the basic condition of survival within the system of capitalist competition.

"The repetition or renewal of the act of selling in order to buy, is kept within bounds by the very object it aims at, namely, consumption or the satisfaction of definite wants, an aim that lies altogether outside the sphere of circulation. But when we buy in order to sell, we, on the contrary, begin and end with the same thing, money, exchange-value; and thereby the movement becomes interminable. . . . The circulation of capital has therefore no limits. As the conscious representative of this movement, the possessor of money becomes a capitalist, and it is only in so far as the appropriation of ever more and more wealth in the abstract becomes the sole motive of his operations, that he functions as a capitalist, that is, as capital personified and endowed with consciousness and a will. Use-values must therefore never be looked upon as the real aim of the capitalist, neither must the profit of any single transaction. The restless, never-ending process of profit-making alone is what he aims at." (Marx, *Capital*, Vol. I, LW pp. 151-3, A pp. 128-31.)

How the Merchant Capitalist made his Profits

The earliest form of capital—long before the development of capitalist production—was merchant capital. The merchant in pre-capitalist times got his profit in a quite different way from the modern capitalist. But this difference is highly instructive.

In ancient and medieval times an important class of merchants lived as it were in the gaps or pores between communities that depended but little on trade, communities that in most things were self-sufficient. These merchants combined trade with piracy and enriched themselves by plunder and violence. In their trading they made profits by buying where there was plenty and selling where there was scarcity; they bought cheaply and sold dearly. The markets they served were normally widely separated and the conditions prevailing in the market where they bought would not be known in the market where they sold. *The merchants thus enriched themselves at the expense of those with whom they plied their trade*, themselves standing apart from the productive activities of the communities from whom they bought and to whom they sold. They themselves were not associated with the production of the surpluses that they appropriated.

Profit in Modern Capitalist Society

In modern capitalist society it, of course, happens that extra profits are made by buying cheap and selling dear, but it is not in this way that the capitalist class as a whole makes its profits.

In modern capitalism exchange is no longer an incidental link between mainly self-sufficient communities, but all production is for exchange; exchange is everywhere. "The wealth of those societies in which the capitalist mode of production prevails presents itself as 'an immense accumulation of commodities' "— that is, goods produced for sale on the market. The bulk of sales are between capitalists; the capitalist whose workers produce raw materials (such as iron ore) sells to the capitalist whose workers produce semi-manufactured goods (such as steel tubes), who sells to another capitalist whose workers produce a finished product (such as bicycles), who sells to a wholesaler, who sells to a retailer. There are at the same time a host of transactions with sub-contractors supplying components (such as bells or brakes), with suppliers of machinery, of fuel, and so forth. It is very evident, therefore, that if a profit is made by buying below value and selling above value, what one capitalist gains another loses, and the capitalist class as a whole is no better off. The capitalist class as a whole cannot overreach itself. The great profits of the capitalists—equal in magnitude to the total of wages paid to the working class—cannot therefore be thus explained.

Transactions which are not between capitalist and capitalist may occur in trade between capitalists and peasants and other non-capitalist producers. An example is the trade between the great European and American combines and the colonial or peasant producers of raw materials. Here powerful firms use their dominating position to gain for themselves extra profits at the expense of small producers. However, these special profits gained at the fringe of capitalist society do not explain the source of profit as a whole; they explain merely a part of the profits of a special group of capitalists. An extra profit of this kind is, as a rule, obtained only where a particular firm, or group of firms acting together, is able to avoid competition from other capitalists who would outbid them.

The only other transactions (leaving aside the labour market, which is dealt with later on) are sales to final consumers. The bulk of the consumers to whom the final products are sold are the workers. Are the workers exploited because they have to buy at disadvantageous terms? Sometimes yes, but this is not the root cause of exploitation in capitalist society. However, this has, in fact, been used as a subsidiary means of exploiting and swindling workers. It was in the fight against this form of swindling that the

Co-operative movement had its origin when the workers of Rochdale started their own shop at Toad Lane in Rochdale in 1844. Again, the Truck Acts which forbade employers to pay workers in kind were intended to protect the worker from this particular kind of swindle; they were, however, repeatedly evaded and, though a Truck Act was passed as early as in 1701, wholesale evasion persistently occurred and was still common in the latter part of the nineteenth century. That swindling in the market is not the basis of capitalist exploitation is evident from the fact that capitalist exploitation continues when the workers buy in a market that is open to all alike. Generally speaking, the market does not—at least under conditions of competitive capitalism—discriminate against any one class of purchasers; and *capitalist profit as a whole in a capitalist society is not derived from buying cheap and selling dear.*

The Cycle of Capitalist Production

"Accompanied by Mr. Moneybags and by the possessor of labour-power", writes Marx, "we take leave for a time of this noisy sphere [i.e. of exchange of commodities, the market] where everything takes place on the surface and in view of all men, and follow them both into the hidden abode of production, on whose threshold there stares us in the face: 'No admittance except on business'. . . . On leaving this sphere of simple circulation or of exchange of commodities, which furnishes the 'Free-trader Vulgaris' with his views and ideas and with the standard by which he judges a society based on capital and wages, we think we can perceive a change in the physiognomy of our dramatis personae. He who before was the money-owner now strides in front as capitalist, the possessor of labour-power follows as his labourer. The one with an air of importance, smirking, intent on business; the other timid and holding back, like one who is bringing his own hide to market and has nothing to expect but—a hiding." (*Capital*, Vol. I, LW p. 176, A pp. 154–5.)

The secret of capitalist profit is not to be found in the sphere of commodity exchange and circulation; it must be sought *in the sphere of production.* It is a distinctive feature of the Marxist approach to economics—in common with the classical economists— that the central focus of its analysis is productive relations; and to explain relations of commodities on the market it breaks out of and goes beyond the sphere of circulation.

When the capitalist sets about production he starts with capital in a familiar form, namely, money, with which he buys the *means of production*. The means which he needs to undertake production normally include a factory in which to produce, machinery and tools with which to fashion his raw materials, and the raw materials themselves, including auxiliary materials such as fuel and oil. However, all this is no more than preparation for production. If he is actually to produce, the capitalist must secure workers and set them to work. The capitalist, then, buys raw materials, hires labour-power, rents (or buys) a factory and machinery—in short, changes his money into various commodities (M—C) which he intends not simply to sell (as did the merchants) but to use in the productive process. He sets the workers to work in the factory using the machinery to shape and re-fashion the raw materials. In the end the commodities with which he started have been transformed into other and different commodities. The process of production has been carried out and completed. The newly produced commodities are then sold and the capitalist has back in his hands money, that is, capital in the same form as that with which he started, but—or the capitalist is a disappointed man—there is considerably more money than he had at the beginning. This whole cycle by which the capitalist has turned money into more money may be expressed in symbols thus:

M	—	C	—	P	—	*new* C	—	M^1
(Money)		(Commo-dities)		(The pro-cess of pro-duction)		(New com-modities fashioned in the process of pro-duction)		(More Money)

The problem to be solved is how does M become M^1, how does money become more money and where does the extra money, the profit, come from?

How the Value of the Product is Made Up

Where, as is usually the case, the capitalist buys from other capitalists the raw materials (including fuel, oil, and other auxiliary materials), the value of these—which it may be assumed he buys at their correct value—is one part of the value of the finished product.

67

A second part of the value of the finished product is the value of the part of the building, plant, and machinery which gets used up in the process of production. Of course, actual bricks and machines do not get swallowed up in one process of production; they become gradually worn out over a period of years. Therefore the capitalist puts on to the other costs an item of "depreciation" based on the average life of such buildings, plant, and machinery as he uses; this depreciation charge is the recognition of the fact that a portion of the value of these items is passed on to the product in the process of production.

The third part of the value of the finished product represents the value "newly added" by the labour of the workers who transform the raw materials, using the plant, etc., into the finished product.

But whereas the value of the raw materials, plant, etc., used up in making the product corresponds with the value which he bought, and passes unchanged into the value of the finished product, the value newly added by the labour of his workers is greater than the value for which he pays his workers. In terms of cash, the workers are paid less in wages than the added value which their labour gives to the product.

Wages

The capitalist thinks of wages as the price paid for labour. Price is value expressed in money. The question to be answered, then, is: "What is the value of labour?"—or so it seems at first sight. However, a little thought shows that this is a meaningless question. Value itself depends on labour and so to ask: "What is the value of labour?" is rather like asking: "What is the heaviness of weight?" "How could we define, say, the value of a ten-hours working day? How much labour is contained in that day? Ten hours' labour. To say that the value of a ten-hours working day is equal to ten hours' labour, or the quantity of labour contained in it, would be a tautological and, moreover, nonsensical expression." (Marx, *Value, Price and Profit.*)

Evidently it is necessary to look more closely into this matter and to try to discover what precisely it is that a worker sells in exchange for the wages he receives. When a worker takes employment, when he "hires himself" to a capitalist, he, in fact, puts at the disposal of the capitalist for a specified length of time—an hour, a day, or a week—his *capacity* to work, that is, the "aggregate

68

of those mental and physical capabilities existing in a human being, which he exercises whenever he produces a use-value of any description." (*Capital*, Vol. I, LW p. 167, A p. 145.) The worker does not sell his labour, but his capacity to labour, his *labour-power*. He puts his labour-power temporarily at the disposal of the capitalist. The capitalist sets the worker to work and may use his capacities well or ill, wastefully or economically. The worker does not sell the actual contribution he makes to the creation of products; he sells his power to work, his labour-power. This distinction between *labour*—the actual expenditure of human skills and energies (on which depends the value of commodities)—and *labour-power*—the capacity or power to work (which the worker sells for wages)—is of great importance.

Wages are the price of labour-power. Since price is the money expression of value, the next task must be to find out how the value of labour-power is determined.

Value of Labour-power

The value of commodities, as has been shown, depends on the labour-time required for their production. This is, in fact, as true of *labour-power* as of other commodities. "The value of labour-power is determined, as in the case of every other commodity, by the labour-time necessary for the production, and consequently also the reproduction, of the special article. So far as it has value, it represents no more than a definite quantity of the average labour of society incorporated in it." (*Capital*, Vol. I, LW pp. 170–1, A p. 149.) The value of labour-power depends, then, upon the amount of labour-time that must be expended in order that labour-power may exist.

Labour-power exists only in living men and women. In order to live men must have the means of subsistence, food, clothing, fuel, shelter, etc. In order that labour-power may continue to exist, the workers must reproduce themselves, must have children; they must therefore have sufficient means of subsistence, not only for themselves, but also for their children. "The value of labour-power is determined by the value of the necessaries required to produce, develop, maintain, and perpetuate the labour-power." (Marx, *Value, Price and Profit.*)

The amount and kind of food, clothing, etc., required varies according to the kind of work done. Therefore the value of

69

different kinds of labour-power will vary. It will vary also because certain types of capacity and skill require a special education or training which takes time during which the worker has to live and on which other expenses may have to be incurred; all these expenses enter into the value of labour-power. Again the worker's "natural wants such as food, clothing, fuel, housing vary according to the climatic and other physical conditions of his country. On the other hand, the number and extent of his so-called necessary wants, as also the modes of satisfying them, are themselves the product of historical development . . . and depend therefore to a great extent on the degree of civilisation of a country, more particularly on the conditions under which, and consequently on the habits and degree of comfort in which, the class of free labourers has been formed. In contradistinction therefore to the case of other commodities, there enters into the determination of the value of labour-power a historical and moral element. Nevertheless, in a given country, at a given period, the average quantity of the means of subsistence necessary for the labourer is practically known." (Marx, *Capital*, Vol. I, LW p. 171, A p. 150.)

At the present time the distinction between "real wages" and "money wages" assumes particular importance since the value of money is liable to fluctuate greatly. By "real wages" are meant wages measured not in terms of money but in terms of the goods they will buy. Movements in real wages are normally measured by comparing the change in the cost-of-living index with the change in money wages.

As explained already in Chapter III,* the existence of a mass of dispossessed workers, "free" to work or starve, is a necessary condition of capitalist production. When there are always other workers to hand to take their place, the capitalist class can in general keep the workers' wages from rising above the subsistence level (as defined above), that is wages do not normally exceed the value of labour-power.

Summing up, therefore, we see that the value of labour-power resolves itself into a definite quantity of the means of subsistence which depends on (*a*) physical needs; (*b*) customary and historically developed needs; (*c*) requirements for upkeep of family; (*d*) expenses of education and training.

* See also Chapter V, pp. 98–9, dealing with capitalism's ever-present army of unemployed the "industrial reserve army".

The Living Standards of the Workers

In general, the capitalist class has gone to extreme lengths to ensure that the worker is not able to sell his labour-power above value, re-enacting often the violence of "primitive accumulation" in order to swell the ranks of the proletariat and to ensure that there are always more workers than jobs, always a "Reserve Army of Labour". If ever, in periods of labour scarcity, the workers are able to force some temporary concessions, the capitalists are certain at the earliest opportunity to take vigorous counter-measures, often using—as after the First and Second World Wars—the right-wing supporters of capitalism within the Labour movement to help them break resistance.

The general law that labour-power does not normally sell above its value is not disproved by national and other differences in wage levels. Historical circumstances, differences in physical needs due to differing productive or climatic conditions, general levels of education and training result in different levels of wages in different countries, different industries and different stages of history. Under such differing circumstances the minimum standard of living and the minimum of goods that the worker must be able to buy will necessarily be different. In order to make exploitation effective in face of changed economic circumstances it may even be necessary to raise living standards. The following extracts from *The Times* (17.12.48) illustrate this and other facts about the conditions of the proletariat in Africa at that time. "Formerly the low productivity of African labour was tolerated because it was cheap and abundant. . . . Natural idleness was checked by physical compulsion. Now development reaches a point where it cannot progress without greater individual effort. . . . Most Europeans have for centuries embraced a religious code which condemned idleness as wicked; his cults and taboos have more frequently taught the African that work is degrading or evil. His universal attachment to the land removes the threat of want if . . . he is prepared to live at a low level of subsistence. Simplicity of needs, together with shortage of consumer goods, robs money wages of their value. . . . Nobody can deny the ugly aspects of mass employment of natives in plantation, industry and mine." However, the African population of 160 millions "by greater effort . . . can produce surpluses which will raise its own standards *and minister to the need of others* [our italics]. . . . The problem, therefore, is how to improve the output of the individual native.

71

. . . First and foremost he must be made physically fitter . . . by means of improved diet. . . . It involves also improved health services. . . . Provision of consumer goods as incentives to labour is important. . . . Education reacts on productivity in many ways. . . . It engenders the desire to compete. . . . It can enable him to rise from the manual to the technical and even professional level. . . . It induces him to want a higher standard of living and therefore to work harder." Here it is argued that wages must be *raised* if profit produced per worker is to be increased.

Wages in the industrial centres of U.S., Britain and Western Europe are today considerably higher than they were in the nineteenth century when the conditions were most fully typical of industrial capitalism before the period of large monopolies and imperialism. In part the higher level of wages today may be attributed to concessions made to pressure from strongly organised trade union movements. In part the resources out of which to make such concessions have been provided by the accumulation of wealth in the main centres of imperialist power; this accumulation of wealth and the enrichment of the centres, has been largely at the expense of the economically more backward countries which were dominated by the industrially advanced. At the same time, productivity has greatly increased and wages viewed as a share of output have not generally increased and in many instances have fallen. Moreover, it is easy to exaggerate the extent to which wages have advanced over minimum needs, which must in contemporary society be regarded as including a much wider range of commodities than in a less developed economy.

In 1946 a wage of £5 15s. was necessary merely to keep a family with three children in health and working capacity (see *Wages Front*, by Margot Heinemann, p. 42). In October 1946 average weekly earnings for adult men *of all grades* were below £5 in flax spinning and weaving, small boot and shoe repair shops and local authorities' non-trading services, and below £5 10s. in woollen and worsted, lace, textile bleaching, dyeing and finishing, boot, shoe and slipper making, laundry service, saw milling and machined woodwork, building and decorating.

"Sir John Orr . . . found", writes Margot Heinemann, p. 42, "by a careful survey of actual family budgets and diets, that families spending less than 9s. per head per week on food in 1935

72

were in practice seriously under-supplied with many of the most important vitamins and minerals necessary to health. This group of families, judging from the available statistics of income distribution, included more than a third of the population. Since that date the increase in the price of food has been of the order of 42 per cent, so that the figure of 9s. in 1935 would be equivalent to 13s. in 1949. Since food expenditure even in the lower groups is seldom more than 40 per cent of income, it would seem likely that a family of five with an income of less than £8 2s. 6d. or thereabouts is likely to be living on a diet deficient in several important constituents." In 1936 the very bare "Rowntree minimum" for man, wife, and three children was 53s.; an official survey of earnings in all industries made in 1935 showed that earnings in general engineering averaged 52s. 6d. This level was exceeded in seventeen industries, the highest being newspaper printing, etc., 100s., and iron and steel smelting and rolling, 66s., and not reached in twenty-six industries, the lowest being wholesale tailoring and dressmaking, 31s.-33s., and cotton spinning, 32s. 6d.

Since 1948 up to 1960, average earnings for men in British manufacturing industry have increased from about £7 5s. a week to £15. and for women from £3 14s. to £7 7s. Average wage rates (as opposed to earnings which reflect increases in overtime working and shifts from lower to better paid industries) have increased less in this period (by 78 per cent for men and 84 per cent for women) and the cost of living rose by 58 per cent. "Real wage rates" (that is, money rates scaled down to allow for the increased cost of living) in this period increased, therefore, by about 15 per cent and "real earnings" by about one quarter. In this same period industrial output per person employed increased by about one third. There are inherent difficulties involved in all measurement of wages and any general statistical comparison should be regarded with great caution; but one may perhaps draw the broad conclusion that during the postwar period of relatively high employment in Britain advances in real wages averaged between 1 and 2 per cent per annum.

The Secret of Surplus Value

The values which workers produce far exceed the value of their means of subsistence, that is, the value of their labour-power, which the capitalist buys by paying wages.

73

The values which the capitalist acquires in the form of raw materials, factory buildings, machinery, etc., produce no new values but are embodied unchanged in the value of the final product. These values remain constant and for that reason this part of the employer's capital is described as *constant* capital. On the other hand the values which the employer devotes to wage payments expand, become more than they were to start with. They vary, and for this reason this part of his capital, namely wages, is called *variable* capital. All turns on the difference between the value of the worker's labour-power that the capitalist buys and the value that the worker creates when he is set to work. Labour-power is, in fact, a commodity which has the peculiar property of creating when it is used value greater than its own value. However free, open, and "fair" the labour market may be, the capitalist still stands to make his profit.

Once this is understood the secret of profit has been grasped; the source of profit is the difference between the value of the worker's labour-power and the value he produces. *The value which the worker produces over and above the value of his labour-power is called surplus value.*

The following figures relating to the cement industry provide a practical example. (The figures are in the main derived from those given in Dr. Rostas' survey in *Productivity, Prices and Distribution*, C.U.P. 1948.) In 1935 wages in the industry were about 65s. a week—rather more than the average for all industries. Cement sold (wholesale) for £2 a ton and the selling price paid to the works (the "factory selling price") was just under 30s. a ton, made up as follows:

	s.	d.	
Depreciation on fixed capital	3	7	} *Constant capital*
Materials, etc.	12	0	
Wages	4	0	*Variable capital*
Total costs per ton	19	7	
"Factory selling price"	29	7	
Margin over costs*	10	0	*Surplus value*

* The 10s. surplus includes 1s. 2d. a ton for payment of salaries of managerial staff, etc., a part of which should be accounted as production costs. In general, the true amount of surplus value is *underestimated* because additional surplus value goes—see Chapter VI—to the merchant out of the margin of 10s. between wholesale and "factory" price.

The Rate of Surplus Value and the Class Struggle

The unceasing aim and mission of the capitalist is to increase his profit, to expand his capital. He struggles, therefore, untiringly, by all and every means to increase his share of the values created by labour and to decrease the share going to the worker as wages. The ratio of surplus value to wages is described as *the rate of surplus value* (or, to express the same thing mathematically, the rate of surplus value equals s/v where s equals surplus value and v equals variable capital or wages). The rate of surplus value is also described as *the rate of exploitation*.

In the example from the cement industry the new values created by the workers' labour amount to 14s. in every ton of cement and a surplus of 10s. is produced on 4s. of variable capital (wages). The rate of surplus value is 10:4, that is 250 per cent (In British industry as a whole the rate of surplus value is at least 200 per cent—see Chapter X).

Of the new values produced a part is "paid for" in wages and a part is "unpaid" surplus value; so we may also say that the working day is similarly divided, thus:

WAGES	SURPLUS
Paid	*Unpaid*

In the cement industry in 1935 the division of seven hours' labour-time was, roughly, 12s. wages: 30s. surplus; or, two hours "paid": five hours "unpaid".

The capitalist ceaselessly strives to increase the rate of surplus value. This he may do in the following ways (which are dealt with more fully in the next chapter):

(i) by extending the working day without increasing wages,

(ii) by reducing wages without reducing the working day or output,

(iii) by increasing output per hour either by (*a*) forcing the worker to work harder per hour for the same wage, or by (*b*) improving methods of production.

The capitalist class struggles by every means to increase its share in the values newly created by the workers' labour. The interests of capitalist and worker are thus diametrically opposed; each struggles to change the division of the working-day in opposite directions, the one to increase wages, the other to increase profits, the one to end the wages-profit system, the

75

other to maintain it. The history of capitalism is the history of conflict between the capitalist class and the working class.

This struggle over the division of the working-day, the ceaseless striving to increase the rate of surplus value, is the economic basis of the class struggle. The class struggle springs, therefore, from the very essence of capitalist exploitation. It takes many forms, some directly economic within the factory, some concerning national policies with regard to social legislation and the social structure as a whole, yet others contesting the whole trend of international policies. The economic situation in which each capitalist finds himself helps to shape the class outlook hostile to any measures that appear likely to reduce the capitalist's share of surplus value. This has tended to create opposition to social progress even where such progress is necessary to the development of capitalism itself. For example, in the last century the capitalists fought against limitation of the working-day to ten hours; they fought against legislation curbing the brutal exploitation in factory and pit of children, not to say infants; they fought against social legislation extending health services, education, and so forth. Today also persistent opposition is offered to every extension in social service expenditure.

The greatest danger to profits and the profit system is united and combined action by those whom the capitalists exploit. They therefore fought for long by legislation to forbid trade union organisation, and when the forbidding of trade unionism was no longer possible they tried to hamper it, as, for example, in recent times with the Trades Disputes and Trade Union Act (1927) in the United Kingdom and the Taft-Hartley legislation (1947) in the U.S.A. When the capitalists feel themselves threatened, they try to enforce the extreme measure of legally outlawing trade unionism. Other types of legislation (for example, taxes hitting the low-income groups) are also used to further the interests of the capitalist class at the expense of the workers.

The exercise of force by the State is but the violent continuation of the domination which finds "peaceful" expression in legislation. Here again and again the use of force by the police or the armed forces protects the interests of the capitalist class. In the most ruthless form of capitalist State, the fascist State, the use of violence and terror against trade unionists and militant workers is resorted to continuously and unremittingly.

Finally, the control of the press and other means of disseminating information by capitalists or those whose outlook is that of the capitalists plays an important part in the class struggle. The workers are misinformed, confused, and misled by organs of propaganda which unceasingly depict events from the capitalist standpoint. In this field capitalist domination of social and economic thought is a matter of no small importance. All these are aspects and manifestations of the fact that whatever class holds the economically superior positions tends to subordinate the whole structure of society to its aims and attitudes.

The class struggle finds its most direct and open economic expression in strikes and lock-outs. "The incredible frequency of these strikes", wrote Engels in his *Condition of the Working Class in England in 1844*, "proves best of all to what extent the social war has broken out all over England". Again at the end of the nineteenth century there was a great new wave of strike struggles, the "match girls' " strike in 1888, then the gasworkers' strike, winning an eight-hour shift and a wage increase, then the great dock strike of 1889, and the formation of new mass unions of the unskilled. "The new unions were founded", writes Engels, "at a time when the faith in the eternity of the wages system was severely shaken." Throughout the period of capitalism's general crisis in the twentieth century, capitalism has been shaken by repeated waves of mass strike struggles. In the three years 1919 to 1921, 6¼ million workers were involved in strike struggles aggregating 150 million working days. In 1926, the year of the General Strike, 2,700,000 workers were on strike for a total of 160 million working days. Between 1929 and 1932, 1,700,000 workers were involved in over 1,600 disputes totalling 26 million working days.

As the crisis of capitalist society deepens the immediate economic demands of the workers become more and more bound up with political struggles. All the heroic battles of the workers within capitalism do little more than hold back the capitalists' attempts to force wages below the value of labour-power. Ought the working class on this account "to renounce their resistance against encroachments of capital, and abandon their attempts at making the best of the occasional chances of their temporary improvement? If they did", Marx answers, "they would be degraded to one level mass of broken wretches past salvation." However, "the working class ought not to exaggerate to themselves the ultimate working of these every-day struggles. They ought not to forget that they are fighting with effects but not with the

77

causes of those effects." (*Value, Price, and Profit.*) The most lasting achievements of the workers' struggles are the strength and experience they gain for new struggles. "They are the school of war of the working men", wrote Engels, "in which they prepare themselves for the great struggle that cannot be avoided; they are the pronunciamentos of single branches of industry that these, too, have joined the Labour movement." Inevitably the political and economic struggles of the workers interlock.

Thus, on the basis of the struggles of the British working class in the early nineteenth century, the Chartist movement developed; and at the end of the nineteenth century the Labour Party was formed in order to further the aims of the trade union movement in the political field. Ultimately the class struggle tends more and more towards aims that look beyond capitalism, necessitating a new type of political party and leadership in that it aims at merging struggle to advance day-to-day interests with the objective of taking State power and using it to effect a revolution in the economic basis, that is to take the key means of production out of private ownership and to replace profit as a motive force of economic activity by direct use of resources (integrated by economic planning instead of by the market) to meet social and individual needs. The trade unions are the *schools* in which the working class first learns not only the economics of day-to-day issues, but also the need to look beyond capitalism towards a fundamentally different type of economic system. Since the immediate results of the day-to-day struggles are necessarily limited, the working class "ought . . . not to be exclusively absorbed in these unavoidable guerilla fights. . . . They ought to understand that with all the miseries it imposes upon them, the present system simultaneously engenders the *material conditions* and the *social forms* necessary for an economic reconstruction of society. Instead of the *conservative* motto: 'A fair day's wages for a fair day's work!' they ought to inscribe on their banner the *revolutionary* watchword: 'Abolition of the wages system!' " (Marx, *Value, Price, and Profit.*)

CHAPTER V

CAPITAL AND ACCUMULATION

"Capital" Implies a Particular Historic Period

The title Marx gave to his main and most lengthy work, namely, *Das Kapital* or *Capital*, indicates the historical period on which his analysis was focused—that stage in the development of human society that is distinguished from others by the dominance of *capital*.

The word "capital" is commonly used with three types of meaning:

(i) as the store of means of production, tools, machines, houses, factories, mines, worked-upon land, stocks of food and raw materials, goods partly worked up, and finished products, etc.—all the various assets that help to further the production of what the community needs;

(ii) as a substantial *sum of money* that may be used to buy instruments of production, to pay wages, or purchase raw materials; in short the "wherewithal" to set up in business;

(iii) as State securities, stocks and shares in companies, etc., which may or may not represent real instruments of production, or money subscribed as shares or loans.

None of these are accurate or complete economic definitions. They describe aspects but not the essence of things. One gets nearer to the essence by considering who the capitalists are and what makes them such. The basic characteristic is membership of that comparatively small class of people who, individually and jointly, own the means of production.

In the United Kingdom in 1946, of the population over 25 years of age, about 1 in 10 only had fortunes over £1,000—and no one with less than that can own much in the way of means required for modern production. This "1 in 10" accounted for four-fifths of all private property in the United Kingdom. Big personal fortunes of £25,000 or over (and nothing less is sufficient to provide significant or influential holdings in most modern businesses) were owned by only 1 in every 250 persons, but between them they owned over one-third of all private property and a much higher proportion of company share-holdings through which today capitalists hold their legal title to the ownership of the main means of production. (Small shareholders, though numerous, are of negligible importance as "owners", being entirely subordinate to the policy prescribed by the major shareholders or financial backers.)

The word "capital" is often used in a general way to describe any forms of property; but what we are interested in is much more than just any property. We are concerned with capital as a central or rather *the* central element in a particular economic system. Property it is true can be turned into money and money into capital, but by performing what function does money become capital? Similarly we need to look beyond "stocks" or "shares" which are simply titles to part ownership of companies which in turn own means of production, have funds in the bank for payment of wages and so forth. In the modern world, therefore, our enquiries need to be directed to the activities of "companies", "firms", "corporations", etc. as the economic organisms through which owners of the means of production operate. This generally must be taken to be our meaning when we speak briefly, for example, of "capitalists engaged in production or commerce".

In themselves the means of production are of no use to the capitalist unless workers are there to work them. However, because the capitalist owns the means of production and the worker does not, he is able to force the worker to work for him. The workers' only alternative is to starve. So the worker does work for him, and when the worker applies himself to the means of production, surplus value is produced, and the capitalist gets an income from his possession of them which he would not get if no one worked on them. An idle factory—no income; a busy factory—£100,000 a year.

Capital Embodies Specific Social Relations and Historic Conditions

Evidently "capital" means something more than the common use would imply. Means of production have existed under all sorts of society and will go on existing; they in themselves have nothing to do with surplus value. Means of production do not become capital until they are owned by a small group in society *and used to extract surplus value*—which, in turn, can only be done because the workers are compelled by economic necessity to work for their capitalists. Capitalists facing workers in a commodity-producing society, capitalists owning money and means of production, workers free to work or starve: that is the essence of the matter. This is the foundation of all the normal capitalist illusions of a "free society". The worker sells his capacity to work in a "free" market; the capitalist buys it, sets the worker to work on *his* means of production, and sells the products in a free market. The capitalist makes profits and is rich; the worker gets his wages and stays poor. Is the worker compelled to produce profits for the capitalist? Of.course not! He is a free man; free to starve if he so prefers!

Capital, then, is not just a sum of money, or instruments of production, or stocks and shares; it is all these things, but under certain very definite historical and social conditions. These conditions are that the means of production are owned by a small group of people—the capitalists—opposite to whom stand the property-less workers compelled by economic and social necessity, because they have no means of working for themselves, to work for the capitalists and so produce surplus value. Capital therefore takes the material form of means of production, etc., but it is not capital by virtue of its material properties but by virtue of the social relation between the owners of means of production and the workers.

Capital as Dead Labour Ruling Over Living Labour

Outwardly the means of production are means of making future production easier. But inwardly what are they? Where did they come from? Did the capitalist make them? Of course not. They were all made by the workers—a week ago or twenty years ago. Therefore they embody workers' time and labour. But the labour they embody is now "dead". A factory without workers produces nothing. A farm with the labourers away produces only weeds. All these things need the human touch to vitalise them. The continuous application of human labour, present human labour, is needed to make them of any use to the capitalist. However, in capitalist society, it is the owners of the dead labour (instruments of production, raw materials, etc.) who dominate and subjugate the living labour. "It is only the dominion of accumulated, past,

81

materialised labour over direct, living labour, which turns accumulated labour into capital. Capital does not consist in accumulated labour serving living labour as a means of new production. It consists in living labour serving accumulated labour as a means of maintaining and increasing the exchange value of the latter." (Marx, *Wage, Labour and Capital*.)

The Turnover of Capital

Like a body of which the flesh and tissues must be continuously renewed if life is to be sustained, the physical substance of capital must continuously assume new forms, if capital is to "keep alive". A factory or machine that remains idle deteriorates and becomes obsolete and brings no profits to the capitalist, but a factory or machine in use gives up its value to the commodities produced and when the commodities are sold the capitalist gets back the values of the dead labour embodied in his means of production (raw material, machines, factory, etc.) plus the new values added by the living labour which repay what has gone into wages and provide him with a handsome amount of surplus value—the value over and above the value he started with. Life for capital means making profit; capital lives by being used. It must ceaselessly go through its cycle of transformations from money into raw materials, machines, and the wages of workers who use up these means of production in making the new commodities which are sold and so transformed back into money which again is transformed into raw materials, wages, etc., and so on until the cycle is again complete.

This process is called the turnover of capital. If the turnover is baulked, then capital is sick; profits are lost, and capital, unable to pursue its career of endlessly repeated transformations, dwindles in value and perishes. Of this sickness of capital, when the turnover is checked and thwarted, more will be said in Chapter VIII, which deals with capitalist crisis. For the moment it need only be shown that the very existence of capital hangs upon this unceasing turnover which, in turn, depends on a most intricate chain of links and interconnections in the market; for not only must the capitalist find workers "free" to sell their labour-power, he must also find other capitalists ready to sell him the machines, the raw materials, the tools, the fuel, the thousand requisites of the productive process; and when all is done, when the products are complete and ready for sale, the purchaser must be found who will give him in money the value of his products so that all may start over again.

Some Bourgeois Notions of Capital

Alfred Marshall, one of the most famous exponents of bourgeois economics, has the following definitions to offer. "The language of the market-place commonly regards a man's capital as that part of his wealth which he devotes to acquiring an income in the form of money. . . . It may be convenient sometimes to speak of this as his *trade capital;* which may be defined to consist of those external goods which a person uses in his trade, either holding them to be sold for money or applying them to produce things that are to be sold for money. Among its conspicuous elements are such things as the factory and the business plant of a manufacturer, that is, his machinery, raw materials, any food, clothing and house-room that he may hold for the use of his employees and the goodwill of his business." (Marshall, *Principles of Economics*, Eighth Edition, Macmillan, 1938, pp. 71-72.) Later he adds: "By far the most important use of the term Capital in general, i.e., from the social point of view, is in the inquiry how the three agents of production, land (that is, natural agents), labour, and capital, contribute to producing the national income . . . and how that income is distributed among the three agents. And this is an additional reason for making the terms Capital and Income correlative from the social as we did from the individual point of view. Accordingly it is proposed in this treatise to count as part of capital from the social point of view all things other than land, which yield income that is generally reckoned as such in common discourse." (p. 78.) That is really all Marshall had to say about the nature of capital, and throughout bourgeois economics the analysis and definition of capital tends to be superficial, amounting generally to little more than Marshall's observation that ownership of property is a source of income and the corresponding definition of capital as that which produces income. For example, a widely used textbook of a later period (*Economics* by F. Benham, Pitman, 1946, p. 138) says: "It is generally agreed that capital is a *stock* or *fund* existing at a given moment, as opposed to income, which is a *flow* over time: so much per week or per year." For any analysis of capital to produce results which are richer in scientific content it is necessary to pay attention to (a) the *historical* setting of the capitalist system and (b) the social and economic relations that make possible the use of wealth as capital.

"Fetishism of Commodities"

Marx, in his chapter on "The Fetishism of Commodities" writes (*Capital*, Vol. I): "A commodity appears at first sight a very trivial thing, and easily understood. Its analysis shows that it is, in reality, a very queer thing, abounding in metaphysical subtleties and theological niceties."

Marx then goes on to show that the relations of men in production (that is, the relation of each producer to the total productive efforts of society, and the relationship of classes in production) appear only in the exchange of commodities on the market, and that there the value of the commodity makes itself felt as though it were a property belonging to the commodity in itself and quite independently of the human being engaged in production. So it is that bourgeois economists see things exclusively in terms of relations of exchange. Their whole theory aims at being a theory of the market, and fails because it does not recognise that relations between commodities on the market must be seen as a *reflection* of the relations of men in production if the real nature of commodity exchange and the laws governing the level of prices are to be understood.

"A definite social relation between men", says Marx, ". . . assumes . . . the fantastic form of a relation between things. In order, therefore, to find an analogy, we must have recourse to the mist-enveloped regions of the religious world. In that world the productions of the human brain appear as independent beings endowed with life, and entering into relation both with one another and the human race. So it is in the world of commodities with the products of men's hands. This I call the Fetishism which attaches itself to the products of labour, so soon as they are produced as commodities." (*Capital*, Vol. I, LW p. 72, A p. 43.)

Men only begin studying the society in which they live when that society has fully developed. The social scientist has therefore to take a course, as Marx puts it, in the opposite direction to historical development. He starts with the results of social development ready to hand before him. Society has certain developed forms and set characteristics which do not seem to be subject to change, but rather to have existed from the beginning of time and to be destined to remain in existence until the end of time.

It is just these set forms which belong to and have developed historically as a part of a particular mode of production (namely, commodity production) that the capitalist economists accept as eternal facts which require no further explanation or analysis. It is this which makes their doctrines superficially plausible and at the same time prevents them from giving a scientific and penetrating explanation of economic realities. "To what extent some economists", writes Marx, "are misled by the Fetishism inherent in commodities, or by the objective appearance of the social characteristics of labour, is shown, amongst other ways, by the dull and tedious quarrel over the part played by nature in the formation of exchange-value. Since exchange-value is a definite social manner of expressing the amount of labour bestowed upon an object, nature has no more to do with it, than it has in fixing the course of exchange." (*Capital*, Vol. I, LW p. 82, A p. 54.) And, says Marx, when they deal with capital their "superstition comes out as clear as day".

Fixed and Circulating Capital

The sums of value (embodiments of "congealed" labour) that figure as capital, assume, as has been seen, a number of different forms—money, shares in companies, machinery, factories, raw materials, etc. Some of these forms merely represent titles to ownership (as a *share* represents a title to ownership of a certain part or share of the capital of a company); some are "real" forms that capital assumes in the course of its turnover. The forms assumed by capital are classified in various ways; there is (and this is of particular importance for the purposes of capitalist accounting) the distinction between *fixed* and *circulating* capital. *Fixed capital* denotes buildings, plant, machinery, etc., all those things necessary to the process of production which are used over and over again and yield up in each cycle of production only a part of their value.

With fixed capital is contrasted *circulating capital*. Whereas fixed capital is used up gradually and yields its value gradually, the material form assumed by circulating capital (leather, for example, used by a shoe-maker) is consumed during the creation of the individual product into which the whole of its value is embodied "at one go". Circulating capital consists broadly of raw materials and wages. It is not "tied up", it turns over rapidly, and at the end of each turnover the capitalist is free to decide what he does with it—he can either put it to the same use as before, or put it to some other use. The *fixed* capital on the other hand is "tied up". It either has to be used for the purpose it was designed to serve or it lies idle, its value wasting away without yielding any profit. The distinction between fixed capital on the one hand, and circulating capital on the other, since it draws attention to the fact that different parts of the capital turn over at different rates, is therefore very important to the capitalist who is calculating all the time how to secure as big profits as he can. However, this distinction, important as it is, masks a more fundamental distinction, that between constant and variable capital, which whilst of little significance to the capitalist who is calculating how to maximise profits, is fundamental to an understanding of how the economic system as a whole works.

Constant and Variable Capital

In order to understand capitalist society and its "laws of motion", it is necessary before all else to grasp the relationship of classes, workers and capitalists. In this the distinction between *constant* and *variable* capital is of fundamental importance. The means of production are not, it has been seen, by themselves of any use; they are only means to produce surplus value. This is true of machinery and equally true of raw materials. The value in them is "dead" and needs the current touch of living labour to be brought to life. Then the value in the machinery (a smaller or larger part of the total value of the machine depending on the length of the life of the machine by comparison with the production period) and the value in the raw materials, value produced by other labour some time in the past, passes—unchanged in size—into the new product. The value of all these commodities, which were produced some time in the past, remains *constant*. *All, therefore, that the capitalist spends on commodities other than labourpower, everything, in fact, that he puts into the productive process, is called constant capital.*

On the other hand, the surplus value that the capitalist aims to get all comes from the living, current labour. He pays out wages (buys labour-power) and the worker produces a value greater than the value of his own labour-power; he adds to the value of the raw materials and machines he uses, a new value greater than that the capitalist pays out in wages. Capital expended on wages therefore does not stay the same, it grows, changes; it is *variable.*

We therefore call the capital expended on labour-power (the wages bill), variable capital. (See also Chapter IV, pp. 73–4.)

Variable capital is the money the capitalist spends on wages. Outwardly wages are, of course, just money. The worker receives his money and spends it on food, clothing, housing, pleasure, and so on; but for the employer all this is a capital investment. It is an investment by him in human labour. If he doesn't pay—then his capital does not go on turning over, it does not keep alive and it yields him no surplus value. If he does—then he gets the worker in his factory; and gets his surplus value. The capitalist does not therefore "give" employment; what he pays in wages is *variable capital which is an investment in human labour*, the advance of food, clothing, etc., to keep the worker alive and active. It is by advancing this variable capital, by using labour power, that the capitalist class get their surplus value.

Absolute and Relative Surplus Value

The motive of capitalist production is profit. The key to increased profit is to increase the unpaid portion of the working day in relation to the paid, to increase the surplus product in relation to the product necessary to supply the workers' means of subsistence or, to say the same thing in other words, to increase the the rate of surplus value (s/v).

The most obvious way of trying to do this is by lengthening the working day without increasing wages. With this aim the early industrial capitalists indulged in the most brutal exploitation of their workers. Women and children were driven as ruthlessly as men to endure hours of work that, literally, killed them. Speaking of the match industry, Karl Marx writes: "Of the witnesses that Commissioner White examined (1863), 270 were under 18, fifty under 10, ten only 8, and five only 6 years old. A range of the working day from 12 to 14 or 15 hours, night-labour, irregular meal times, meals for the most part taken in the very workrooms that are pestilent with phosphorus." (*Capital*, Vol. I, LW p. 246, A p. 230.)

The history of Britain a century ago is crammed with innumerable examples from every industry of the most horrible exploitation by extending the working hours to the very limits of human endurance; indeed, beyond the limits in so far as countless workers were driven by the exactions of capital to an early death. A halt was called to this industrial murder only after long years of struggle by the workers, in which the Chartist movement played a big part. "Capital is reckless of the health or length of life of the labourer, unless under compulsion from society." (*Capital*, Vol. I, LW p. 270, A p. 255.) Compulsion did not become effective until 1860; at last the Government began to provide for adequate enforcement of laws limiting the working day. (The many laws enacted in earlier years had been largely ineffective since no inspectorate had been provided to see that the provisions of the laws were observed.)

As today the tendency of those who support the capitalist system is to fear any measures that might cut into profits and so to oppose—unjustifiably, relatively to technical advance—expenditure on social progress or raising living standards, similarly in the past fear of anything that might reduce surplus value led to arguments justifying the degradation and murder of countless proletarians by intolerable lengthening of work into all hours of the day and night. For example, Nassau W. Senior, Professor of Political Economy at Oxford, used his authority to fight against the agitation for a ten-hour working-day, and solemnly wrote that in a typical cotton-mill "the whole net profit is derived from the last hour". (Senior, *Letters on the Factory Act, as it Affects Cotton Manufacture*, London, 1837.)

Senior's contention was soon given the lie by events themselves. Capitalism had to accept the Ten-Hours Act (1874) and turned to new ways of increasing its profits. As usual, capital had been blinded by greed, and evidence was soon to be forthcoming that the product of the reduced working hours was in fact as great as that of the longer hours.

Since the middle of the nineteenth century the main effort of the capitalist class has been to increase surplus value by getting more out of a limited number of working hours rather than by ruthless extension of the working time. This change in emphasis has not, of course, prevented the capitalists from fighting against reducing and for lengthening the working day as and when opportunity has offered. The main emphasis has, however, been on packing more and more productive effort into each minute of the seven, eight, nine or ten hours of the "normal" working day which each worker spends in the factory. In short, the main thing has been to increase the *intensity* of work.

Clearly, if an employer can get his workers, without extra pay, to do as much in each hour as before they did in two (by, say, getting workers in the weaving industry to supervise twice as many looms) he is as well off as if he had doubled the working day.

There are a number of devices which help the capitalist to increase intensity of work. These include (1) *Strict supervision and discipline*, that is, fines for lateness or absences (such as going to the lavatory) during working hours, curtailment of meal-times, etc. (2) *Methods of wage payment*. The forms of wage payment become a battleground between the employer and the trade unions. Piece-wages, that is, wages based on ouput, provide the capitalist with a means of forcing the worker to work hard throughout the working day, since on this depends how much the worker takes home at the end of the week. At first sight it might seem that the payment of piece-wages contradicts what has been said previously about wages and the value of labour-power approximating to the value of the worker's means of subsistence. Payment "by the piece", that is, according to output, suggests that when production goes up wages will go up correspondingly. This is only true in the very short run. Workers' experience through many decades has shown that piece-wages are always in the end fixed at prices which are based on time-wages and the sum of goods that the worker must buy in order to live. If production increases sharply the piece-rates are soon cut. Piece-wages for a full day's work may, it is true, tend to work out at a little more than the time-rate for the day, but against this must be set the fact that greater intensity of the work increases the worker's needs. However, it pays the capitalist to pay more for piece-work since the extra exertion called forth increases the amount of surplus value produced by an amount that considerably exceeds any little extra paid in wages.

The capitalist pays the worker "by the piece" in order to make him stretch himself, but he takes good care to see that the total wage he pays approximates to the value of the worker's labour-power. What the worker earns has, therefore, little to do with the value that he produces.

(3) *Conveyor-belt and other speeding-up systems*. Not all productive processes are equally adaptable to piece-work. Capital in the past sought by a variety of means to get the advantages of the piece-work system even where it was not applicable; for example, jobs in which the output of each individual worker could not be assessed were sub-contracted to the leader of a team of workers

(as in the butty system in the mines). In modern factory organisation the conveyor-belt and similar systems have been adopted
over an increasingly wide range of industries. In the conveyor-
belt system "the job" is carried along on a moving belt and each
operation must be carried out at the speed dictated by the belt.
The worker cannot, therefore, ease off when he feels inclined to
do so.

(4) *"Cajoling" methods.* As the workers have increased their
political strength and have improved their organisations, the
capitalists have needed more and more to supplement brute
force and the threat of the sack by "cajoling methods". Many
capitalists try, by providing minor amenities, to "appease"
their workers and so to get more out of them. By introducing
such devices as profit-sharing* and pension schemes they hope
to mask exploitation and to give their workers a material incentive to stay in their employ.

To sum up, then, the capitalist may increase the unpaid
labour that he appropriates either by lengthening the working
day or by increasing the intensity of work. Both methods "get
more out of the worker", both methods add to the amount of
surplus value that the worker produces, directly and simply
because he does more work for the capitalist.

The capitalist would also increase the rate of surplus value if he
forced a reduction in wages. This he repeatedly tries to do but
here a limit is imposed by the minimum necessary to maintain the
workers in a fit condition for work. There are, however, other
ways in which the unpaid portion of the working-day (the surplus)
may be increased relatively to the paid portion (wages). For
example, if by improved methods of production the worker's
output is increased, the capitalist's surplus relatively to wages
will increase. His surplus will also increase, if the value of labour-
power falls because the value of the worker's means of subsistence
falls (for example, if the labour-time required to produce a bushel
of wheat falls and the value of bread falls correspondingly). In
these latter cases the surplus increases, even if the length or the
intensity of the working-day is not increased; although there is no
absolute increase in the amount of effort expended by the worker,
his share in the product of his working-time is *relatively* less. The

---

* Detailed analysis of profit-sharing schemes operating in Britain in the
1920s and 1930s showed that wages plus profit shares in firms operating such
schemes averaged less than wages paid by other firms in the industry.

distinction between the method of increasing surplus value described in this paragraph (*relative surplus value*) and that described in the preceding paragraph (*absolute surplus value*) is of considerable importance.

The following is Marx's definition: "The surplus value produced by prolongation of the working day, I call *absolute surplus value*. On the other hand, the surplus value arising from the curtailment of the necessary labour-time, and from the corresponding alteration in the respective lengths of the two components of the working day, I call *relative surplus value*." (*Capital*, Vol. I, LW p. 315, A p. 304.)

Relative and absolute surplus value are often found going hand in hand. In the early nineteenth century the very machines that increased productivity at the same time made possible the ruthless extension of the working day of the machine-minders and the merciless depression of wages as more and more unskilled women and children were employed. In the twentieth century the conveyor-belt and "stop-watch" methods of increasing the intensity of work have gone hand in hand with technical developments.

Relative Surplus Value

Relative surplus value arises from increased productivity due to better machinery, better organisation, and other technical advances that the capitalist may introduce; but—if we go to the root of the matter—only in so far as these result in cheapening the workers' necessaries of life. The capitalist who improves methods of production is compelled not by a desire to lighten the work of the worker or to enrich the community at large, but by the categorical imperative governing his existence as a capitalist that he must try always to increase profits. The economic situation of the capitalist compels him, whether he wishes it or not, to be an instrument of technical progress. When he introduces improved methods of production he does so because he hopes to get a greater output per worker and to reduce costs per unit of output. The capitalist calculates his costs against the market value, which is determined by the *average socially necessary labour-time*. By introducing a new and improved technique he will reduce his labour-time per product below the social average and will reap an extra profit accordingly so long as this happy state of affairs lasts. The lure of extra profit unceasingly stimulates technical change, particularly under conditions of unfettered competition between capitalist and capitalist. Under these circumstances the advanced technique does not for long remain advanced and above the social average. Therefore the reduced labour-time of the one or two advanced capitalists becomes general and the average socially necessary labour-time falls and with it the market value. In this way the extra surplus value will be lost and with it the higher rate of surplus value, unless the value of labour-power also falls. However, it is more than probable that the improved methods of production will directly or indirectly reduce the value of the workers' necessaries of life and therefore reduce the value of labour-power. If this happens, the paid portion of the working-day will be reduced and the surplus increased for the capitalist class as a whole, and there will be a relative increase in surplus value. The rate of exploitation in modern capitalism is in fact often increasing in this way; for example, during the boom in U.S.A. in the 1920s when wages were rising fast, profits rose even more rapidly and the rate of surplus value as indicated by Census of Production figures (the true rate was higher) rose from 106 per cent in 1921 to 152 per cent in 1929.

The way in which increased productivity increases the rate of surplus value is illustrated from the cement industry in Britain to which reference has already been made in Chapter IV (p. 74). Using Dr. Rostas' figures as a basis, we may make the following comparison which shows how the rate of exploitation increased between 1924 and 1935.

Cement: Costs and Surplus
per ton

	1924	1935
(1) Materials	21/-	12/-
(2) Depreciation of fixed capital ..	6/-	3/6
(3) Wages	8/-	4/-
(4) "Factory" selling price* ..	43/-	29/6
(5) Surplus	8/-	10/-
(6) Rate of surplus value [(5):(3)] ..	100%	250%

During this period of eleven years output per worker increased greatly—from 370 tons a year in 1924 to 783 tons in 1935. The industry was "rationalised" and technically developed (horse-

* Wholesale prices per ton were £3 in 1924 and £2 in 1935.

power per worker was even by 1930 more than double what it was in 1924). Despite the huge increase in output the weekly earnings of the workers hardly changed. (Average hours of work increased 4 per cent and average earnings per hour by 1 per cent.)

Total operatives employed fell from 12,450 in 1924 to 8,300 in 1935, but output increased from 3.2 million tons to 5.9 million tons. Applying the figures in the table above to the total output figures we get the following picture for the industry as a whole:

		£ million		
Constant Capital		*1924*	*1935*	
used up in the ∫	Fixed Capital	.96	1.03	Fixed Capital
year: ⎰	Materials	3.36	3.54 ⎱	Circulating
Variable Capital:	Wages	1.28	1.18 ∫	Capital
	Surplus	1.28	2.95	
	Total	6.88	8.70	

These figures show that, whilst wages stayed much the same, the surplus was more than doubled as a result of the increased productivity. Dr. Rostas' analysis also shows how works with lower labour-time per ton output (usually the larger ones) got a bigger share of the surplus value than works in which labour-time per ton output was above the average (usually the smaller firms). Output per head in eight establishments employing between eleven and forty-nine workers was 560 tons and "the gross margin" (the surplus plus depreciation on fixed capital) was 10s. 5d. a ton. Output per head in ten establishments employing between 200 and 750 workers was 731 tons and "the gross margin" was 14s. 7d. a ton.

Accumulation and Capitalist Competition

It is a commonplace observation, now as in the past, here or in other capitalist countries, that a capitalist, whatever profits he may be making, is always struggling for more. But it is a quite wrong, upside down procedure to attribute the character of the system to greed for money; on the contrary, the greediness with which its agents behave must be attributed to the economic system. The hotter the rivalry between competing capitals the more is single-mindedness in the pursuit of profit a necessary condition of survival as a capitalist. The natural laws of capitalism tend to eliminate those who do not seek continuously to increase their wealth. In general only a portion of the surplus value will be consumed by the capitalist on his means of living; the balance is used to buttress him in his unceasing fight against his rivals. This balance he turns into new capital which in its turn will enable him to appropriate additional surplus value. This process of turning surplus value into new capital is called *accumulation*.

Surplus value which is turned into capital may be used in a number of different ways. It may be directly "put back into the business" and used to expand the scale of production to support additional wages and material costs involved in the expansion of production or to buy new plant. One of the leading firms in the cement industry, for example—the Associated Portland Cement Manufacturers—reinvested in plant £3.8 million out of the surplus produced between 1924 and 1935 and their capacity is estimated over this period to have increased from 1,280,000 tons a year to 2,240,000 tons a year. Accumulated surpluses may also be used to form money reserves which through the banks and the financial system generally will be loaned to other capitalists at an appropriate rate of interest (see Chapter VI, pp. 121–3). Such funds, when the moment is opportune, may be taken back to finance new expansions in production under the direct control of the capitalist undertaking in which the surplus was produced. Alternatively, the accumulated surplus may be removed altogether from the undertaking in which it was produced and be invested far afield. The period of monopoly capitalism has, in particular, brought many changes in the *forms* of capital accumulation. Banks, insurance companies and other financial institutions serve as agencies for collecting on a wide social scale "savings", accumulations of profits and other unused funds. These are then made available for use as capital in other fields. This centralisation of funds is an important factor in relation to the development of monopoly capitalism and imperialism, which is dealt with later. In this period (particularly at the end of the nineteenth and beginning of the twentieth centuries) much of the accumulated capital was directed away from Britain to seek more profitable fields of investment in colonial and other territories.

The Organic Composition of Capital

As technical methods improve it is clear that, in addition to the greater expenditure on machinery, etc., the amount of raw materials that each worker uses up in the course of his day's work greatly increases. Consequently (even though the relative value of raw materials, etc., may fall), in the course of time wages tend, as capitalism develops, to form a smaller part of the capitalist's outlay—that is, the ratio of variable to constant capital becomes smaller. Of course, conditions in separate industries differ greatly but under the pressure of capitalist competition and accumulation the over-all tendency inevitably is for the amount of constant capital in capitalism as a whole to increase relative to variable capital. This ratio, constant : variable capital (c/v) is described as the *organic composition of capital*, and the smaller variable capital (wages) is in relation to constant capital (machinery and raw materials, etc.), the *higher* is the organic composition said to be. (Whilst the general notion of the *organic composition of capital* is not difficult to grasp as the relationships between capital used to buy labour power and capital used to buy means of production, between *living* and *dead* labour, the reader should be warned that the *measurement* of this relationship involves considerable theoretical as well as practical difficulties. Currently, profound theoretical work is being done on this problem by P. Sraffa of Cambridge; see, for example, his *Production of Commodities by Means of Commodities*, C.U.P. 1960.)

The Concentration and Centralisation of Capitalism

Closely allied to the technical developments in methods of production which are instigated by competition between capitalists is the tendency for the capital used in production to be concentrated in larger and larger amounts.

On the one hand the technically most advanced firms will tend to make the greatest profits and the funds available to them for accumulation will tend accordingly to be the greatest. On the other hand, the larger firms will be in the best position to adopt new methods of production requiring highly specialised and costly machinery, large-scale organisation, etc., and also to raise funds for expansion. There will therefore be a tendency for the larger productive units to get larger still. In some branches of industry (such as steel towards the end of the nineteenth century or artificial silk in the twentieth century) it will be hopeless for capital below a certain size to compete. The small capitalists will be crushed out, or must find means of operating in branches of industry where small-scale production is better able to carry on. In such industries, however, they will face the competition of a host of other small capitalists in the same predicament as themselves and will confront the everpresent danger that large-scale production may succeed in invading their territory. In times of economic crises a host of small capitalists will be bankrupted or forced to sell out to larger capitalists. Thus, in addition to the enlargement of individual capitals out of their own accumulated profits, etc. (the *concentration* of capital), individual capitals again and again lose their independence and are brought under centralised control (the *centralisation* of capital); capitalist, says Marx, expropriates capitalist.

The development of banking and credit will further speed both the concentration and centralisation of capital. Thus the capitalist mode of production necessarily leads to the development of larger and larger capitals. (The consequences of this important law of capitalist development are dealt with in Chapter IX, on Imperialism.)

Social Consequences of Capitalist Accumulation

Capital never stands still. It either marches forward extending its power, growing richer, replacing old plant and equipment with new, acquiring new undertakings and new markets, or else it is crushed or absorbed by rivals who have fared better in the ruthless and ceaseless competition between capitalist and capitalist. The small capitalists are in this way continually being broken and driven out of business, and the influence and wealth (particularly the share in ownership and control of the means of production) of the big capitalists increase at their expense.

The small capitalists are not, however, wiped out of existence. Periodically their numbers may actually increase as new capitalists set up in business, but the share of production in the hands of the small capitalists tends to decrease, their weight and say in economic affairs become less; they are more and more at the mercy of the big capitalists.* At the same time, small non-capitalist traders and "business men" such as craftsmen working on their own, peasant-farmers (not in Britain but in colonial countries and in Europe in great numbers), small shopkeepers, "one-man firms" continue in existence. Despite constant additions to the numbers of the small firms, the share all these people have in the business to be done is a constantly diminishing one. There

---

* Small firms tend to become more and more dependent on sub-contracts from large firms, and so to be put at their mercy.

is an unceasing inflow to their ranks as one or another individual makes a bid to get away from the situation of a proletarian and to escape the material and personal restrictions that go with selling one's labour-power. But the dice are loaded against success in this venture and the inflow is always matched by an outflow into the ranks of wage earners and "down and outs". So the tendency is for many of the small firms to collapse and for one-man businesses to produce only miserable incomes more precarious and often less than those of wage earners.

Over great areas of the world in colonial and former colonial territories and in "peasant countries" generally, small commodity production, that is production for the market by individuals or individual families using such means of production as are available to them, is imposed by lack of any economic alternative, by the absence of all opportunity for employment in larger scale and more modern economic enterprises. On the many hundreds of millions so situated the concentration of production and centralised accumulation of capital in the industrially advanced centres of capitalism makes its impact felt as, for them, a persisting economic crisis from which they are unable to escape to any alternative. That is, viewed on a world wide scale, the concentration of capital leads to an expansion throughout the world of economic activity by the most wealthy capitalist organisms, but it does not lead to the absorption of more than a minute fraction of the millions who are nonetheless directly or indirectly affected in a most severe way by the impact of big capital. The millions whose markets and whose economic way of life is destroyed by the growth of modern industries and techniques elsewhere, are hardly at all absorbed *within* the industrial system on which the world wide power and influence of big capital is based.

What are the fortunes of the workers as the mass and power of capital increases? "It is questionable", said John Stuart Mill in his *Principles of Political Economy*," if all the mechanical inventions yet made have lightened the day's toil of any human being." Mill said that a hundred years ago; however, it is still questionable, at least if we add Marx's qualification that Mill should have excluded the well-to-do idlers whose number machinery has greatly increased. Marx comments that the aim of capitalist application of machinery is not to lighten human toil. "Like every other increase in productiveness of labour, machinery is intended to cheapen commodities, and, by shortening that portion

97

of the working day in which the labourer works for himself, to lengthen the other portion that he gives, without an equivalent, to the capitalist. In short, it is a means for producing surplus value." (*Capital*, Vol. I, LW p. 371, A pp. 365–6.)

The measurement and comparison of standards of life at widely separated times is not an easy matter; but certain broad tendencies are clear. Even in the era of capitalism's greatest prosperity in the nineteenth century, the numbers of workers seeking jobs always exceeded the number of jobs available. From the middle to the end of the nineteenth century unemployment, now rising, now falling, averaged about 5 per cent of those seeking work. In England the position of the working class was exceptionally favourable in comparison with other European countries (the fruit of trade union organisation and of England's industrial supremacy in the nineteenth century); but though real wages probably rose by 50 per cent in the latter half of the nineteenth century, ouput per worker increased by at least 100 per cent. The relative position of the workers therefore deteriorated considerably.

The progress of capitalist accumulation inevitably swells the industrial reserve army of unemployed labour. As the total social capital is increased, the organic composition of capital rises and the investment in the form of wages (variable capital) decreases relatively. This tendency may be illustrated with figures taken from the U.S. Census of Production; the total annual turnover of capital (including only the "used up" portion of fixed capital) increased from 8.8 billion dollars in 1899 to 18.9 billion dollars in 1914—an increase of 115 per cent. The variable part of this capital (wages) increased from 2.0 to 4.1 billion dollars over the same period—an increase of only 105 per cent.

Growth in the working population coupled with the forcing of new recruits into the ranks of the proletariat as capitalism invades the territory of non-capitalist production (including, in particular, that of craftsmen and peasant-producers) brings a more rapid increase in the numbers of the "propertyless" seeking jobs than the number of jobs created by the expansion of capitalist production. Thus capitalism creates an army of unemployed, what Marx termed the industrial reserve army. This reservoir of unemployed creates the illusion of over-population; it seems that there are more men than can be provided for from available economic resources. In fact, however, it is not the case that the physical resources are insufficient, but simply that under capitalist conditions of production and property ownership the numbers of those who can live only by selling their power to work necessarily tend more and more to exceed the numbers that capitalism will employ. "The greater the social wealth", writes Marx, "the functioning capital, the extent and energy of its growth, and, therefore, also the absolute mass of the proletariat and the productiveness of its labour, the greater is the industrial reserve army. . . . The greater this reserve army in proportion to the active labour army, the greater is the mass of a consolidated surplus population, whose misery is in inverse ratio to its torment of labour. The more extensive, finally, the lazarus-layers of the working class, and the industrial reserve army, the greater is official pauperism. *This is the absolute general law of capitalist accumulation.* . . . Accumulation of wealth at one pole is, therefore, at the same time accumulation of misery, agony of toil, slavery, ignorance, brutality, mental degradation, at the opposite pole, i.e. on the side of the class that produces its own product in the form of capital." *(Capital,* Vol. I, LW p. 644–5, A pp. 659–61.)

For the capitalist the "reserve army" of unemployed seems a heaven-sent blessing. In times of prosperity it provides for him the additional workers he requires; in times of depression it enables him, because of the ever-present threat of unemployment that faces the worker, to cut wages and so, he hopes, to recoup his dwindling profits.

However, all is not as it seems. The capitalist method of production is caught in a contradiction from which it cannot escape. Each capitalist strives to increase his profits and in doing so strives to cut the worker's share in the values he produces. He strives to increase output and at the same time reduce "his labour costs". Capitalism grows and expands; it subjects to itself an ever greater part of the world. In the end everywhere the very masses whom it exploits to gain its profits have become the main market to whom it seeks to sell its products. Each capitalist wishes his own workers poor so that his profits may be high, and the rest of the world rich so that they may buy his products.

The impoverishment of the masses, however, brings its own vengeance. The workers, whom capitalism has brought together in the great factories and towns that it creates, stand together in unity and learn, as the laws of capitalism work themselves out, that they must oppose the operations of these laws and the policies of those who defend the system from which they spring.

In the upshot capitalism is unable to reach a state of economic or social stability and plunges in every country from one round of economic and political crises and wars to the next. All the machines and modern means of production, whilst they remain in capitalist ownership, are governed in their use by the aim of increasing surplus value. If they serve to lighten man's toil, it is either an incidental by-product of other motives or else the result of demands pressed by the workers against or in spite of the workings of the economic system. They do not lead directly to the result that one might be led to expect, namely, that technical command over nature would automatically lead to improved conditions of life and ease the economic and social tensions of the system. On the contrary, the development of the means of production within the capitalist system has generated processes which cause its social and political tensions to become more acute. It is not difficult to see that this is so when all is reckoned in the account—not only what wages will buy, but also mass unemployment for years on end, the strained speed of modern production, drudgery and boredom at work, insecurity, anxiety, poverty, colonial exploitation and the repeated scourge of war.

"In all countries," said Marx in his inaugural address to the first International Working Men's Association (1864), "it has now become a truth demonstrable to every unprejudiced mind and only denied by those whose interest it is to hedge other people in a fool's paradise, that no improvement of machinery, no appliance of science to production, no contrivances of communication, no new colonies, no immigration, no opening of markets, no free trade, nor all these things put together, will do away with the miseries of the industrious masses; but that, on the present false base, every fresh development of the productive powers of labour must tend to deepen social contrasts and point social antagonisms."

This remains true of capitalist society today, though the social contrasts and antagonisms assume constantly new and unexpected forms. In one country or another as a result of the strength of the workers' movement coupled with an expansion in the surplus value available to the capitalists (as, for example, in the industrially advanced countries of the imperialist powers), material conditions for the workers have improved, if the comparison is made over considerable periods of time. But despite changes in the quantity of material goods available to employed wage-workers and improvements in social services in some places, it is clear that insecurity, acute social tensions and the degradation and perversion of man's working activity remain. One must conclude, as is evident from events in the century since Marx spoke the words quoted above, that the economic processes of capitalist development tend to increase social instability and to degrade the condition of man.

CHAPTER VI

THE DISTRIBUTION OF SURPLUS VALUE

"The capitalist", says Marx, "who produces surplus value—
i.e. who extracts unpaid labour directly from the labourers, and
fixes it in commodities, is, indeed, the first appropriator, but
by no means the ultimate owner, of this surplus value. He has to
share it with capitalists, with landowners, etc., who fulfil other
functions in the complex of social production. Surplus value,
therefore, splits up into various parts. Its fragments fall to various
categories of persons, and take various forms, independent the
one of the other, such as profit, interest, merchants' profit, rent,
etc." (*Capital*, Vol. I, LW p. 564, A p. 576.)

We may now consider the principal economic laws which
determine how the total surplus value produced by the productive workers as a whole is divided out between capital in
different branches of industry and between different kinds of
capital, such as commercial capital and loan or bank capital.

The Rate of Profit and the Rate of Surplus Value

"Surplus value" and "the rate of surplus value" (s/v) are
economic concepts that are not used by economists who proceed
from the capitalist standpoint, because they serve no practical
purpose in the conduct of a capitalist undertaking. The institu-
tional unit of a capitalist economy is "the firm" (i.e. establishment, factory, company, etc. that functions and is managed as a
unit). For it "surplus value" is seen always in the form of profit
and there are no practical reasons for enquiring what lies beyond
this form in which it makes its everyday economic appearance.
The importance of the concept of surplus value arises when the
system as a whole is being considered and the fundamental
relations characterising the system as a whole (for example,
the basic class relations between workers, capitalists, landowners;

or what might be called "sub-class-relations" such as those between small capitalists and large, and between industrial capitalists and capitalists in commerce and finance, the position within the system of professional workers, workers "on own account", simple commodity producers, etc.). Such analysis makes it possible to consider the movement of the system as a whole, and brings to light the basic contradictions within the capitalist system; it also makes it possible to see with precision the specific forms that economic exploitation assumes within capitalist society, and in so doing focuses attention on the economic roots of class power and class struggle. These aspects of economic analysis, dealing with the movement of the social system as a whole and the basic class relations within it, bring into evidence the basic causes of class conflict within capitalism and point to the conclusion that the movement of the system will tend towards disintegration and loss of social coherence rather than towards a new stability.

Such analysis of historical trends is of great practical importance, evidently, to the political movement of the working class that is looking for social progress and change. It gives to the socialist movement and to the workers as a class, that is, to the Labour movement as a political force, a confidence that the course they are following is not only socially realistic but coincides with the needs of the people in the widest and most general sense, if social progress is to continue to be made.

Adam Smith's analysis of capitalism as a whole, as an economic system, made in the 18th century when the industrial revolution was just beginning and strong opposition from the landowners had to be faced, gave to the capitalist class a confidence in its future. One may compare this to the impetus that Marx's economic theory gave to the socialist movements of the working class a century later. It would be foolish to expect such analyses to be promoted today by the institutions of a capitalist society which requires such damaging theory for no practical purpose of its own nor in the current conduct of economic affairs. Marxist theory comes into bitter conflict with the interests of the capitalists as a class. It gives them no historical future; and naturally, the institutions of established capitalist society prefer schools of theory more flattering to the established order. Such situations are not uncommon when truth and political power conflict.

The analysis of profit can in no way replace the analysis of surplus value; but study of the relations between surplus value and profit and of the forms assumed by profit in the functioning of the capitalist economic system, is of great importance.

Profit to capitalists is what capital produces, the reason for which they invest their capital, the motive of all their activities. Capitalists are not concerned with the ratio between the surplus they produce and the wages they pay (the "rate of surplus value") but with the ratio between the surplus they get and the total capital employed. This ratio is the rate of profit. Thus the *rate of profit* may be defined as *the ratio of surplus value (s) to total capital [which consists of constant capital (c) plus variable capital (v)]* whereas the rate of surplus value is the ratio of surplus value to variable capital: in short,

$$\text{Rate of profit} = \frac{s}{c + v}$$

$$\text{Rate of surplus value} = \frac{s}{v}$$

This definition of the rate of profit applies only if we are considering an economic system *as a whole*. In making it we are talking in terms of general and fundamental economic relations, and we need to build a number of "bridges" before we can pass over to consideration of typical individual firms. But here we approach a general concept that is of great importance in the operation of the capitalist system, namely, *the average rate of profit*, the underlying relationship between the total capital socially employed and the total surplus value produced.

To the capitalist, what he spends on wages (variable capital) and what he spends on plant and raw materials (constant capital) are equally costs of production, and the extra he gets by selling above costs is his profit.

What, considering the matter first from the standpoint of the individual firm or capitalist, determines the rate of profit? (1) *First, of course, the rate of profit depends on the rate of surplus value.* For example, a capitalist invests £1,000: £900 on raw materials, etc., and £100 on wages. If the rate of surplus value is 100 per cent, profit will be equal to wages, that is £100; if the rate of surplus value is increased to 150 per cent profit goes up accordingly to £150. The rate of profit is calculated *per annum* and if we assume that the figures given above represent capital invested in a turnover of production that takes a year, the capitalist's rate of profit will be 10 per cent when the rate of surplus value is 100 per cent and 15 per cent when it is 150 per cent.

Now suppose that the turnover of capital is speeded up and two cycles of production are completed in the course of the year, then (assuming 100 per cent rate of surplus value) he will get a profit of £100 twice in the year and make a profit of £200 on his capital of £1,000, which is a rate of profit of 20 per cent. (2) *In the second place, therefore, rate of profit depends on the speed of turnover of capital.*

There is a third important fact on which the rate of profit depends. Suppose that the rate of surplus value is 100 per cent and the capital turns over only once in the year, but that the capitalist lays out only £700 on raw materials, etc., and the remaining £300 on wages. If the rate of surplus value is 100 per cent, surplus value will equal wages (£300), and the capitalist will make £300 on £1,000, which is 30 per cent. *Therefore (3), the rate of profit depends on the ratio between variable and constant capital, i.e. the organic composition of capital.*

Conclusion (3) at first sight seems strange. Can the capitalist increase his profit simply by spending more on wages and less on materials? It would be easy if he could do this as and when he pleased but, of course, in practice this is not so. The amount of raw materials, labour, and plant that he employs depends largely on technical considerations. If wages are low, the inducement to introduce costly machinery to increase productivity will not be strong. Much will depend on the prevailing social and economic conditions, but in general a capitalist who uses more than the average *socially necessary* labour-time will not get, in exchange, values corresponding to the labour-time that has been expended on his products. To survive a capitalist must, broadly speaking, use a competitive technique which is up to the social average. At all events he cannot arbitrarily determine the proportion of variable capital to constant capital and, if he tries to, it will get him nowhere if he fails to maintain output per man hour. It is no contradiction to this fact that, if wage-rates are low, it often will not be worthwhile to introduce new machinery; but with wage-rates at a given level, the ratio between wages and other costs will be broadly fixed by technical considerations.

Profit and Productivity

Changes are, of course, continually occurring in the organic compositions of individual capitals, and generally the process works on the following lines: the capitalist struggles to increase output and to this end introduces new techniques which lead to a reduction of wages in relation to other costs. Immediately he gets an extra profit because his improved methods reduce his factory's "labour-time per product" in relation to the social average labour-time which determines the market value of the product. However, as more advanced technical methods begin to be adopted generally, his advantages over other capitalists disappear and the rate of profit tends to fall, as a result of the higher organic composition of capital that has now become general. It should be noted that though the *rate* of profit tends to fall the total *amount* of profit does not necessarily tend to fall since the total amount of capital may and probably will increase. (The historical tendency for the rate of profit to fall will be dealt with further in Chapter VIII.)

The points made in the preceding paragraph may be illustrated numerically. Suppose three firms A, B and C are producing chairs as follows:

TABLE

Firm	Materials £'000	Machinery £'000	Costs: Other £'000	Wages £'000	Total Costs £'000	No. of workers	No. of chairs produced ('000)	Total Receipts from Sales £'000
A	50	10	10	30	100	100	130	130
B	40	5	5	50	100	170	110	110
C	55	15	10	20	100	60	150	150
Total for Industry	145	30	25	100	300	330	390	390

The average rate of profit in the industry is 30 per cent, but firm C makes 50 per cent and B only 10 per cent. C gets a big extra profit as a result of his better technique; and he gets this at the expense of the more backward firms in the industry—in this illustration firm B. Suppose now that the backward firms improve their technique up to C's standard; then ouput will be increased, employment reduced, and the rate of profit will be higher for the industry as a whole. But, obviously, things could not rest so. If production increased in this way, and if such exceptionally high rates of profit were obtainable for some time, attracting new capital into the industry and so further increasing production, the market would be over-supplied and prices would slump, setting opposite trends in motion, reducing profits, employment and output. After that a new unevenness would develop, oscillating round a new level, based on average technical standards that were now much higher, say, more like those of Firm C than Firm A. The price of chairs would then be such—17s. 6d. say—as to accord these firms an average rate of profit comparable to that earned in other industries.

The example taken serves to illustrate the profound process of change generated by the changes in productivity which rivalry between competing capitals compels. Consideration of the complex process, from which such a simplified example extracts only the barest outline, helps one to form a mental picture of the manysidedness and the conflicting, contradictory character of the trends and counter-trends through which the motion of the whole economic system is effected.

Different Compositions of Capital in Different Industries

Leaving aside, however, the over-all differences in the organic composition of capital at different points of time and the differences in the organic composition of individual capitals in the same industry, one needs to recognise that in different industries, for purely technical reasons, the *average* organic composition differs widely. Coal-mining, for example, does not involve working up a raw material purchased from another industry, but only the actual extraction of a raw material from the earth. Wages therefore necessarily form a large part of total costs; the organic composition of capital is relatively low. Does this then mean that the rate of profit in coal-mining is necessarily exceptionally high? This would indeed be a strange conclusion, but what has been said above would suggest that this must be so. However, the facts are that the rate of profit in coal-mining was in the twenty years prior to nationalisation below the average rather than above.

The following table (based on the 1935 Census of Production) shows roughly—columns (2) and (3)—the size of the wages bill in relation to production costs in five industries:

Percentage Division of Value of Output

Industry	Cost of Materials	Wages	"Gross Profits"*
(1)	(2)	(3)	(4)
Grain Milling	82	5	13
Seed Crushing	80	6¼	13¼
Linoleum	50	15	35
Chemicals, Dyestuffs, and Drugs	46	14	40
Coal-mines	15	62	23

The table above shows differences in the materials: wages ratio which in the main are neither temporary nor accidental. Consider, for example, the 46:14 ratio in chemicals, as against the 15:62 ratio in coal-mining, and note that over-all "profits" in chemicals are three times the wages bill and in coal-mining half the wages bill. Clearly it is not the case that the industries with low organic composition of capital make exceptionally high profits and vice versa. It is necessary, therefore, for economic theory to explain how differences in the organic composition of capital affect the ability of different industries to make profits. Here we must disregard all the temporary fluctuations in general economic and market conditions (which have a great effect in the real world as depicted in current statistics) and look only for the underlying economic laws.

Equalisation of the Rate of Profit

Suppose that industry is divided into three branches, A, B, and C, and that the organic composition of capital in these three branches is as follows:

	Constant Capital	Variable Capital
A ..	80	20
B ..	70	30
C ..	60	40

* Including other production costs, e.g., executives' salaries, depreciation, repairs, advertising, rent and, in the case of coal-mines, royalties.

Suppose that the rate of surplus value in all industry is 100 per cent and that the capitalists in each of these branches of industry sell their products at full value. Then the rates of profits earned will be as follows:

		Constant Capital	Variable Capital	Surplus Value	Value of Products	Rate of Profit %
A	..	80	20	20	120	20
B	..	70	30	30	130	30
C	..	60	40	40	140	40
Totals	..	210	90	90	390	30*

Suppose this actually did happen in the period of competitive capitalism. Suppose industry C earned 40 per cent. What then would happen? Capitalists always seek the most profitable investment for their capital and obviously they would rush to invest their capital in industry C, and would begin taking their capital out of industry A as quickly as they could. What then would happen? Clearly a lot more of industry C's goods would be produced and a lot fewer of industry A's. There would be over-production in one line and under-production in the other; a glut here and a scarcity there, and, as a consequence, products C would sell below value, and products A above value, which would mean that industry C would no longer earn so high a rate of profit, whereas industry A would earn a higher rate of profit.

Our study of capitalist economy is now passing to a new stage. Having analysed the basic economic relations (the class relations of labour and capital in a market, commodity-exchange economy whose means of production are privately owned), we now go beyond these essentials to consider relationships between different industries and different sectors of the capitalist class. Here we begin to see what effects the profit motive has on the economic balance between industries. We have already noted that the firm with better technique gains an advantage over the firm with poorer technique, getting a greater profit. In the rest of this chapter we shall be considering only the *average* techniques of the various industries, dismissing further consideration of

* Average rate of profit for all industry.

differences *within* industries and dealing only with differences *between* industries (as if each industry were one big firm of average technical performance).

If equal amounts of capital tend to get equal profits, that is, if the rate of profit tends towards a uniform level as between the different fields in which capital is employed, then prices will tend to equal the sum we get by adding the average rate of profit to capital used. This would mean, reverting to the example on page 106 above, costs per chair of about 15s. 5d. (i.e. £100 divided by 130) plus a profit on this of 4s. 7d. (i.e. 30 per cent of £100 divided by 130). This would give a price of £1 per chair. Seen this way it may seem that prices are determined by costs plus whatever profit the capitalist chooses to add. *This, however, is not so.* A capitalist is not free to choose the level of profit that suits him. He is subject to economic forces which he does not control, penalising him either by losing markets or by losing profits if the margin of profit that he takes does not accord with conditions imposed upon him by the economic system as a whole. In short, the average rate of profit is fixed *by relationships that apply to the system as a whole.* The most important of these relationships are (*a*) the relationships between the total (previously produced) stock of capital used and the new product created in each cycle of production, (*b*) relationships between the capitalist class and the working class, and (*c*) the balance between what is produced and what is required (the "output" and "intake") by the different branches of industry.

(*a*) Net new product or *national income.* Suppose the total stock of goods used in carrying through a cycle of production represents the output of 10,000 million labour-hours and that a labour force of one million workers expends 2,500 labour-hours per worker in this new cycle of production, then the ratio between the new product and the previously produced goods used in its production is, measured in labour time, 2,500 million divided by 10,000 million, that is 1:4.

(*b*) Of this new product, part will go to the workers in wages and the rest will be a surplus out of which profit and other non-producers' incomes will be paid. (To simplify the picture we will assume that the whole surplus becomes profit). The total amount of profit will thus depend, firstly, upon the total size of the new national product—(*a*) above—and, then, upon the relationship between the working class and the capitalist class as a whole, of which the most important economic measure is the general level of real wages. This relationship will determine the average rate of profit. If wages take, for example, four-tenths of the new product (which we assume, as in our example above, to be equal to one-quarter of the stock of goods used in its production), profit will be $\frac{6}{10}$ of the new product and the *rate of profit*, that is (profit) $\div$ (capital used) will be $\frac{6}{10} \times \frac{1}{4} = \frac{6}{40}$, i.e. 15 per cent.

If wages advanced to take half the new product, the rate of profit would fall to $\frac{5}{10} \times \frac{1}{4} = 12\frac{1}{2}$ per cent. If wages fell to $\frac{1}{3}$ of the new product, the rate of profit would advance to $\frac{2}{3} \times \frac{1}{4} = 16\frac{2}{3}$ per cent.

(c) The technical conditions of each industry determine the balance of products and requirements, that is, of "output" and "intake". Through a groping process of trial and error, with many surpluses or many shortages, the system as a whole establishes the balances between what the different branches of industry supply to and require from one another. At one end the materials taken from nature supply the beginning of the process of production; at the other end final consumption removes products from the interchanges of the economic system in which the main and determining factors are the transactions between producers. These conditions of production determine relative prices in the sense that some prices are above values in terms of labour time, these being counterbalanced by the prices that fall below value. The level towards which prices tend over the course of time will be such that equal capitals earn equal rates of profit. The result will be that prices tend towards costs (i.e. capital expended) *plus* the average rate of profit, as determined by factors (a) and (b) described above.

This tendency towards the equalisation of the rate of profit operates within capitalist production, shaping the broad distribution of capital between different industries, although in detail obscured by the differences in efficiency and the shifting fortunes that ceaselessly affect individual capitalists; *the tendency is for capital to be so distributed* between different branches of industry that all capitals earn an equal rate of profit, namely, the average rate of profit for capitalism as a whole.*

---

* So far as there is free mobility of capital, which in the case of capital in agriculture there in fact is not, as will be explained in the next chapter. The free movement of capital in industry is also hampered in the period of monopoly capitalism.

In a fully developed capitalist economy, as a result of the tendencies described above, commodities sell not necessarily at their values but at a price which equals cost (that is, broadly speaking, constant capital plus variable capital) plus the average rate of profit. This price Marx calls *the price of production*.

"Prices of Production" and the Critics of Marx

Critics of Marx, and in particular Böhm-Bawerk, have used this "Prices of Production" law (explained by Marx in Vol. III of *Capital*) to attack Marx, maintaining that it contradicts the value theory used by him in Volume I. "The Prices of Production Law", say the critics, proves (*a*) that, after all, commodities in fully developed capitalism do not exchange at their values as determined by the labour-time embodied in them, and (*b*) that the prices at which they actually do exchange depend on demand and supply.

It is necessary to remind the critics that Marxist theory never said that commodities *always* exchange at their values, but only that in and through numerous fluctuations up and down they *tended* to exchange at value. Now this statement that was broadly true of simple commodity production is modified in order to bring it into line with the conditions prevailing in fully developed capitalist production. Under such conditions commodities tend to exchange at value only on the assumption that capital of average organic composition is employed, and, to deal with production in which capital of other than average composition is employed, a new economic law is formulated which does not contradict but exemplifies a particular application of the law of value. This new law says that *in fully developed capitalism commodities tend to exchange at their prices of production*. It is important to note that the "Prices of Production" law depends on the principle that value is determined by labour time. The average rate of profit is determined by the relationship of wages to surplus value (that is, the ratio of the labour time spent on producing the share taken, through wages, by the workers, to the labour time spent producing the surplus over and above this). This relationship is determined in the economy as a whole, as is also the relationship of the new product (the product of "living labour") to the stock of goods used in production ("dead labour"). Moreover, when viewing the economy as a whole, Marx is not concerned with differences in the relationships between different sectors of the economy. Examination of the typical "average" case where goods exchange at value is, therefore, correct and necessary if the argument is to hold for the system as a whole. The "Prices of Production" law does not contradict the law of value but takes it as its starting point in moving on to consider the relationships between different sectors of the economy.

It is a strictly scientific method of work to modify general laws in order to apply them to particular circumstances. The natural scientist does this over and over again; and in dealing with the latest stage of capitalism, namely, monopoly capitalism, it will be necessary to modify still further the "Prices of Production" law.

Consider now point (b). Some capitalist economists try to explain exchange-values solely in terms of supply and demand. Is not the line of argument here a surrender to their point of view? This is not so. The "Prices of Production" law shows how prices are determined by conditions of production. A certain balance needs to be established between the requirements of the different industries, between the goods they supply and the goods they take. Prices of production will tend to be such as to establish this balance in such a way that equal capitals earn equal profits. Up to this point, the effect of "excesses" or "deficiencies" of "supply" or "demand" does not need to be considered or introduced. One may assume that supplies match requirements as determined by the conditions of production. But one gets lost and starts "chasing one's own tail" if the attempt is made to explain exchange values from the outset in terms of supply and demand, without having first laid the foundations for economic analysis using the assumption that supply and demand balance. This is essential, since excesses of supply and demand express only *relative* excesses within the economy and cannot constitute the fundamental principle for the working of the economy as a whole. "The exchange or sale of commodities at their value", writes Marx, "is the rational way, the natural law of their equilibrium. It must be' the point of departure for the explanation of deviations from it, not vice versa, the deviations the basis on which this law is explained." (*Capital*, Vol. III, LW p. 184, K p. 221.) He adds: "If demand and supply balance one another, they cease to explain anything, they do not affect market values, and therefore leave us even more in the dark than before concerning the reasons for the expression of the market value in just a certain sum of money and no other...." (*Capital*, Vol. III, LW p. 186, K p. 223.)

Commercial Profit

In Chapter IV it was explained that in capitalist societies surplus value (and therefore profit) does not originate from trading, buying and selling. It is indeed true that a particular capitalist often makes a profit by buying cheap and selling dear, but when he does so, it is at the expense of the capitalist from whom he buys, or to whom he sells. The *source* of profit is not in exchange, nor in buying and selling; but although the *source* of profit is not to be found in buying and selling, it is of course an evident fact that the commercial capitalist, who merely buys and sells, none the less makes profits. How does he do so?

The point is to explain how the merchant continues to enrich himself from commerce within capitalist society. The merchant is, of course, much older than capitalist society. As has already been explained, in the ancient world of Greece and Rome and in medieval times, the merchant flourished wherever commodity exchange had developed to any substantial extent. Then the merchant (in addition to piracy and the use of force) enriched himself by buying cheap in one market and selling dear in some distant market. He traded with communities who depended on exchange only for a smaller number of goods, mainly luxuries. The merchant knew where there was scarcity and where there was plenty and guided his trade accordingly. He was the dominant figure in the field of commodity exchange, and merchant's capital was then the main form of capital. With the development of the capitalist mode of production, the position of the merchant alters radically. Merchants' capital becomes secondary to productive capital and the conditions which determine what profits the merchant gets are greatly changed. Here we need to consider these new conditions under which the merchant functions in a fully developed capitalist society.

The productive capitalist must, in order to realise the new values his workers have created for him, sell his products. If, for example, he is a manufacturer of boots he must sell his boots in order to get money to buy more leather, to pay his workers' wages and his overhead charges. If he cannot turn his products into money he cannot start a new turnover of production and his capital lies idle, giving him no profit until he has succeeded in selling his products. The sale of his products is therefore vital, and the more speedily this is effected the better it is for him.

The early capitalists were often (see Chapter III) merchants who had embarked on production in order to expand their supplies of commodities for sale. At this stage the merchant and producer are usually one, but as capitalist production develops the several activities which the production and exchange of commodities involve become specialised. Productive capital becomes more important than merchant's capital and the productive capitalist gives first attention to the use of his capital in the productive process. At this stage it becomes worth his while to sell below value to a merchant. In this way he will get his money back quickly and this will speed the turnover of his capital. The merchant on the other hand will establish contacts in all likely markets and see that the value of commodities is realised by sale as soon as possible. Throughout the epoch of capitalism the task of selling commodities tends to be handled by capitalists who specialise in this activity until the present stage of vast monopolies and trusts is reached and a further change occurs, in that the trusts are often able, because of the huge scale on which they operate, to increase their profits by undertaking their own marketing.

The commercial or merchant capitalist must obviously have capital with which to operate. He needs this not only to enable him to buy the goods that are offered to him, but also to pay for the handling of the goods and for the costs of book-keeping, offices, sales assistants, etc. On the capital he uses he will, of course, expect to get the average rate of profit. If merchant capitalists do not get the average rate of profit they will begin to seek more profitable investments elsewhere.

The commercial capitalist is, then, a specialist in buying and selling, to whom the productive capitalist surrenders a part of the surplus values produced in the factory in order that the last stage in the turnover of his capital may be achieved and his profits realised accordingly. The values surrendered by the productive capitalists must be sufficient to enable the commercial capitalists to earn the average rate of profit, or else capital will be removed from commerce into industry.

Wages of Commercial and Distributive Workers

Since a commercial undertaking produces nothing, it creates no values, and all its profits and the wages, etc., of its employees come out of the surplus value produced by the workers directly engaged in production. All the values distributed derive from the point of production in the factory; but, of course, the commercial capitalist will see that the wages paid to his clerical and distributive workers are as low as possible, so that as much as possible of the surplus value represented by the difference between the "factory-gate" price and the final selling price may come to him as profits.

It is clear then that capitalists do all they can to cut down the wages paid to those whom they employ on realising the values which are produced in industry. Nevertheless capitalism wastes a vast amount of manpower in "socially unnecessary" sales organisations (including, of course, advertising) and commercial transactions designed to push individual products at the expense of someone else. This fight for markets to which the productive relations of capitalism give rise, causes a tremendous waste of resources.

The Co-operative Movement

A century ago, in order to escape from the excessive prices and adulterated products which the capitalist retailers had forced on them in the industrial areas of Manchester, the workers started their own "Co-operative" shops. From small beginnings the Co-operative movement has grown into a vast organisation of retail shops, handling about one-eighth of the nation's retail trade. Through this organisation (although it is influenced by capitalist ideas and by the capitalist relations of production that prevail in society generally) the workers recover for themselves a small part of the surplus value which they produce and which otherwise would be appropriated by the merchant capitalists. The Co-operative movement, starting in the sphere of retail trade, has spread into the field of wholesale trade where the Co-operative Wholesale Society and the Scottish Co-operative Wholesale Society operate in a fairly big way; they have moreover spread their activities, on a much more restricted scale, to the field of production. Within a capitalist society Co-operatives, whether in trade or production, cannot and do not change the basis of capitalist exploitation. However, they provide a powerful organisation embracing the mass of the working-class and lower middle-class consumers through which economically and politically the struggle against monopoly capitalism can be conducted, a struggle which necessarily finds reflection in the internal conflicts within the Co-operative movement between those who seek to accommodate their activities to capitalist society and those who seek to unite the struggle for Co-operative aims with the struggle for the overthrow of capitalism as a whole and the building of a socialist society.

Interest

In any form of society in which commodity exchange has developed to any considerable extent, money brings power for those who have it over those who lack it. In pre-capitalist societies, such as feudal and ancient society, the exaction of interest on loans (usury) is commonly to be found. "The most characteristic forms", writes Marx, "in which usurers' capital exists in times antedating capitalist production are two. I say purposely characteristic forms. The same forms repeat themselves on the basis of capitalist production, but as more subordinate forms. These two forms are, first, usury by lending money to extravagant persons of the higher classes, particularly landowners; secondly, usury by lending money to the small producer who is in possession of his own means of employment." (*Capital*, Vol. III, LW p. 581, K p. 697.) These pre-capitalist forms of "usurers' capital" of course continue to play an important role in the modern world, particularly in countries in which capitalist production has developed only to a limited extent (e.g. much of Asia, S. America and Africa and, pre-1917, Russia, and, pre-1949, China). In capitalism, however, loan capital and interest assume a new status. No longer is interest branded (as it was, for example, by the moralists of feudal times) as an unjust exaction; instead, the capitalist moralists and economists see interest as a just and necessary part of the social order of things. The reason for this change is to be found in the changed relations of men to one another in production and in the fact that capitalism provides a basis which makes it possible for interest-bearing capital to enjoy a more continuous existence. Usury in its modern form (the ugly word is no longer used) accords with the interests of the dominant capitalist class, since the capitalist who borrows money can use it to produce surplus value out of which the interest on the borrowed money can be paid to the mutual advantage of both the borrower and the lender. Interest-bearing capital is thus an integral part of the capitalist system; indeed, it is the most typical form of capital, money which generates more money all by itself! Such anyhow is the appearance, for in the case of interest the reality of exploitation which generates the extra money is hidden far from sight.

Interest is Payment for the Use of Money Capital

Suppose that a capitalist actively engaged in industry or commerce earns on his capital the average rate of profit, say 20 per cent; and, let us suppose that he borrows £100 to extend the scale of his business. "If this man (i.e. our 'active' capitalist) should pay, say, £5 at the close of the year to the owner of the £100, out of the produced profit, he would be paying for the use-value of the £100, the use-value of its function as capital, the function of producing £20 of profit. The part of the profit that he pays to the owner is called interest. It is merely another name, a special term, for a certain part of the profit which capital in the process of its function has to give up to its owner, instead of keeping it in its own pockets." (Marx, *Capital*, Vol. III, LW p. 333, K p. 398.)

Interest-bearing capital (unlike commercial capital) does not therefore enter into the formation of the average rate of profit, which depends on the relation between the total amount of surplus value and the total social capital. Whether a particular bit of capital in an industrial or commercial undertaking is owned by the "working" capitalist or by someone who has made him a loan does not affect the total of social capital. If the capital is loaned, the only difference is that two persons have different titles to the same capital and the profit produced by it. The "owning" capitalist is entitled to a specified rate of interest; the "active" capitalist to such profit as the capital makes over and above the rate of interest. It is worth here noting that in the modern limited liability company the various forms of shareholding (referred to in Chapter X) provide a range of intermediary forms of "legal title" to a share in the profit, which lie between interest proper on loans or debentures and the "working" capitalist's profit. Interest in its most typical form is a payment for capital in money form.

What determines the rate of interest? To this question there is no clear-cut and simple answer. Obviously, in normal times, the rate of interest must be less than the average rate of profit or it would not be worthwhile for the "active" capitalists to borrow, but even this generalisation may not have been true in certain periods of crisis when payments were due and capitalists who were unable to sell the goods they had produced were exceptionally eager to come by capital in its money form. However, broadly speaking, one may say (1) that the rate of interest will bear some relation to the average rate of profit, and (2) that the relation of the rate of interest to the average rate of profit will depend upon the demand by "active" capitalists for extra capital and the supply of capital to lend by owners of capital who do not wish to use it "actively" themselves. In a fully developed capitalist society supplies of money capital come, in the main, from the banks (in close association with other large financial institutions such as insurance companies, investment trusts, etc.), whose policy can to a certain degree control the amount of money available to borrowers. In the stage of development that modern capitalism has now reached, interest rates are greatly affected by government action in the sphere of finance, by new government borrowing and by the management of the National Debt.

It must be added that the particular rate of interest charged to a particular borrower will vary from the general rate of interest according to the length of time for which he wishes to borrow, the security for repayment that he can afford, the risk, and so forth. Indeed, there is a whole hierarchy of interest rates geared to the "bank rate".*

Capitalist Theories of Interest and Profit

The standpoint of bourgeois economics is in many respects the reverse of what has been set out here. Interest is what capital "earns", just as wages is what labour earns (and likewise rent is what land "earns"). According to bourgeois theory the three "factors of production", capital, labour, and land, divide out the product of industry in such a way that each gets such share as supply and demand conditions enable it to command; which, indeed, says little more than that each "factor of production" gets what it gets. However, the importance to capitalism of putting things this way is that it disguises the reality of capitalist exploitation and suggests that capital has every bit as sound a claim to interest as labour has to wages. On this theory profit is but a special form of interest, and interest the fundamental thing, the payment due to capital.

F. H. Knight, an American economist who commands considerable respect in capitalist circles, argues in his book *Risk*,

* The Bank Rate is the officially advertised rate at which the Bank of England will discount short-term bills for members of the money market. Other rates of interest, above or below it, tend to change in step with it; but the Bank and the Treasury also influence interest rates by controlling the *amount* of money available to the money market.

Uncertainty, and Profit that profit (as distinct from interest which is the "normal" reward of capital) is the reward for unforeseeable, uninsurable uncertainty and he seems to suggest that on balance the capitalist class probably makes more losses than profits! In short, the capitalist class does not make profits; capital simply "earns" interest. Bourgeois economists also argue that a part of what the worker normally considers to be profits is properly a reward for managerial enterprise which the capitalist earns by virtue of his skill in this art. (By contrast our contention is that many salaries paid to capitalist directors far exceed the wages which they might have earned for managerial duties and are in fact disguised forms of surplus value.) Thus the bourgeois economists explain away the surplus value that is paid out to various classes of capitalist and are left with interest as "the reward of capital".

For what service is interest a reward? "For the use of capital", replies the capitalist economist. The fact that it is the capitalist himself who normally uses capital does not worry the bourgeois economist. Interest, he says, is a reward to the capitalist because he does not straightaway consume the values of which he is the owner, but instead abstains and puts them at the disposal of the community in order that they may be used to facilitate more lengthy processes of production which result in the community getting (after waiting all this while) a greater volume of production. The capitalist holds back from immediate consumption and uses his capital to feed the masses (to whom he pays wages whilst the lengthy productive process proceeds) and is rewarded with interest. The picture of a millionaire capitalist abstaining from immediate consumption of his vast fortune is, of course, ludicrous and the only truth behind this theory is that it reflects the fact that the capitalist as owner of capital and of the means of production can hold up the community to ransom and extract great wealth for himself from the toil of the masses. However, this idea is much more clearly and precisely expressed in the Marxist doctrine of surplus value, which provides an effective instrument for carrying out a full analysis of the economic structure of society.

Banks

The final stage in the capitalist cycle of production is achieved with the sale of the commodity produced (C—M) which enables the capitalist to recover the capital which has temporarily been embodied in commodities and to realise the surplus value which has been produced. In developed capitalist society payment is normally made by cheque through the banking system. The banks in this way collect for the capitalists the revenue that comes to them from the sale of their commodities. They also hold for them that part of their capital which is for the time being in money form. These funds which the banks hold are the deposits credited to the accounts of their business customers. Thus one of the main functions of the banks is to hold the money capital and surplus value realised in the course of the turnover of capital. Another main function of the banks used to be to issue the notes which serve as currency for cash payments. (The issue of notes is in Britain now restricted mainly to the Bank of England, and the total amount of notes which may be issued is provided for by legislation. The note always represented in "normal" capitalist conditions a definite weight of gold for which it could be exchanged and the number of notes issued bore a definite relationship laid down by statute to the amount of gold held by the Bank of England. Since "going off the gold standard"—originally in the First World War and again in 1931, after a partial return in 1925—no fixed relationship between notes and gold has existed.) A third main function of the banks is to lend capital in money form.

The earliest bankers were goldsmiths who held funds in safe keeping for merchants and other wealthy persons. The origin of the note was the receipt promising to repay the gold deposited with the goldsmith, which naturally came to be used in place of the gold in making payments. The early "goldsmith-bankers" also were a usual source from which those in need of money capital sought loans. Thus the three main functions of the bank date back to earliest times. What, however, is new about the banks in fully developed industrial capitalism is the fact that in their hands are concentrated virtually all the monetary transactions of capitalist society. They collect funds, they lend funds, they settle payments, and they serve as a clearing house for all industry's transactions.

Banks, therefore, bring together as it were all surplus funds available for use as capital, and make it available (against interest payment) for use as capital by industry and commerce. With the development of the banking system loan capital assumes, says Marx, "more and more the character of an organised mass" under the control of the bankers. On the one hand the bankers hold deposits (idle capital deposited with them); on the other, they issue loans to capitalists. And a very profitable business this is, since they use money left in their keeping to make money for themselves. The chief function of the bank's own capital is to inspire confidence in customers; what they lend is other people's money. However, the bigger the business a bank does, the greater the confidence it inspires. Thus the bigger a bank gets the easier it is for it to grow still bigger and as its custom grows bigger, so its profits grow bigger.

A simplified example will show how banks organise the distribution of loan capital and make big profits for themselves. Numerous capitalists deposit their idle funds with, say, Bank X (the size of the funds themselves may depend largely on the policy pursued by the banks). This they may do by the mere process of paying their receipts into the accounts they run at Bank X. Suppose that these deposits come in all to £200 million; Bank X will pay a low rate of interest on many of these deposits, say, £1 million in all, that is on an average ½ per cent. Now Bank X will know that not all its depositors will want their money back at the same time and will lend this £200 million to other capitalists, in some cases on a short-term basis so that it can get the money back quickly if necessary, and in some cases for a longer term. In practice most banks keep about 10 per cent in cash (in hand and at the Bank of England) and lend up to about 90 per cent of the total sums deposited with them. The rate of interest that Bank X receives will be considerably more on the average than it pays its depositors. Supposing it gets on the average 3 per cent on the £200 million it has to lend, it will collect £6 million, whereas it pays out to its depositors only £1 million. It has not only organised and distributed the loan capital available to the capitalist class it has also pocketed £5 million for itself. So the banks and countless other commercial and financial institutions suck up a considerable share of the surplus value produced by workers in industry, mines, agriculture, etc.*

---

* This description of the activities of the banks is, necessarily, rather simplified, not to say over-simplified. In particular, it has not been possible within the compass of a text-book such as this to describe the far-reaching changes that have taken place in the monetary and financial system of capitalism within the period of its general crisis, that is, since the First World War. These changes would need to be dealt with in some detail in order to explain how the total of funds at the disposal of the banks is determined, the extent to which the banks are able to "create" credit, how they control the distribution of credit and financial resources generally, and how their activities affect the

Rent, Interest, and Profit—the Capitalist Trinity

Part of the surplus value produced by the workers also goes to the landowning class as rent, in a manner which is explained in the next chapter. Rent, Interest, and Profit—the "Holy Trinity" of capitalism—are the main forms in which surplus value is distributed to the exploiting class. These basic forms assume, however, many different appearances.

value of money. Here it must suffice to list some of the new factors that have an important bearing on the activities of the banks, as follows: the highly concentrated monopoly power of the greatest financial interests, the intertwining of their activities with those of the State, the inconvertibility of currencies (into gold) and State regulation of foreign exchange transactions, the huge and growing proportion of "capital assets" held in the form of Government securities (the "National Debt"), the vast scale on which the State itself borrows, spends and receives money in the form of taxation.

CHAPTER VII

RENT AND CAPITALISM IN AGRICULTURE

Ground rent is a toll exacted by the owners of the land from those who use it; it is almost as old as private property in land, and at different stages in the development of human society has assumed a considerable variety of forms. In typical capitalist conditions rent is paid in money, coming out of surplus value produced by wage labour.

The roots of rent reach back far into the past. The landowning class is the relic of what before capitalism was the dominant ruling class. In Britain, the most capitalist of capitalist countries, the landowners have become almost completely merged with the capitalist class, but in the world as a whole, and not least in the British Empire, old pre-capitalist forms of landownership and exploitation continued to have a great importance.

Agriculture is an essential basis of social life. From farming and the cultivation of the land come man's food and materials from which other necessities of life are made. The vast majority of the world's population live and work on the land. Whereas the industrial population of the "advanced" capitalist countries such as Britain and the U.S.A. is counted in tens of millions, the peasantry of China and India is counted in hundreds of millions. In India, three-quarters of the population depend for their living on agriculture or pastoral pursuits. In Eastern Europe the position was before the Second World War much the same (for example, Rumania 78 per cent, Yugoslavia 71 per cent, Poland 63 per cent); it is, however, now rapidly changing. Likewise in South America, Africa, the Near East, and in all the colonial and ex-colonial territories of the world, the masses of the people live upon the land, oppressed by ancient forms of exploitation on to which the yoke of capitalist imperialism was superimposed. In the colonial and semi-colonial territories, the struggle for national freedom has often combined with a struggle for land reform.

Dominated by industrially powerful countries, their own industry developed only slowly and with the greatest of difficulty. Usually their agricultural production, obstructed by lack of capital, required tremendous expenditure of effort in return for persistently poor prices.

Land-Ownership in Pre-Capitalist Economies

In the first dawn of human history man lived by hunting and gathering the foods that grew wild. No one "owned" the land and no one exacted rent for the use of the land. The several tribes claimed certain territories as their hunting grounds (and, when necessary, defended their claims in battle), but it would be stretching words to say that they "owned" such territories. Private ownership in land did not develop until the cultivation of the soil and the raising and tending of cattle had developed; even then, the concept of tribal ownership for long tended to be dominant, private ownership of land, as we today understand it, only appearing where commodity production and exchange had developed to some considerable extent. Even when the division of society into exploiting and exploited classes (see Chapter I) had become firmly established, the ruling kings or priests (as in Egypt) justified their exactions by claiming that the right to dispense and control the property of the tribe or community of tribes was vested in them as custodians of the communal or tribal interests (often symbolised by the tribal god). In feudal society the rights of the feudal lords were but an extension and development of the rights of the tribal chieftain; the feudal lord claimed to represent the community of his subjects. However, these claims and so-called rights of the exploiters over the exploited had become the opposite of that from which they had originated, the rights of the community had been turned into the rights of a privileged class used against the community, and once established, the privileged exploiting classes used their power and all the religious and legal trappings in which they dressed their power to appropriate wealth produced by the impoverished peasants or serfs who worked the land.

The tenure of land in feudal times is, therefore, radically different from the primitive tribal conditions of land tenure, but at the same time property in land in the form that developed under the influence of capitalist conditions had not yet made its appearance. Under feudal conditions land was not originally saleable. The conditions of land tenure reflected the relationship between lord and serf. The basis of the feudal lord's power was the land over which he was lord and those who lived on this land. Custom, force, and personal control of the courts of law ensured to the lord labour and dues from those who were subject to his rule; the serfs on his land could not leave the land or dispose of their rights in it, they had to seek his permission to marry, and were in other ways subject to his control. On the serfs who worked for him depended the power and circumstances of the lord; on the other hand, those who lived on the land established for themselves by custom and struggle certain accepted rights as regards tenure of their farms, use of common land and so forth. There was in all this still a considerable gulf between, on the one hand, "the rights" of the feudal lord and his subject and, on the other, the capitalist idea of property rights.

Today the world is littered and encumbered with the relics of ancient forms of exploitation. In India the zemindars, who in the times before British rule had been the collectors of taxes paid by the cultivators of the communally owned land to their kings or rulers, were turned by the British conquerors into landlords and at the same time compelled to pay over a substantial share of their revenues from the land to their new British masters. Between the zemindar and the peasant stretches a long chain of exploiters. "In some districts", says the Simon Report (Vol. I, p. 340), "the sub-infeudation has grown to astonishing proportions, as many as fifty or more intermediary interests having been created between the zemindar at the top and the actual cultivator at the bottom." Thus the agricultural communities of India, still bearing the traces of tribal organisation, have had superimposed in historical sequence a series of later forms of exploitation. In Japan or the Philippines (much as in pre-1949 China), the peasants, unable to get a living elsewhere than on the land, are forced to pay over to the owners of the land all that they produce in excess of the barest essentials of life. Generally speaking, the rent to be paid is a percentage of the produce (which was in China and Korea about 60 per cent) paid in kind and sold by the landlord. In Iran the produce is divided into five equal parts in payment for land, water, tilling cattle, seed, and labour, which means that the well-to-do peasants who provide their own seed and cattle receive no more than three-fifths of their produce, whereas the poorest peasants must eke out an existence on one-fifth of their produce. In many colonial countries tribal ownership still continues.

The Development of Rent in Capitalist Society

How did rent in its modern, typically capitalist form develop? In feudal society, the serf made payment to his overlord by giving of his labour. Part of the week he worked his own land, the rest he worked for the landlord. The landlord received *labour rent*, that is the owner of the land exacted his toll by making the serf labour for him. A new form of rent develops when, instead of being forced to divide his working time between his own fields and those of his lord, the producer is made to divide his product, part going to the landowner and part being kept for himself. *Rent in kind* is then paid; a form of rent which no longer assumes a serf working under the eye and whip of his lord, but a producer who is at work his own master but is compelled by legal enactment to surrender a part of his produce. With the growth of commerce and commodity exchange, a further change in the form of rent develops. In place of rent in kind, the money equivalent, the price of his product, is paid over as rent. In short, *money rent* is paid. "The transformation of rent in kind into money rent", writes Marx, "taking place first sporadically, then on a more or less national scale, requires a considerable development of commerce, of city industries, of the production of commodities in general, and with them of the circulation of money." (*Capital*, Vol. III, LW pp. 777–8, K p. 926.)

Marx further points out that the transformation of rent in kind into money rent is only possible when a more or less definite market price has become established for the serf's products. Such money rent (that is rent in kind converted into its money equivalent) is the last form of what one might call "feudal rent", that is a payment that represents the unpaid surplus labour that the serf is forced to give to his lord. However, once money rent has been introduced, it is a clear sign that the old feudal forms of exploitation are being superseded by new forms. Labour rent was the normal form of exacting surplus value in feudal society; the replacement of labour rent and rent in kind by money rent shows that ground-rent is ceasing to be the prevailing and normal form for the appropriation of surplus value.

In Chapter III reference was made to the changes in feudal society which paved the way for capitalism. It will be remembered that with the development of trade, the desire of the feudal lords to have wealth in money form increased. This often led to conversion of feudal dues into money payments (although at times the feudal lords found that they stood to gain more by themselves selling the products received by the more direct forms of exploitation). The sale of estates to merchants and townsmen (who looked for revenues in money form) also developed as a result of the growth of trade and the desire of the feudal lords to lay their hands on money.

The development of money rent necessarily stimulates more fundamental transformations. "With the coming of money rent the traditional and customary relation between the landlord and the subject tillers of the soil . . . is turned into a pure money relation fixed by the rules of positive law. The cultivating possessor thus becomes virtually a mere tenant. This transformation serves on the one hand, provided that other general conditions of production permit such a thing, to expropriate gradually the old peasant possessors and to put in their place capitalist tenants. On the other hand it leads to a release of the old possessors from their tributary relation by buying themselves free from their landlord, so that they become independent farmers and free owners of the land tilled by them." (Marx, *Capital*, Vol. III, LW p. 778-9, K pp. 927-8.)

The dispossession of the smaller peasant farmers and the creation of a landless, propertyless class who, to live, must hire themselves for wages (to which reference has already been made in Chapter III) was an important symptom and also an important cause of the dissolution of feudal relations in the countryside. The driving of the peasant from the land is always accompanied by the emergence or forcible imposition of capitalist production relations and is important alike for the growth of capitalism in manufacture and in agriculture itself. In England the enclosure of the land in the fifteenth and subsequent centuries hastened the dispossession of the weaker peasantry; elsewhere usury has played a major role in the destruction of the small independent proprietor. Forced in years of bad harvest, or when prices slump in years of glut, to have recourse to the money-lender, the peasant falls into his grip and has in the end to sell his land. In colonial countries the usurer has ever been a cause of ruin, supplementing the direct use of legislation (as in Kenya) as a means to evict the peasant from his land. At the same time the small agricultural handicraftsman is ruined by the competition of capitalist products.

The advent of the trader and the money-lender and the creation of a propertyless class on the land, the rural proletariat, hastens the development of class differentiations within the peasantry. Whilst some are ruined, their employment as hands speeds the enrichment of the more well-to-do peasant farmers (such as the kulaks in Russia).

This process, which is repeated wherever capital invades the "natural economy" of backward semi-feudal countries, or of native farmers or pastoralists, began to take place in Britain some five centuries ago. Capital from the cities moved into agriculture; in sixteenth-century Britain this movement was given great impetus by the growing market for wool which attracted capital in sheep-raising. There thus arose new relationships in agricultural production, and rent acquired a new character, that of ground-rent within a capitalist mode of production. Describing this new stage, Marx writes: "When the capitalist tenant farmer steps between the landlord and the actual tiller of the soil, all relations which arose from the old rural mode of production are torn asunder. The farmer becomes the actual commander of these agricultural labourers and the actual exploiter of their surplus labour, whereas the landlord maintains a direct relationship, and indeed simply a money and contractual relationship, only with this capitalist tenant. Thus the nature of rent is also transformed. . . . From the normal form of surplus value and surplus labour, it becomes a mere excess of this surplus labour over that portion of it which is appropriated by the exploiting capitalist in the form of profit." (*Capital*, Vol. III, LW p. 779–80, K p. 929.)

Rent as a Share of Surplus Value

We explained in the last chapter how in one industry the outlay of capital on raw materials, plant, etc., in relation to the outlay on wages will be considerably more or less than in another, and how in these circumstances commodities tend to exchange at their "price of production", and how the total values produced tend to be divided out so that each capitalist (assuming average technique, efficiency, etc.) receives for his products a price equal to capital used in the production period plus the *average rate of profit*. The average rate of profit determines how the total surplus value produced is divided out between the several capitals, that is it determines the division of the "unpaid labour". Where and how does *rent** come into this dividing out of the surplus value? Is it part of the average rate of profit as, for example, interest is? Is it, indeed, a part of the surplus value extracted by the capitalist? What is it, and where does it come from?

Rent is clearly unearned income. The landowner does no work, and he sells no labour-power; he receives his rent simply because he is by legal title the owner of land. However, the money that the landowner receives for allowing someone else to have use of his land is just as good money as that which the capitalist receives when he makes a profit out of the worker; money paid in rent can buy the products of other men's labour just as well as any other money. The landowner is very obviously not a recipient of wages, and what comes to him as rent cannot come from anywhere else but out of the product of unpaid labour. It cannot be anything but *surplus value*.

Rent, then, is a part of the surplus value created in agriculture; moreover, it is something over and above the average rate of profit which the capitalist farmer, like all other capitalists, expects to get on the capital he employs. But how is it that the landowner is able to get something over and above the surplus value which provides the average rate of profit on the capital actually employed? It has already been shown how equal amounts of capital tend to earn equal amounts of profit. The rate of profit tends to be equalised according to the amount of capital engaged. This process of equalisation takes place because if capital employed in one branch of industry tends to earn more than capital employed in other branches of industry, more capital will be invested in the exceptionally profitable industry, as a result of which more goods will be produced and as supply increases relative to demand, prices will fall. This process will go on until this industry earns no more than the average rate of profit. Another way of describing this process is to say that the products of industries with high organic composition of capital will tend to sell above value and those with low organic composition will tend to sell below value.

Surplus value created in industries with capital of low organic composition flows away into industries of high organic composition. Agriculture is an industry of low organic composition. Is it

* By *rent* is meant ground-rent and not rent as it is commonly used covering both rent for land—ground-rent—and payment for use of buildings on the land.

therefore correct to say that surplus value created in agriculture tends to flow away and be distributed elsewhere in other industries? It has been shown above that this redistribution of surplus value and equalisation of the rate of profit takes place as a result of the "flow" of capital into industries which get more than the average surplus value. Is there any reason why extra capital should not go into agriculture and cause the surplus value produced there to be equalised out in the same way as it is for other industries of low organic composition? At first blush it would seem that additional capital can as well go into agriculture as into any industry; but in fact this is not so.

Agriculture is *cultivation of the land, and the land is privately owned. This private ownership of the land acts as a barrier* preventing the free flow of capital into agriculture, and preventing also the outflow of surplus value produced on the land. The "extra" surplus value which results from the low organic composition of capital in agriculture is not, therefore, distributed and "equalised" between other branches of production. An example will show some of the differences. If one owns a shoe-factory and wishes to double the amount of capital invested, a second factory can be built identical to the first; no special problems will be involved. But if one is a farmer and wishes to double one's scale of operation, things will be different. The most obvious way of doubling the scale of operation would be to buy a second farm; but this would not in fact increase the industry—it would merely extend one man's farm at the expense of another farmer. In short, there is not a limitless supply of accessible and reasonably good land and therefore an expansion of the agricultural industry either involves bringing new poor land into cultivation or else a greater investment of capital and more intensive farming of land which is already under cultivation. But the free flow of capital into farming is hampered, not only because the area of cultivable land is limited, but also because conditions of land-tenure and ownership militate against new investments of capital in farming. For example, a farmer holding land under the typical short-term lease will after improving the land have part of the extra yield of the land sucked away as a result of an increase in rent. For this reason the farming community have long agitated for more certain conditions of tenure and for compensation for improvements on the termination of a lease.

The private ownership of land which prevents the easy inflow of capital into farming also hampers the free flow of surplus value from agriculture into other industries. This does not, of course, mean that farmers get unusually high profits. Any theory that led to such a conclusion would be nonsensical. The extra surplus value which does not flow away from agriculture, flows away, however, from the farmers' pockets. It goes into the pockets of the owners of the land, who can appropriate a part of the surplus value produced on the land by virtue of the fact that they own what land there is and can stipulate the terms on which it will be used. They have a monopoly which they exploit by appropriating a part of the surplus value produced on the land in the form of *rent*, and by raising the rent as and when the surplus value increases (either as a result of the farmer applying more capital, or of social developments or other causes raising the price of the product).

Adjusting the table used in Chapter VI to show how the distribution of surplus value is equalised, we may show how in the case of agriculture it is not equalised, as follows:—

				Surplus Value	
		Surplus	Value of	Capitalist	
C	V	Value	Product	Profit	Rent
50	50	50	150	30	20

How is Rent Determined?

For simplicity's sake we assume here that the land is worked by a capitalist farmer who gets on his capital the same rate of profit as any other capitalist. But in making this assumption we should not forget that in fact, even in Britain, which economically is farther removed from feudalism than any country in Europe, farming is a down-trodden small-scale industry crushed between landowner on the one side and powerful industrial and commercial trusts on the other; these, in addition to the landowner, suck off a portion of the surplus value created by the agricultural workers, so that what is left to the capitalist farmer is often less than the average rate of profit.

Absolute Rent

Some pieces of land are more fertile than others, and some more accessible, and it is to be expected therefore that such land will command higher rent than the less fertile and the less accessible.

First of all, however, it is necessary to leave aside the differences between the best and worst land and to ask whether all and any land, including the worst, commands a rent. Once asked, this question is easily answered. Clearly where there is private property in land the owner will not allow someone else to have the use of it for nothing. The very existence of a landowning class implies that the owners can determine how the land is used and will only relinquish the use of the land to any other person on their own terms.

If nothing but commercial considerations enter into the land-owner's calculations, he will expect the appropriate normal rent. The basic minimum rent which must be paid for all land, even the worst, is called *absolute rent*, in contrast to the extra rent paid in respect of advantages in fertility or location which is called *differential rent* (see below).

The amount of rent that is paid for the use of any acre of land, even the worst land (namely, the *absolute* rent), depends ultimately on the availability of land and the demand for agricultural produce. In densely populated territories where there is little or no chance of the would-be farmer being able to satisfy his "land-hunger" from virgin land which is fertile but as yet untilled, the monopoly position of the landowning class will be strong and the amount of absolute rent exacted will be correspondingly greater. For example, the industrialisation of Britain which began in the latter half of the eighteenth century greatly increased the demand for agricultural products to feed the growing numbers of town workers, and the monopoly position of the landowners was to this extent strengthened. However, this monopoly was at the same time weakened by the development of virgin land in America. The fight to maintain import duties on corn, such as those imposed by the "Corn Laws" (which were repealed in 1846) was the last desperate attempt of the landowning class to maintain the full strength of its monopoly. In so far as the old feudal relationships had not completely disappeared in the countryside, and capitalism in agriculture was still only developed to a limited extent (such conditions existed prior to the Second World War in Eastern Europe and still are to be found in colonial and semi-colonial territories), the amounts to be paid in rent derived in some measure from the payments made of old when the feudal dues paid by serfs to their lords were commuted into money payments. However, with the development of capitalism on the land (which began in England on a considerable scale as early as the sixteenth and seventeenth centuries) the influence of this historical or customary element in rentals, which dated from feudal times, became less and less significant and the absolute rent tended primarily to be determined by the demand for land in relation to the strength or otherwise of the landowners' monopoly.

The capitalists are aware that the landowners' monopoly baulks the development of productive forces in agriculture. In the hey-day of capitalism the more radical bourgeois economists (such as Henry George) advocated State ownership of the land. Such public ownership of the land would make possible the abolition of *absolute rent* and would stimulate improved and cheaper methods of growing food. In no country, however, did the capitalist class push to extremes a claim for public ownership of the land (though division of the land amongst the peasantry was effected by the French Revolution of 1789). In practice *no radical change in the ownership of the land has ever been effected except as the fruit of social revolution*. Therefore, despite "theoretical advantages", capitalism is not prepared to strike at the ownership of the land; such a revolutionary measure as expropriation of the landowners is too much akin to the revolutionary claim put forward by the workers, that the capitalists themselves must surrender into public ownership the means of production that they own. The question of taking the land into public ownership tends, therefore, to be glossed over and the capitalists content themselves with merging their interests with those of the landowners by themselves acquiring a substantial share in the ownership of the land.

Differential Rent

Absolute rent is that basic rent which any piece of land commands regardless of the relative fertility or accessiblity of the land. On the worst land the rent paid will be absolute rent and nothing more. Moreover, it is on the worst land that the price of production of agricultural products will be determined, since the economies in production costs which derive solely from better location or higher fertility pass to the landowner as rent. This rent deriving from differing fertility, etc., is called *differential* rent.

It is not hard to see how the owner of the land is able to reap a *differential rent* in addition to an absolute rent. A farmer of normal efficiency will expect to receive approximately the average rate of profit on his capital. If he were fortunate enough to be able to rent land of high fertility for the same rent as the worst land, he would clearly make considerably higher profits than the farmer farming the worst land. However, the landowner will know what his land is worth (by testing the market, if necessary), and the rent that he will be able to charge will be such as to put into his pocket any extra profits due to the fertility of the land; that is competition of the farmers will fix the rent at a level which will enable the farmer of average skill to earn the average rate of profit which the farmer on the worst land earns after paying the landowner only the *absolute rent*. Differential rent therefore goes to the landowner and the price of production (that is, costs plus average profit) is determined on the worst land.

One may illustrate the point in figures as follows (assuming that the average rate of profit earned generally by capital is 30 per cent—and that the farmer gets this average rate, and assuming that the area of land considered in each instance is the same): suppose the farmer on the worst land lays out £500 on constant capital; £500 on variable capital, wages; pays £100 in rent; and produces 140 units of produce. Assume that he will not continue in production unless he gets 30 per cent (£300) on his capital outlay of £1,000. Then, if this worst land is to be farmed at all, the produce of 140 units must yield £1,400, that is the price per unit of produce must be £10. Produce grown on the more fertile land will, of course, command the same price and for the lands of differing fertility matters will work out thus:

	Worst Land	Medium Land	Good Land
(1) Produce in units ..	140	160	180
(2) Value of produce at £10 per unit	£1,000	£1,600	£1,800
Costs			
(3) Constant Capital ..	£500	£500	£500
(4) Variable Capital ..	£500	£500	£500
(5) 30 per cent Profit on Capital	£300	£300	£300
(6) Absolute Rent	£100	£100	£100
(7) Difference appropriated by landowner as Differential Rent ..	Nil	£200	£400

Marx uses as a means of illustrating how differential rent arises from monopoly ownership of natural advantages, the example of land on which a waterfall happens to be located. The owners, he writes, "may exclude others and prevent them from investing capital in the waterfalls. They can permit such a use or forbid it. . . . Therefore the surplus profit, which arises from this employment of waterfall, is not due to capital but to the harnessing of a natural power, which can be monopolised and has been monopolised. . . . Under these circumstances the surplus profit is transformed into ground-rent, that is, it falls into the hands of the owner of the waterfall. . . . It is evident that this always is a differential rent, for it does not enter as a determining factor into the average price of production of commodities, but rather is based on it". (*Capital*, Vol. III, LW p. 630, K p. 756.)

Differential rent may arise from advantages in location or advantages in fertility. Of course, these two factors may work against one another; the gains from extra fertility may be negatived by long distances for transport to market towns. Many other combinations of factors enter in, but for present purposes there is no need to examine all of them in detail. It is, however, important to note that the fruits of increased investments of capital in the land may be appropriated in part by the landowner in the form of differential rent. As has been explained already, the landowner will be able, on the termination of a lease, to increase the rents of land which has been improved (for example, drainage or use of fertilisers, etc.). Moreover, a part of any additional surplus value derived from a general increase in the amount of capital invested in the land goes in the end to the landowners. The appropriation in these ways of the fruits of improvements to the land and of more intensive cultivation acts as a check to investment and retards the development of agriculture.

Differential rent arises from monopoly in the *use* of land and must continue to exist so long as the mode of production is capitalist and the land is farmed by individual capitalist enterprises. If land is privately owned the landowner appropriates this differential rent, leaving the capitalist his average rate of profit. *Absolute rent*, on the other hand, arises from monopoly in the *ownership* of land. It exists so long only as there is private ownership in land. "Can we assume," writes Lenin, "that the landowner will permit the farmer to exploit the worst and most badly located land which only produces the average profit on capital, gratis? Of course not. Land ownership is a monopoly, and on the basis of this monopoly the landowner demands payment from the farmer for this land also. This payment will be *absolute rent*, which has no connection whatever with the difference in productivity of different investments of capital and which has *its genesis in the private ownership of land*. . . . We are actually dealing with a two-fold monopoly: in the first place, we have monopoly of enterprise (capitalist) on the land. This monopoly originates in the limitation of land, and is therefore inevitable in any capitalist society. *This* monopoly leads to the price of grain being determined by the conditions of production on the worst land; the surplus profit obtained by the investment of capital on better land, or by a more productive investment of capital, forms differential rent. This rent arises quite independently of private property in land, which simply enables the landowner to take it from the farmer. In the second place, we have the monopoly of private property in land. Neither logically nor historically is this monopoly inseparably linked with the previous monopoly. This kind of monopoly is not *essential* for capitalist society and for the capitalist organisation of agriculture. . . . It is absolutely necessary to distinguish these two kinds of monopolies; and consequently it is also necessary to recognise that absolute rent which is *engendered* by private property in land exists side by side with differential rent." (Lenin, *The Agrarian Question and the Critics of Marx*, Chapter II.)

The Selling Price of Land

For political economy the key facts about land in modern capitalism are: (*a*) it is privately owned; (*b*) its area is limited; (*c*) it has, in the Marxist sense, no value (except in so far as labour has been put into it).

Land has no value since it is not the product of human labour. In so far as land has "socially necessary" labour-time expended upon its improvement, as on a drainage scheme, enrichment with fertilisers, fencing, hedging, clearing, etc., it contains a value in the true sense of the word. In effect, such improvements are no different from buildings built upon the land; their value derives from the average socially necessary labour-time required for their production. But the land, apart and distinct from improvements to or buildings on it, though in the strict sense it has no value, most certainly has a price, as frequent sales and purchases

137

of land in capitalist society clearly demonstrate. The following example shows how the price of land is determined. A man who buys a title to land buys a property right which enables him to appropriate a definite amount of surplus value. Suppose that this is £100 a year. Then the owner of this title is similarly placed to a man who has lent a sum of money on which he receives £100 in interest. If the prevailing rate of interest is 5 per cent that sum of money is £2,000. It is therefore just as good to own the title to the land as to own £2,000. The price of the land is then simply the *capitalised rental* (that is the capital sum which would yield interest equal to the rental). From this it follows that if interest rates fall, the price of land goes up; in our example, if interest rates fall to 2½ per cent the value of the land will tend to rise to £4,000.

Effect of Capitalism on Agriculture

The first effect—first, that is, in point of time—of captalism on agriculture was an increase in the yield of the land. The old three-field system (itself a great advance on the primitive methods of farming that had preceded it) was the typical method of farming in feudal times. The land which the feudal peasants tilled was divided out into three great "fields" in which each of the peasants held a number of strips of land about an acre each in area. The three great "fields" were tilled in rotation, one under wheat, say, one under oats, and one fallow. These traditional feudal methods of farming, enshrining in rigid custom the wisdom of earlier times, left no room for the application of new knowledge to the art of farming, and gave little scope to improved methods of cattle-raising. Moreover, they cost a deal of energy to peasant-farmers who tended widely separated strips. The compact farms and the new property and productive relations which capitalism brought made possible the introduction of modern methods of farming and released new productive potentialities; this was the progressive element in the brutal process by which the common lands were enclosed and the fabric of feudal life was torn asunder, forcing the serf or feudal peasant (save for the few who themselves became capitalist farmers) to leave their lands and seek work for wages either for an employer in town or else still on the land as a hired farm-worker.

Improved knowledge of crop rotation was applied, the land was "fed" with marl; new implements, better ploughs, reapers, threshing machines (invented 1784) were introduced, new knowledge was applied to the breeding of cattle, and so on, and as a consequence of all these developments the land yielded a substantially greater produce. (For example, beeves which in 1710 average 370 lb., in 1795 reached 800 lb. and sheep reached 80 lb. against an average of 28 lb. in 1710.)

Alongside of all this there were important changes in the relationships of men in production. The feudal manor was largely self-supporting. It bought little and sold little. The peasants' needs for food, clothing, and protection from the weather were in the main met by the efforts of the peasants themselves. It has already been shown how an important part in the breakdown of feudal society was played by the growth of the market, and how the growth of the market also led to capitalist production methods both in agriculture and industry. These developments caused in due course a complete transformation in social conditions and the manner of life. The countryman was no longer growing food with the prime object of feeding himself and the small community to which he belonged. Now he produced to sell; he produced for the market, and the conditions of his life were more likely to be disturbed by the uncertainties of the market than by the uncertainties of weather and disease which (leaving aside the temper of his feudal master) had hitherto been the countryman's main concern. Life changed in other ways besides. Capital in agriculture, though in its early days it counted for something and was profitable, came in the eighteenth and nineteenth centuries in Britain to be overshadowed by capital in industry. Though the division of labour and the concentration of wealth played its part in the development of capitalism in agriculture, the scope for increasing profits from the bringing together of more and more capital, the division and sub-division of processes of production, and the introduction of new productive methods was limited. Private property in land, though it had initially released new productive forces, soon began to act as a fetter on further advance.

In industry increases in surplus value due to the investment of capital in improved plant and machinery go in full to the capitalist; in agriculture, as already explained, long-term improvements to the land have meant more surplus value for the landowner rather than for the farmer. Moreover, the parcelling out of the land into comparatively small units and the lingering rights of feudal times have served as obstacles to the development of large-scale and scientific farming. When capital has been invested in agriculture in a big way it has usually gone where the fetters of private property were less likely to hamper its large-scale development—in the Americas, for example, or the Dominions where there were big tracts of sparsely populated lands and fewer age-old property rights, or in colonial territories where the old conditions of land tenure were, with conscious purpose, brutally destroyed and the natives driven from the land to supply the needs of the invading capital.

In Britain farming technique has been slow to develop, and whilst the tendency towards the concentration of capital that plays a highly important part in industrial development is seen also in agriculture, its effects are far less pronounced and agriculture remains generally in the hands of the small-scale capitalist and the family farmer.

Though the farm-labourer was wretchedly exploited, working long hours for a wage that bought only the barest necessities of life, the farmer himself was not much better off. Forced to pay high rentals and heavy rates of interest to the banks from which he had from time to time to borrow, the British farmer between the First and Second World Wars did not generally make high profits. His products had to compete with imported foods, and the large combines which monopolised the market for his goods took generous profit margins for themselves at his expense. The farmer had also to buy from monopolies, at the high prices which monopolies can enforce, such things as fertilisers, cattlefeed, and so forth. With so many people battening on such a backward industry it is not to be wondered at that the farmer fared poorly. The agricultural industry between the wars was allowed to sink into decay; and if in the twenty years since the outbreak of the Second World War, the situation in British agriculture has been somewhat better, it is due to the necessity to expand home production during the war, coupled with political pressure after the war which succeeded in securing large subsidies for British agriculture.

The Antithesis Between Town and Country

Because the investment of capital in the land runs into obstacles under conditions of private ownership, the scale of production in Britain (and indeed all Europe) carried on by each unit has remained very small. (In Britain in the 1940's, for example, when something over a million persons were employed on the land, there were some 400,000 individual farms.) Large-scale farming has developed mainly in sparsely populated lands and lands less encumbered by the encrusted rights of landed aristocracy. There is, therefore, in Europe particularly, a marked difference between the social conditions in manufacturing and heavy industry and the social conditions on the land. On the one hand, there is large-scale production, tens of thousands of workers employed in single factories, huge and dirty concentrations such as London, Birmingham, Glasgow, Newcastle, or Manchester; on the other hand, the quiet but stagnant life of the countryside with its small farms and villages. Corresponding to the economic contrast between town and country, is the difference in outlook and habits between the townsmen and country folk.

Backwardness of British Agriculture and its Problems Today

Agriculture in Britain will remain backward in relation to industry so long as small-scale farming remains the rule and so long as the technical and scientific possibilities of the present day are not exploited to the full. The vast profits that the industrial capitalists accumulated in the course of the nineteenth century were not invested in British agriculture. Not only did the property rights and exactions of the landowners militate against this, but also with the growth of imperialism there was more or less conscious opposition from the capitalists themselves, since they saw in food and raw material imports one of the main means by which interest payments on their vast overseas investments would return to Britain. Such imports represented to the big capitalists with imperial interests a means of realising their profits from overseas investments. The economic policy of British imperialism hit British agriculture a double blow; first as an investment home agriculture was passed over in favour of more profitable overseas investments and, secondly, the produce of colonial peasant labour living on the brink of starvation was drawn into commodity markets centred in Britain and other metropolitan countries. The vast colonial populations, on whom the advent of powerful foreign capital imposed the necessity of producing commodities for sale in overseas markets, constantly—and inevitably—oversupplied the metropolitan markets to the serious disadvantage of themselves and the agricultural producers of the metropolitan countries.

Britain in this way became dependent to an excessive and unnecessary degree on overseas supplies of food. Food accounted for about half of our total imports in 1946, less than half of our food supplies being met from home production. One of the most vital long-term problems is to redress the unbalance of capitalist economy (which fosters urban industry to excess) and to give greater technical and economic emphasis to development, both social and economic, in the countryside. Private property is the real obstacle to tackling this problem in a serious way, and social ownership and planned use of resources in the economy as a whole is the necessary precondition to any complete solution. Clearly also the problem of agriculture is linked with that of town and country planning. Political pressure in the post-war years had led to improvements in town and country planning and also in British agriculture, but the measures taken have shown at the same time what formidable obstacles private property in land and means of production puts in the way of any lasting and thorough solutions.

Rent Other Than Rent for Agricultural Land

The "rent" that people are most familiar with is house-rent. In the main this is not rent at all in the sense in which the term is here used; for in the main house-rent is payment for a part of the use-value of a commodity (namely, a house, which is a product of human labour, and which takes many years to consume or use up). But ground-rent constitutes a considerable part of the rent that a worker pays for a dwelling or a capitalist pays for a factory or office. Building land commands considerably higher prices than agricultural land because the differential rent due to location is high. Sites in or near towns which are suitable locations for housing estates, blocks of flats, office and commercial buildings, factories, etc., are limited and in heavy demand, but the advantages of locating a factory, for example, near other related industries, near railways and other transport centres, and so forth, are very considerable and mean big economies in working costs. Similarly, a shopping centre, if it is to do good business, must be near to residential, industrial, or commercial buildings, that is in some place where potential customers congregate. Workers' houses must be reasonably near factories or factories near workers' houses. In these ways one urban development leads to another, and the industrial expansions of the last century and a half have led to great increases in the price of land in and around the great industrial centres and to the vast enrichment of the owners of such land. The Marquess of Bute, for example, the owner of 117,000 acres of land, in 1938 disposed of an estate covering half of Cardiff and worth £20 million plus reversionary rights worth twice as much. The Duke of Westminster's estate included a square mile of London, mostly in Belgravia and Pimlico. The Duke of Devonshire, like many other property owners, assumed the anonymity of a limited company—Chatsworth Estates Ltd.—which is the "landlord" of a number of immensely valuable properties. The Church is another great urban landowner, whose revenue from property in 1939 totalled £1,822,000 (including £345,000 from houses and premises in or near London, £84,000 from the Paddington Estate, £693,000 from ground-rents on leases over fifty years, £337,000 from royalties, and £237,000 from farm lands and buildings). Land and property owners in Britain drew in 1946, for example, unearned income totalling, despite the effects of rent restrictions, £386 million.

Differential rents are also paid for other advantages to be reaped from the use of particular areas of the earth's surface or of its sub-soil, such as royalties for mining rights, wayleaves, enhanced rentals for land on which water supplies are to be found or on which electricity can be cheaply generated from water-power, land offering special attractions to tourists, and so on. Wherever there is private ownership of the land, speculative racketeering is liable to occur. This is particularly likely, as in Britain in the fifteen years after the Second World War, when prices and money incomes are tending to rise. The rise in land values due to the general rise in price levels, leads to speculative purchases of land which in turn stimulate further rises in land-values, particularly in towns, where the need for housing, factory and office space is imperative and continues to be met at constantly rising costs.

Production Relations in Agriculture

Production relations in agriculture are complex and various. The capitalist farmer is the exception rather than the rule in the world as a whole, though the hand of capitalism and monopoly capitalism makes itself felt wherever food is grown for sale. It may therefore be useful here to summarise the main types of economic and production relations that are to be found in agriculture.

I. The actual *working of the land* may be undertaken by

(*a*) a peasant-farmer employing no labour-power other than his own or his family's;

(*b*) a small capitalist farmer employing, perhaps, three or four "hands", and himself a "working farmer" (typical of much English farming);

(*c*) the "gentleman farmer", not himself working, but living from the surplus value derived from a large farm;

(*d*) large-scale ranch or plantation farming, involving big capital (mainly in the colonies and North and South America);

(*e*) co-operative farming, which may assume a wide variety of forms, ranging from joint working of the land to joint use of machinery and marketing of produce (mainly on the Continent of Europe).

II. *Ownership* of the land may be

(*a*) by an old feudal or landowning class exacting rents, dues or share of produce, usually from peasants or small farmers;

(*b*) by capitalists or property owners who have invested their capital in land and may or may not have an interest in the undertaking using the land;

(*c*) small farmers or peasants owning their own land, which is, however, frequently mortgaged and therefore in the virtual ownership of the mortgagee (usually a bank or other financial institution).

III. *Sale of produce* is for a very wide range of agricultural produce to large monopolies; for example, in the United Kingdom Ranks and Spillers (flour), in Africa Unilever (palm-kernels, etc.). Purchase of supplies (such as fertiliser from Imperial Chemical Industries) must also be made from monopolies for a considerable range of goods. The agricultural producers (most of whom are peasants and small men) are thus squeezed from either side by monopoly capitalism, with the result that a considerable part of the values produced on the land are appropriated by monopolies who can fix high selling and low buying prices.

CHAPTER VIII

REPRODUCTION OF CAPITAL AND CRISIS

Accumulation, without limit, is made inevitable by competition between capitals; since more capital is ultimately the only ammunition against rival capitals, there is no limit to the need to make profit, because there is no limit to the amount of accumulated profit deemed to constitute a sufficient reserve of economic strength. Profit as a means to more profit is, therefore, the constant aim. The satisfaction of the needs of the masses of the people is not the aim of capitalist production, nor even the provision of luxury goods for the propertied classes. The aim is profit.

Anarchy of Capitalist Production

Capitalist production is without plan or order; it is "anarchic". Each capitalist employer decides what and how much is to be produced, whether output should be increased, maintained, or cut down, whether a factory should be closed or a new factory built and set to work. His decisions are guided by his ability or otherwise to sell his products at profitable prices and his expectations of finding profitable markets in the future. Such order as exists in capitalism is therefore the order imposed by the laws of the market, not the purposeful order of a conscious plan (such as exists in socialist production). "Anarchy", writes Engels, "reigns in social production. But commodity production, like all other forms of production, has its own laws which are inherent in and inseparable from it; and these laws assert themselves, in spite of anarchy, in and through anarchy. These laws are manifested in the sole form of social relationship which continues to exist, in exchange, and enforce themselves on the individual producers as compulsory laws of competition. . . . They assert themselves apart from the producers and against the producers, as the natural laws of their form of production, working blindly. The product dominates the producers." (*Socialism, Utopian and Scientific*, Chapter III.)

145

The Turnover and Reproduction of Capital

As long as capitalist production continues without interruption, capital is being "turned over" and reproduced, and profits are being reaped. The turnover of capital is the "life process" of capitalism and deserves therefore some further consideration, supplementing what has already been said on this subject in Chapters IV and V. The basis of capitalist economy as a whole is industrial or productive capital, that is capital which is used to produce new commodities embodying values and surplus values. This capital must endlessly pass, if it is to keep "active", through a series of changing forms. Starting with money the industrial capitalist buys (*a*) means of production, buildings, machinery, raw materials, etc., (*b*) labour-power. Then follows the productive process, and the labour-power is set to work using the machines and raw materials to produce new commodities. However, if raw materials are not available, the turnover of capital is interrupted; production cannot go on until a source of supply for the missing raw materials has been found. Again, if machines or replacement parts cannot be purchased production is held up and the turnover of capital is interfered with or interrupted until supplies are obtained. Again, if labour-power is not available—if, for example, the workers go on strike—the turnover of capital cannot proceed until a supply of labour is forthcoming. Thus in order that the turnover of capital may continue, the capitalist must continuously be able to purchase the labour-power and means of production that he requires. In terms of the formula $M—C..P..new\ C—M^1$ (Money—Commodities..Production.. new Commodities embodying increased value—increased amount of Money), the successful completion of the stage M—C presupposes that the commodities required are available. It will be clear from what has been said above that if the scale of production is to be expanded, the capitalist needs not only an increased amount of money at the start of the new cycle of production, but he must also be able to purchase additional supplies of means of production and labour-power. If these are hard to obtain the expansion will be impeded.

When the process of production is completed the capitalist has in his hands commodities embodying old values previously contained in the means of production and new values created by the workers' labour. At this stage of the turnover his capital has assumed the form of commodities and it must speedily complete

146

the next stage of the turnover if it is to keep alive. The commodities produced must be sold (new C must become M¹). This is only possible so long as there are purchasers willing and able to buy—at profitable prices—the commodities which the capitalists produce. The turnover of capital depends therefore on the goods produced being sold. If this does not happen, the turnover is baulked and interrupted.

The whole problem of capitalist crisis is to explain why the turnover of capital is impeded or interrupted. The explanation of economic crisis falls therefore into three parts:

First, the study of the turnover of the social capital as a whole, which involves considering the relationship between the different branches of industry. This process involves the continual reproduction of capital, and is described therefore as *simple reproduction* if the total capital stays the same and as *expanded reproduction* if the total capital is increased. The study of simple and expanded reproduction shows what conditions need to be fulfilled if the market is to supply the goods that are required and to take up the goods that production supplies. From this study we see how disproportions between different branches of industry *might* disturb the balance of industry and hamper the turnover of capital.

Secondly, the study of the factors determining the level of demand in the economy as a whole, in relation to productive capacity.

Thirdly, the study of long term trends which tend to influence the course of development and structure of the capitalist economies and to intensify social contradictions wherever capitalism operates.

Simple Reproduction

In order to consider the balance between different branches of industry in its most simple—and fundamental—form, we divide all industry into two main groups: (I) industries producing goods used in the production of other goods, that is "means of production", and (II) industries producing goods which pass out of the field of production to be consumed in satisfaction of some human want—that is "consumers' goods", also called "means of consumption". (Of course, there are some goods which may be used either as consumers' goods or as means of production, such as coal, which may be used for heating homes or as industrial fuel. Such industries must be considered as falling partly under (I) above and partly under (II).) What balance must exist between these two departments of production in order that the turnover of capital may continue smoothly? It will be convenient first of all to consider *simple reproduction* of capital, that is the mere replacement of the capital used without any new capital being created out of the surplus value produced; or, in other words, reproduction without accumulation.

Capitalists producing means of production (Department I) buy raw materials, plant, etc., and hire labour-power which when set to work produces in addition to its own value a surplus value. The products of all these industries will therefore have a total value that contains (i) the value of the constant capital consumed (raw materials, part of machinery used up in the production period, fuel, ancillary materials, etc.); (ii) the variable capital (wages); and (iii) the surplus value, i.e. total value less (i) and (ii). The total value produced may be represented as $(c+v+s)$ where c is constant capital, v variable capital and s surplus value.

Similarly the total values produced in the consumption goods industries (Department II) contain (i) constant capital consumed; (ii) wages; (iii) surplus value.

The capitalists in Department I have at the end of the process of production a mass of "means of production", only a part of which they can themselves use in the next cycle of production. If their workers are to live, they cannot feed themselves on "nuts and bolts" and the other means of production they have produced. To live they must buy consumers' goods—food and clothing—the products of Department II. Likewise the capitalists who, it is assumed, do not accumulate but spend all their surplus value on means of consumption, will wish to buy goods produced by the other group of capitalists in exchange for their surplus value that has been embodied in such commodities as machines, steel, "nuts and bolts", etc., that is means of production. The capitalists and workers in the consumer goods industries, on the other hand, can get their means of living from the products of their own group of industries, but the machinery and raw materials which they need for the next cycle of production will have to be bought from the capitalists of Department I producing means of production.

If, therefore, requirements and supplies of consumers' goods and producers' goods respectively are in balance, the means of production offered for sale by the producers' goods industries (over and above what they take for themselves) exchange for the consumers' goods offered for sale by the consumers' goods industries (over and above what they take for themselves). Since simple reproduction is here being considered (that is, it is assumed that there is no accumulation of capital), the condition implied in this exchange is that the prices of the consumer goods sold by Department II equal in total the prices of the producer goods sold by Department I. This gives: wages plus surplus value in producer goods industries equal constant capital used up in the consumer goods industries; that is: $(v+s)$ in Department I equal c in Department II.

Expanded Reproduction

Expanded reproduction means reproduction of capital on an increased scale. This is done by using a part of the surplus value produced in the course of one "turnover" of capital as new, additional capital in the next "turnover". The surplus value accumulated (that is turned into new capital), will partly be spent on raw materials, machinery, etc., forming constant capital, and partly on the wages paid to the additional workers employed by the new capital. If production is to match requirements, and vice versa, under these circumstances, the consumer goods required by Department I must exchange against the producer goods required by Department II. However, Department I requirements of consumer goods will not be the same as in simple reproduction. As before, these requirements will be for personal consumption by wage workers and for personal consumption by capitalists, but this time to the original wage workers' consumption must be added that of new workers employed as a result of new investment of capital. (This naturally will be only one part of the new investment.) On the other hand capitalists' consumption will not equal the whole surplus value produced in Dept. I because that part of the surplus value which is accumulated (the *whole* new investment) must be deducted. Also Dept. II's requirements for machinery, raw materials, etc., will have changed and now to the replacement of the constant capital consumed there must be added such part of the new investment out of surplus value as is expended on raw materials, machinery, etc.—that is in the form of new additions to constant capital. In short, consumer goods from Department II go to Department I for (i) the old labour force (ii) the new labour force and (iii) capitalists' personal consumption; and producers' goods come from Department I to Department II (iv) to replace means of production used up and (v) to expand means of production. (If the total prices of items (i) above are represented by the symbol V_I, (ii) by SvI, (iii) by SxI, (iv) by C_{II}, and (v) by $ScII$, then $V_I+SvI+SxI=C_{II}+ScII$.)

How these Proportions are Established

It is not difficult to see that in the thousands of sub-branches of industry (such as production of timber, steel, machine-tools, bread, luxury foods, etc.) goods produced and goods used, supplies of products and requirements of means of production, must be properly proportioned if a balance between the two departments is to be achieved and surpluses and shortages are to be avoided. In fact, these proportions are never established with any precision. Each producer feels his way towards making the best profits he can by judging the state of the market, and so the market in a clumsy and socially costly way governs and corrects the balance of production between the main and subsidiary sectors of industry. The aim of a socialist economy is to remove the control of private property and profit and to substitute the conscious, deliberate control of an economic plan. The plan is designed to shape the main proportions of production (reflected in "production targets") and its implementation requires an appropriate balance of prices to facilitate the realisation of the plan.

The essential difference between a socialist and capitalist economy is to be found in the economic forces by which the main direction and purpose of the producers is governed. Of course, the aim of consciously and purposefully determining the use of resources and the main proportions between sectors of production does not preclude use of "markets" and "market techniques" as instruments within the general framework of a plan. A "market economy" on the other hand, is one in which "the market" is the governing factor and implies a predominance of private ownership and control of means of production. A "planned economy" is one in which a consciously determined plan is the governing factor and implies public ownership and social control of the means of production.

In unplanned capitalist society thousands of privately controlled businesses decide what will be produced without knowing what other capitalists in their own or other countries are going to produce. Each assumes that market conditions will be such as to absorb his products when they are ready for sale. The network linking producers and users is, in fact, very complex, for the balance to be struck is not only between means of production and means of consumption in general, but also between the many sub-divisions of each industry; for example, there must be a certain proportion between the production of textile goods and textile machinery, between the output of the engineering industry and the supply of iron and steel, etc., etc.

The disproportions that afflict capitalist production are never easily overcome. Overproduction here will lead to falling prices and bankruptcies. Shortages there will temporarily result in extra profits which may lead to expanded production and attract new capital. So crudely, blindly, bringing in their train unemployment and idle machines and plant, the laws of the market and the laws of commodity exchange under capitalism assert themselves. As technique changes, further changes occur in the balance between industries, and so endlessly adjustments and readjustments become necessary. However, the disproportions linger on, impede the turnover of capital and incessantly cause endless waste of productive resources.

Crises of Relative Over-production

What has so far been said may be summed up as follows: the anarchy of capitalism causes ceaseless waste and dislocation, the subtle proportions between the different branches of production that make up the complex network of modern industry are only established in the ebb and flow of capital which takes place so long as there are disproportions causing products to be sold above or below their values (or, more accurately speaking, *prices of production*). However, as the historical experience of capitalism shows, the crises that occur are much more than partial crises, that is, in addition to surpluses, unemployment, unused capacity in some industries and scarcity and shortages in others, there occur again and again general crises affecting all branches of production, creating what would seem, had it not so often in fact occurred, an absurd impossibility, namely, over-production, unemployment, surplus and excess all round in virtually all branches of industry. How does this absurdity come about, this *general* inability to use existing means of producing wealth in a world of poverty? Below we shall consider how decline in one part of an economy tends to spread by generating decline in other parts; but first we will consider a basic aspect of capitalism which predisposes the economy as a whole to general crises.

It is first necessary to consider how *relative over-production*, namely, production in all branches exceeding effective demand, is possible. Over a century ago those whom Marx called "the vulgar economists" (such as J. B. Say, the French economist) asserted that over-production was impossible since every sale represented a purchase and every purchase a sale. (They recognised the unity but failed to recognise the contradiction implied in purchase and sale.) This line of argument, which reappears again and again in bourgeois economic theory, runs generally as follows: every sale creates income for the seller, who in return distributes the proceeds as wages, profits, interest, rent, etc., which represent the purchasing power which constitutes demand. Therefore total output necessarily equals total demand. This conception of things became so deeply imbedded in capitalist economic theory that when Keynes in the 1930's (still working within the basic assumptions of modern capitalist theory) maintained that market and monetary forces left to themselves would not necessarily result in the full and optimum utilisation of economic resources, his views were for some years regarded as dangerously heretical by most other capitalist theorists, and it is only since the Second World War (see below p. 173 ff.) that his theories have become firmly established as the "new orthodoxy".

The theoretical refutation of Say is not difficult. Its plausibility derives from the fact that whenever some one sells a commodity someone else is paid. If payment were made in goods, if, that is, barter prevailed, it would, of course, be true, not to say obvious, that for all goods given in barter a corresponding amount of goods are received in barter; here, if you like, supply must equal demand. But when money intervenes, it is not at all necessary that demand should equal supply or for every sale to represent a purchase *of another commodity*.

"Nothing can be more childish", writes Marx, "than the dogma, that because every sale is a purchase, and every purchase a sale, therefore the circulation of commodities necessarily implies an equilibrium of sales and purchases. If this means that the number of sales is equal to the number of purchases, it is mere tautology. But its real purpose is to prove that every seller brings his buyer to market with him. Nothing of the kind. The sale and the purchase constitute one identical act, an exchange between a commodity-owner and an owner of money, between two persons as opposed to each other as the two poles of a magnet. . . . No one can sell unless someone else purchases. But no one is forthwith bound to purchase because he has just sold. Circulation bursts through all restrictions as to time, place, and individuals, imposed by direct barter, and this it effects by splitting up, into the antithesis of a sale and a purchase, the direct identity that in barter does exist between the alienation of one's own and the acquisition of some other man's product. . . . If the split between the sale and the purchase becomes too pronounced, the intimate connection between them, their one-ness, asserts itself by producing—a crisis." (*Capital*, Vol. I, LW p. 113, A p. 87.)

Wherever commodity exchange has developed, the *possibility* exists that commodities produced for sale may not find a purchaser. The values produced *may* not be realised. When capitalism has developed, this eventuality is not merely possible, it is inevitable, for reasons that will be explained in the next section. Here, however, it may be pointed out that in developed capitalism the capitalist will buy goods and labour-power—that is he will re-invest the capital and surplus value which he gets back in money form from the sale of his products—only in so far as *re-investment promises to be profitable.*

The Inevitability of Crisis in Capitalist Production

The purpose of capitalist production is to increase capital by producing and *realising* surplus value in exchange.

In the process of reproduction capital has to pass through three stages: (i) money capital is transformed into productive capital (machinery, raw materials, labour-power), (ii) productive capital by the process of production is transformed into com-modities of a higher value than the capital used up, (iii) commodities (including the "surplus") are reconverted into money again. Without this continuous transformation, capital remains idle; it cannot produce surplus value.

Why is it *inevitable* in this capitalist process of production that there should periodically be crises of over-production, in which productive capacity and the production of goods for sale outstrips the effective demand?

Consider first why and how each capitalist is trying to expand. Clearly, the larger the scale of production, the greater the potential profit, and the larger the profit, the greater the resources out of which to expand production; and so a capitalist would like it to go on *ad infinitum*. The capitalist who instals new plant and introduces new methods, reaps on every article produced extra profits at the expense of his rivals who have less advanced methods of production. On the other hand, the capitalist who does not build up his productive resources is liable to be forced out of business by his rivals. The drive for ever more accumulation and ever more productive power is, therefore, inseparable from capitalist production. Marx speaks of "the tendency of capitalist production to develop the productive forces as if only the absolute power of consumption of the entire society would be their limit." (*Capital*, Vol. III, LW pp. 472-3, K p. 568.)

So long as this process of accumulation is going on generally throughout the economy, the expanded production and stock-building of the capitalists is providing a larger market, more raw materials are bought and used, new machines are installed and the very fact of shortages sharpens the desire to build up stocks. However, the scramble to expand proceeds without order or prevision of where the economy as a whole is heading. Lack of balance is bound to occur at one point or another, causing breaks in the market. When this occurs, a break in the market in one place will have repercussions elsewhere. Furthermore, there are many other circumstances (e.g. technical change, changes in overseas markets or "price relativities") that may upset such balance of supply and requirements as exists; but since all the time each capitalist is looking for every opportunity to increase profits relatively to costs, this must mean restraining mass consumption relatively to total production. If wages and other non-capitalist incomes go up, for example by 5 per cent and total production by 10 per cent, the share of profits in the national income, if it was, say, 50 per cent to start with, will rise to 52.3 per cent and that of wages and other income will fall to 47.7 per cent. So once the upsurge of accumulation is interrupted, as it inevitably must be sooner or later in socially anarchic production, the consumer market, which stands at the end of the chain of sales and purchases between capitalists, inevitably proves itself restricted and inadequate to sustain the general level of the market. It cannot compensate for a falling off in the demand of capitalists for producer goods; it soon begins itself to fall as here and there the level of production, and with it employment, is cut back.

In a fully capitalist country such as Britain, the money that is spent on consumption will, in the main, be either the wages of workers or else will come out of surplus value. Of these two sources of expenditure on consumers' goods the wages of the workers is much the more important. Capitalists' expenditure on consumer goods, though higher per head, is in total much less because they are far fewer in number. Moreover, as already explained, the proportion of surplus value spent on consumption tends to get less, since it is of the essence of capitalism that as concentration and centralisation of capital proceeds an ever greater part of profits is accumulated by the capitalist class as a whole.

It follows that the decisive element, the main factor ultimately determining the level of demand for consumers' goods is, in a capitalist country (under normal conditions) the sum total of wages paid to the workers. The incomes of traders and many others are, directly or indirectly, dependent very largely on the purchasing power of wage-earners. Since, however, the motive force of capitalist production is profit, and since the lower the share of wages in the output, the higher the share of profits, there is a constant tendency for capitalist society to undermine its own mass market. This contradiction between the expansion of production and the relative restriction of the mass market for consumer goods finds expression both in the "boom" and "slump" phases through which the cycle of production tends to pass in capitalist society. Expansion always implies an expansion of profits, and so expansion of accumulation and an expansion of purchasing power in which the main emphasis is on producers' goods. Prices generally rise, bank advances and deposits rise, the money supply made available through the banks expands; and because prices rise, the advantage of increased mass purchasing through increased wages is counteracted by the decreased purchasing power of each pound and shilling in terms of goods. Mass purchasing power, though higher in money terms, in real terms remains somewhat restricted, at all events relatively restricted. The longer the expansion continues, the stronger these inflationary trends become; but once the expansion and the inflation stop, employment and wage payments are reduced and mass purchasing in money terms shrinks.

The inevitability of capitalist crisis derives from the contradiction between the social character of production and the private appropriation of the values produced by the capitalists who use them solely with the aim of appropriating more profit. The thirst for profit causes each capitalist on the one hand to expand without limit his productive resources and, on the other hand, to restrict ever more and more the share in the product going to the worker. The same motive—profit—stimulates these mutually contradictory tendencies. "The last cause of all real crises", writes Marx in the passage already in part quoted above, "always remains the poverty and restricted consumption of the masses as compared to the tendency of capitalist production to develop the productive forces as if only the absolute power of consumption of the entire society would be their limit." (*Capital*, Vol. III, LW pp. 472–3, K p. 568.)

Crisis and the Struggle for Markets

The contradiction that leads the capitalists to crisis also drives them to try to escape crisis by winning new markets. Capitalist goods invade the territories of all the older modes of production, destroying handicraft and peasant production. Large-scale production calls for expanded markets and new outlets are sought overseas. However, as capitalism spreads over ever larger sections of the world, the contradictions of capitalism appear not merely as contradictions within each national economy, but as contradictions of world economy. An ever wider range of independent producers and the many millions of peasants and handicraft workers in colonial and backward countries are with the spread of capitalism drawn into its market. But whilst this process undermines their pre-existing economic conditions, the dominance of the industrially developed capitalist powers obstructs, economically and politically, their own development and advancement. So again in this way also the expansion of capitalism restricts the development of mass purchasing power on a world scale. Everywhere capitalist production establishes itself abroad, the employment that it provides tends to go with disruption of the pre-existing economy and to create greater masses of under- or unemployment elsewhere. In short, where capitalism goes it creates poverty undermining the purchasing power of the very people that it has drawn within its orbit.

A Century and a Half of Recurring Crises

Crisis is the violent expression of the fundamental contradiction of capitalist production, the contradiction between social production and private appropriation of the product. All depend on all, and all are linked to all in modern capitalist society (that is to say production is *social*), yet decisions on what shall be produced, when, where, and how, are taken by the relatively small number of capitalists in the light only of their *private* interests of profit and power. With ever-increasing intensity this contradiction has expressed itself in general crises of over-production which have recurred roughly every ten years since the beginning of the nineteenth century. "For many a decade past", wrote Marx and Engels in the *Communist Manifesto* of 1848, "the history of industry and commerce is but the history of the revolt of modern productive forces against modern conditions of production, against the property relations that are the conditions for the existence of the bourgeoisie and of its rule. It is enough to mention the commercial crises that by their periodical return put the existence of the entire bourgeois society on its trial, each time more threateningly. In these crises a great part, not only of the existing products, but also of the previously created productive forces, are periodically destroyed. In these crises there breaks out an epidemic that, in all earlier epochs, would have seemed an absurdity—the epidemic of overproduction. Society suddenly finds itself put back into a state of momentary barbarism; it appears as if a famine, a universal war of devastation had cut off the supply of every means of subsistence; industry and commerce seem to be destroyed. And why? Because there is too much civilisation, too much means of subsistence, too much industry, too much commerce. The productive forces at the disposal of society no longer tend to further the development of the conditions of bourgeois property; on the contrary, they have become too powerful for these conditions, by which they are fettered, and so soon as they overcome these fetters, they bring disorder into the whole of bourgeois society, endanger the existence of bourgeois property. The conditions of bourgeois society are too narrow to comprise the wealth created by them."

157

Sir William Beveridge, in his *Full Employment in a Free Society*, analyses the course of industrial activity in Britain for over a century and a half, and concludes that "fluctuation of industrial activity in Britain in periods of an average length not very different from those of the modern trade cycle can be traced over the whole time for which data of construction industries are available, i.e., from 1785" (p. 309). He records (p. 281) the following years of boom and slump:

Crests	Troughs
1792	1797
1803	1808
1810	1816
1818	1821
1825	1832
1836	1842-43
1845-46	1849-50
1853	1858
1860	1862
1865	1867
1874	1879
1882-83	1886
1889	1893
1899	1903-04
1906-07	1908-09

A boom followed the 1914-18 war, giving way to slump in 1921, a new boom in 1929 was followed by slump that reached its lowest point in 1932. In 1938 industrial activity was falling off sharply, but the normal course of a new crisis that was developing was interrupted by the arms race and preparations for war.

Since the Second World War, industrial production in Britain rose up to 1951, the index – 1954 = 100 – being 79 in 1948 and 91 in 1951. In 1952 there was a slight decline, by 2 per cent. Then a three years rise, carrying the index of industrial production to 105, was followed by 4 years of stagnation till 1958 when a new rise began, which again came to a halt in 1961.

Unemployment in Britain has since the Second .World War remained relatively low (1.5 per cent in 1949 rising to 2 per cent in 1952, falling to 1.1 per cent in 1955 and rising again to 2.1 per cent in 1958). The course of unemployment in the preceding 80 years is depicted in the diagram below.

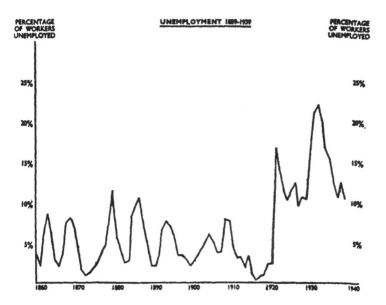

From the 1840's on, this same cycle of production repeats itself not merely in Britain but also in Europe and America; the crisis of over-production becomes a world crisis of over-production.

Since the Second World War the sharpest industrial fluctuations have been in the U.S.A. where there were marked declines in industrial production in 1948-49, in 1954 and in 1958. Unemployment in the U.S.A. has also been considerable and tending to rise. (In 1961 it was nearly 7 per cent.)

The Trade Cycle

The contradiction of capitalist production makes itself felt, not in the form of a prolonged steady over-supplying of the market, but in *periodical* crises. In a slump orders will be cut and the low level of production will be supplied largely from existing stocks; but in time replacement becomes necessary and productive activity increases. Capitalists find that the demand for their products is improving. Many therefore decide with each new turnover of capital to extend their scale of operations; they buy more raw materials, perhaps install some new machines, and employ more workers. This increased activity at certain points

159

within the capitalist system has important consequences for capitalism as a whole. For example, more workers will be employed and as a result more wages in total will be paid. This will mean a more lively demand for food, clothing, furniture, and for all the other goods that enter into the consumption of the working class. The suppliers of these goods will feel the demand for their products increasing, prices will probably go up and this will encourage them to produce more than before. However, as well as—and more important than—the increase in the wages bill will be the increased demand for equipment and for raw materials, leading to rising prices and expanded production of these "producers' goods". Everywhere *the market* expands—and in particular the market for producers goods which is the mainstay of every expansion in capitalist production.

As expansion at one point in the system stimulates expansion elsewhere, giving rise to yet further expansions, demand begins to outstrip supply; business looks up and all seems to go well. But how long does this go on? In this stage of recovery the increased demand will be both for producers' goods and consumers' goods; but the emphasis at this stage will tend to be on producers' goods. New modern methods of production in which labour costs are relatively low (and constant capital relatively high) will go ahead fastest; also extra raw materials and machines, etc., must be ordered and obtained first before expanded reproduction can go ahead. It will take time, in some cases a year or two, for these goods to be produced and delivered; but at last they will come forward in increased quantities and begin to be converted into other products. Ultimately the values they represent will be embodied in "consumption goods"; a piece of steel, for example, is made into a petrol lighter *or* into a machine tool which in turn begins to gradually give up its value in use and to embody it in the numerous goods produced through its agency, be they petrol lighters, pencils, or other machine tools—which in turn form a link in a chain of production that normally will end in the production of "consumption goods.".

After a period of expansion there always begins a period of slump, the onset of which is generally cataclysmic, since once the threat of glutted markets and falling prices is seen, every capitalist hastens to save what he can. Some quickly cut production and try to sell while they may the goods they have on hand; or they will try to maintain prices by destruction of stocks and means of production. In a few months production has dropped down to a low level of activity. A period of stagnation follows—the "depression"—which may continue for a matter of years. After a time when many factories have been closed down, when others have continued production at a low level without renewing their equipment, when stocks have been sold out or destroyed, a stage is reached when the meagre supply of commodities has fallen below the reduced demand. Things do not, after all, come to a complete standstill even in the worst crisis; there remains a certain minimum demand that is "effective" and has to be satisfied. Necessary repairs and re-equipment of plant are postponed as long as the crisis is acute. When prices are slumping nobody buys if he can wait until they have touched bottom. In the end, however, orders will be placed. Eventually production and employment begin to rise again and demand for goods begins to increase in step with the increased incomes of newly employed workers. The economic system gets back again to the stage of recovery. So the cycle continues.

In the nineteenth century, the period of the cycle tended to be about 10 years or thereabouts. After the Second World War in the U.S.A., the tendency was for the cycle to be considerably shorter. Apart from the 1945-46 downturn arising out of the switchover from arms to civil production, industrial production dropped in 1948-49, 1953-54, 1957-58 and 1960-61. That is the cycle period in these 15 years was roughly 5, 4, and 3 years successively. A feature of the post-war American cycle was the relatively high level of final consumption maintained through the cycle; and it is worthy of note that this, without an expanding demand for producers goods, is insufficient under the conditions of capitalist production to sustain the overall level of economic activity. Often—and this is true of the past as well as of recent years—the precipitating cause of a downturn is a chance event or external factor that shows up the lack of momentum that has already developed in the system, and, once generally seen, this causes, all round, decisions to contract production and stock building. The rising boom is like a tower in which every structural weakness becomes more and more dangerous as the height increases.

Fixed and Circulating Capital and the Trade Cycle
It was explained in Chapter V that the essential difference

between *fixed* and *circulating capital* is to be found in the different rates at which they turn over, and the fact that fixed capital yields up its value gradually and circulating capital "at one go" (see p. 85). Circulating capital (capital devoted to the purchase of raw materials, etc., and the payment of wages) normally completes the cycle Money—Commodities—Money in a matter of months, whereas it is a matter of years or even decades before fixed capital (capital invested in machinery, factory buildings, etc.) has yielded its full value and returned into the hands of its owner in the form of money.

In analysing and explaining the course of the trade cycle, it is important to bear in mind this distinction between fixed and circulating capital. If production is to continue, circulating capital must continually be replaced; wages must continue to be paid, and raw materials must continue to be provided. If circulating capital is not replaced in full, then production cannot continue at the same level as formerly. The position with regard to fixed capital is very different: machines and buildings need not, and indeed usually will not, be steadily replaced as they wear out.

When the first signs of crisis appear, capitalists who in the boom had been tumbling over each other to buy new machinery and build new factories, immediately stop doing so and scrap their plans for expansion. Their expenditure on fixed capital is limited to provision, severely reduced, for repairs and maintenance.

Fluctuations in construction and machinery production are therefore far more violent than in industry generally. The replacement of fixed capital does not follow a smooth course but goes by "stops and starts" in rhythm with the cycle of boom and slump. Marx, writing in 1870 on the turnover cycle of capital, says: "If the development of fixed capital extends the length of this life [of industrial capital] on the one side, it is on the other side shortened by the continuous revolution of the instruments of production. . . . This implies . . . the necessity of continuous replacement . . . long before they are worn out physically. One may assume that this life cycle, in the essential branches of great industry, now averages ten years. However, it is not a question of any one definite number here. So much at least is evident that this cycle comprising a number of years, through which capital is compelled to pass by its fixed part, furnishes a material basis

162

for the periodical commercial crises in which business goes through successive periods of lassitude, average activity, over-speeding, and crisis. . . . A crisis is always the starting-point of a large amount of new investments. Therefore it also constitutes, from the point of view of society, more or less a new material basis for the next cycle of turnover." (*Capital*, Vol. II, LW pp. 185–6, K p. 211.)

The following figures illustrate the relatively more violent oscillations of industrial activity in construction and production of machinery in the great crisis of 1929:

Index of Industrial Activity
(*Full Employment*, Beveridge, pp. 312-13)

			Construction and Instruments	Other Industries
1929	..	..	133.9	113.3
1930	..	..	119.8	109.3
1931	..	..	74.9	99.1
1932	..	..	51.1	95.0
1933	..	..	75.9	95.4
1934	..	..	100.2	100.3

Tendency of the Falling Rate of Profit

In the nineteenth century crises the typical course of price movements was as follows. As the depression gives way to recovery prices begin to rise. With the onset of the boom prices rise still further, then, auguring the slump that must follow the boom, prices begin to weaken and sooner or later the crash comes and prices tumble headlong down. These price movements are not the cause, but the consequence, of the trade cycle. In the period after the Second World War (when, in effect, all capitalist countries had left the gold standard) the persistent, "creeping" inflation of prices, though more pronounced in boom periods, continued in many instances even through periods of decline.

Through the ups and downs of the trade cycle a number of long term processes tend to make themselves felt and to shape the more general course of economic development. The process of accumulation of capital, with improving technique, involving less labour in the production of each unit, reduces the exchange value of each unit, and so should reduce the price. But in fact, no capitalist reduces his price until the market compels him to do so. While in the period of boom the technique of an enterprise or industry may be rapidly improving, the big demand usually enables the capitalist to maintain the old price (or even increase it) in spite of the reduced value of each unit. It is only when the crisis comes that there is a "shake-out", a compulsory adjustment of prices to the reduced value of the products. For the capitalist, when prices are high and demand is brisk, it will be easy to earn a high rate of profit; this will encourage him to new investment and production on an expanded scale which, in the short run, will help to sustain the boom but in the long run when contraction begins, will leave a wider margin of unused capacity.

The weakening of prices or of demand, once contraction begins at some points in the system, causes capitalists elsewhere to retrench and "draw in their horns", since lower prices must mean a lower rate of profit. The cutting back of production in one place leads to cutting back elsewhere. The crash starts. Prices tumble down and profits fall, sink for some capitalists to nothing, and for others turn to losses. With this rise and fall in prices in the course of boom and slump the rate of profit oscillates violently, rising sharply in the boom and dropping steeply in the slump. This upswing and downswing of profits does not, of course, reflect changing rates of exploitation, but changing relations of prices and values which arise from the changing conditions of demand and supply in the successive phases of the trade cycle.* However, behind the oscillations in the rate of profit that reflect the changing market conditions in the cycle of boom and slump, long-term forces are at work. As capitalism "shakes out" of each crisis, it emerges changed.

The structure of the economy as a whole is changed. Old plants have gone out of use, new plants are coming into use. Methods of production have changed. Probably, concentrations of some productive units have occurred; and by reason of these various changes the balance of capital invested in different forms, that is for payment of wages, purchase of materials, purchase of plant and equipment, has also changed.

* In the boom prices *in general*, that is all prices, tend to be above value; in slump they tend *in general* to be below value. Price is the *money* expression of value; a general price rise means, therefore, a fall in the value of money and vice versa. In the course of the trade cycle, there are sharp reversals (at the peak of the boom and trough of the slump) in the exchange relationship as between commodities in general on the one side and the money commodity on the other.

The dynamic factor in these changes is always the change in productive techniques. The capitalist entrepreneur knows he can increase his own capital if he can get a greater output out of his workers without costs being correspondingly increased. He is therefore looking always for new methods of production, new technique, new plant and equipment, which will reduce his costs. His interest is not in productivity for its own sake, but in póssible ways of increasing profits. Naturally, if wage rates are very low, the inducement to introduce costly labour-saving machinery will be less strong. Again, in "monopolised" industries which are not exposed to the full blast of cut-throat competition, capitalists may delay the introduction of new plant and technique in order to safeguard the value of the equipment which they already possess. However, even with cheap labour or monopoly conditions the drive towards technical advance (though weaker and slower) nevertheless persists. Moreover, in the upswing of the trade cycle wages tend to rise and this necessarily acts as an additional stimulus to technical improvement.

Reduction of costs and the measures necessary to this end seem from the capitalist's standpoint plain common sense. He would, for example, calculate that, with wages at such and such a rate and the cost of machinery, etc., being such and such, he could produce more at a lower cost per unit and make a good extra profit. There is, however, more in all this than meets the eye. The capitalist has laid out capital on machinery and his new machinery will, because it increases productivity, involve as a rule greater consumption of raw materials per man employed. His outlay on constant capital will therefore increase greatly by comparison with wages (variable capital) not only on account of the cost of the improved machinery but also because of the additional consumption of raw materials. Suppose that he now expends £80 on constant capital for every £20 on variable, whereas before he expended £50 on constant for every £50 on variable. What effect will this have on the rate of profit? If in the first instance the rate of surplus value was 100 per cent, the overall rate of profit would have been 50 per cent, thus:

$$c + v + s$$
$$50 + 50 + 50 = 150 \text{ and}$$
$$\text{the rate of profit} = \frac{s}{c+v} = \frac{50}{100} = 50 \text{ per cent}$$

However, after the introduction of the new machinery, even though the rate of exploitation is increased to 150 per cent, the rate of profit falls to 30 per cent. Now £80 goes on constant capital for every £20 on variable, and the whole calculation works out as follows:

$$c + v + s$$
$$80 + 20 + 30 = 130, \text{ and}$$

the rate of profit $= \dfrac{s}{c + v} = \dfrac{30}{100}$ and is therefore 30 per cent.

This is indeed a startling result, which seems so opposed to everyday industrial experience as to be hard to believe. The capitalist only adopts technically improved methods of production when—and because—they will bring him more profit.* The analysis given above seems to prove quite the opposite. The point, however, is that the immediate consequences for the industrial capitalist are altogether different from the ultimate consequences for capitalist society and the capitalist class as a whole. "No capitalist", writes Marx, "voluntarily introduces a new method of production, no matter how much more productive it may be, and how much it may increase the rate of surplus value, so long as it reduces the rate of profit. But every new method of production of this sort cheapens the commodities. Hence the capitalist sells them originally above their prices of production, or perhaps above their value. He pockets the difference, which exists between these prices of production and the market-prices of the other commodities produced at higher prices of production. He can do this, because the average labour-time required socially for the production of these other commodities is higher than the labour-time required under the new methods of production. His method of production is above the social average. But competition generalises it and subjects it to the general law. Then follows a fall in the rate of profit—perhaps first in this sphere of production, which gradually brings the others to its level—which is, therefore, wholly independent of the will of the capitalist." (*Capital*, Vol. III, LW p. 259, K p. 310.)

* Once expensive new plant has been installed, once workers have been trained to particular methods, and so forth, heavy financial loss will be involved if a capitalist introduces new methods before the old have earned their keep. Technical development as between different firms, different industries and indeed different countries is for such reasons necessarily uneven: now one goes ahead and now another.

The position is that the conclusions of the theoretical calculation given above have a certain validity as representing a tendency within the economy considered as a whole over a period of time—the tendency, in Marxist terminology, for the rate of profit to fall. The tendency is for the introduction of more advanced techniques to depress the average *rate* of profit in the economy as a whole. Despite the fact that the firms first introducing new techniques may increase their rates of profit, others also soon go over to more advanced techniques and as a result of competition the average rate of profit, in time, falls. At the same time the more backward firms lose markets and make considerably lower rates of profit, though the various firms may not feel the full impact of their new situation until the slump and depression phase of the trade cycle is reached.

Mass and Rate of Profit

This tendency for the rate of profit to fall is a highly complex one and in its operation is dependent upon particular social and historical circumstances; and this should be clearly borne in mind in considering the oversimple numerical illustration below, designed only to make more intelligible the general concept of the long term changes liable to occur in the economic structure. The rate of profit tends to fall as the technique of production develops, since improved technique involves usually a greater outlay of capital on machinery and raw materials; in short, the *organic composition of capital* tends to become higher. The division of a typical £100 of capital at three successive dates might, for example, be as follows:

		Constant Capital	Variable Capital
1860	..	50	50
1870	..	60	40
1880	..	70	30

Suppose that the rate of surplus value was 100 per cent in each year, then the profit on this £100 of capital would have been 50 per cent in 1860, 40 per cent in 1870 and 30 per cent in 1880. The rate of profit would have fallen. But would the total profits of the capitalist class have fallen also? This by no means follows from the fact that the *rate* of profit has fallen. The total *amount* of profit going to the capitalist class depends not only on the *rate* of profit but also on the amount of capital on which profit is being earned. This, as the processes of accumulation proceed, increases. Thus the very process which raises the *organic composition of capital* and causes the *rate* of profit to fall, at the same time increases the total *amount* of capital. As a consequence the total *mass* of profit will tend to rise at the same time as the *rate* tends to fall. An example will make the point clear. Total capital in Britain probably increased by about two-thirds between 1893 and 1913 (when it was—at a very rough estimate—about £8,500 million). Suppose that in the earlier year a rate of profit of 12 per cent was earned on £5,000 million and in the latter 10 per cent on £8,500 million, then, despite the fall in the *rate*, the mass of profit would have increased from £600 million to £850 million. (In fact figures for total profits given by national income statisticians —which include profits on overseas investments—show a greater increase; however, available statistics on capital and profits are very inadequate and do not provide sufficient information from which to calculate the true rates of "home-produced" profit.)

Causes Counteracting the Tendency of the Rate of Profit to Fall

Marx was careful not to speak categorically of a falling rate of profit but of a *tendency* for this to happen. The law, he says, becomes "more of a tendency, that is, a law whose absolute enforcement is checked, retarded, weakened, by counteracting influences." (*Capital*, Vol. III, LW p. 229, K p. 275.)

The counteracting influences listed by Marx include:

(i) *Raising the intensity of exploitation.* The capitalist in pursuit of higher profit drives his workers the harder and if a lengthening of hours cannot be enforced, seeks the same end by speeding up the rate at which the machinery operates. At the same time improvement in technique leads to an increase in relative surplus value (as assumed in the example given above) and even though real wages stay at the same level they tend to fall in relation to the values produced by the worker.

(ii) *Depression of wages below value.* Again and again the capitalists try to fight against falling profits by cutting wages (as in 1921 and 1931).

(iii) *Cheapening of the elements of constant capital.* Increased productivity of labour means that the labour-time embodied in given amounts of raw materials, machinery, and other forms of constant capital falls. Therefore a doubling or trebling (because of improved technique) in the *amount* of cotton, for example, worked up by a textile worker by no means necessarily involves a doubling or trebling of its value, since productivity in the growing and transportation of cotton may well have increased also.

(iv) *Relative over-population* (that is more workers than jobs) results from the tendency for variable capital (and, therefore, the number of workers employed) to decrease relatively to constant capital. The "reserve army" of unemployed grows greater; such is the underlying tendency. But the underlying tendency for variable capital to decrease relatively to constant is to some extent counteracted because a plentiful supply of cheap labour retards the introduction of machinery and stimulates luxury trades, for example, in which wages are the main item of costs.

(v) *Foreign trade* and "super-profits" of overseas investments give special advantages to the capitalists of an industrially advanced country (see also Chapter IX on Imperialism). "The favoured country", writes Marx, "recovers more labour in exchange for less labour" (*Capital*, Vol. III, LW p. 233, K p. 279), the surplus being pocketed by the capitalist class of the "advanced" country (who get good prices for their manufactures and buy raw materials and foods at relatively low prices).

In all forms of society far reaching consequences result from technical change. In capitalist society the rate of technical change is high by comparison with any earlier forms of society. The long-term structural changes here being considered clearly set in motion a whole series of conflicting processes out of which sharp social and economic tensions develop as the effects of the changes are felt. "The periodical depreciation of the existing capital", writes Marx, "which is one of the immanent means by which the fall in the rate of profit is checked and the accumulation of capital-value through the formation of new capital promoted, disturbs the existing conditions, within which the process of circulation and reproduction of capital takes place, and is therefore accompanied by sudden stagnations and crises in the process of production." (*Capital*, Vol. III, LW p. 244, K p. 292.)

The Tendency of the Rate of Profit to Fall and the Law of Motion of Capitalist Society

The rate of profit tends to fall because the organic composition of capital (the ratio of *constant* to *variable* capital) tends to increase. This process creates counteracting processes which in themselves sharpen the contradictions of capitalism. When times are good, every capitalist who can hastens to operate on a bigger scale, to buy new machinery, to enjoy the advantages of mass production. In short, a basis is laid for improved technique and capitals of higher organic composition. Then comes the slump, which brings the plans of hundreds to nought; but in the slump the capitalists with the biggest resources and the firms with the most advanced technique are the most likely to survive. These strong capitalists use the opportunity of the slump to devour their weaker rivals; many smaller firms either become bankrupt or go out of business or else are bought up and absorbed by the larger firm. In the depression prices are low, and in order to make a profit the capitalists strive to cut down costs by reducing wages and increasing productivity. Each new cycle inaugurates, therefore, a new stage in industrial re-equipment (which leads to a general rise in the organic composition of capital). Each cycle brings also further concentration and centralisation of capital. Capitalist society thus moves forward to a new stage in which there have developed even sharper contradictions between the productive power of industry and the purchasing power of the masses, between private ownership and the social character of production.

It is not, therefore, hard to recognise the profound significance of the law of the falling tendency of the rate of profit in shaping the development of capitalist society. In this tendency and the counteracting forces that it excites, expression is given to the ceaseless struggle by each capitalist concern *individually* to increase its profits, but this very struggle tends *socially* to make the rate of profit fall. This in its turn stimulates efforts to increase profits, and these very efforts magnify still further the factors which cause the rate of profit to fall and sharpen still further the contradictions of capitalism.

Economic change (and with it social changes affecting profoundly all aspects of life) is constantly galvanised by the revolutions—great and small—that transform the techniques of production. These imply great disturbances for each capitalist organisation—the costly writing off of capital tied up in older plant and equipment, new and untried methods, different deployment of the labour force, etc. Naturally, there is much reluctance to making such changes, but in the end the rivalry of competing capitals compels them—though, as will be seen later, the concentration of production leads to attempts (which are never more than temporarily successful) to escape these painful processes by the formation of restrictive associations and monopolies.

Also with the advancement of science—which in itself implies a vast "socialisation" of technical knowledge—larger and more specialised productive units tend to be required. The economic fragmentation that private ownership of the means of production implies, obstructs and makes difficult the application of scientific knowledge. In such ways the progress in productive techniques (for which capitalism in its early days was, in contrast to dying feudalism, the most suitable vehicle) develops to a point at which the capitalist economic structure becomes altogether unsuited and an obstacle. An economic effect of changing productivity (of which the tendency for the rate of profit to fall is an important expression) is constant movement and instabilities in the structure of capitalist society.

The individual efforts of the capitalists thus lead collectively to ends which none of them consciously envisaged or aimed for. Capitalist production moves forward, only to be blocked—again and again—by unseen barriers. "Capitalist production", writes Marx, "is continually engaged in the attempt to overcome these immanent barriers, but it overcomes them only by means which again place barriers in its way on a more formidable scale. *The real barrier of capitalist production is capital itself.* It is the fact that capital and its self-expansion appear as the starting and closing point, as the motive and aim of production; that production is only production for *capital*, and not vice versa, the means of production are not mere means for a constant expansion of the living process of the *society* of producers. The limits within which the preservation and self-expansion of the value of capital resting on the expropriation and pauperisation of the great mass of producers can alone move, these limits come continually in conflict with the methods of production which capital must employ for its purposes, and which steer straight toward an unlimited extension of production, toward production as an end in itself, toward unconditional development of the social productivity of labour. The means, this unconditional development of the productive forces of society, comes continually into conflict with the limited end, the self-expansion of existing capital. Thus, while the capitalist mode of production is a historical means by which the material forces of production are developed and the

world market required for them created, it is at the same time
in continual conflict with this historical task and its own corresponding relations of social production." (*Capital*, Vol. III, LW
p. 245, K p. 293.)

Bourgeois Economists on Crisis

In general, the explanations of crisis by bourgeois economists—
that is, economists whose method of analysis is derived from the
mainstream of bourgeois theory—have all in common the fact
that they do not regard crisis as inherent in the system, as spring-
ing from essential relationships of capitalist economies as such.
However, in other respects, bourgeois theories of crisis are very
much at variance amongst themselves. Each tends to focus attention on one aspect of the crisis and, neglecting the interconnections between this and other aspects, to regard it as the fault
that needs correcting. For example, in a period of boom credit is
expanded and deposits held by the banks increase. If, say some
economists, the availability of money was restricted, the boom
would be held within bounds and crisis could be prevented.
From this aspect of the trade cycle, the *monetary theories* of crisis
are evolved (such as those of Hawtrey and Irving Fisher) and
the new monetary policy applied in the United Kingdom—
with far from fruitful consequences—in the decade 1951-61.

Others (such as Professors Hayek and Robbins) note that the
money available to capitalists is spent on vast expansions of
productive resources and when the slump comes many of these
expansions are interrupted before they are completed and before
they have come to fruition. These economists argue that the
crisis is due to *over-investment*, that the expansion schemes were too
ambitious and were not matched by savings and cutting down on
current consumption on a scale sufficient to finance the vast
capital expansion that was started. The remedy proposed is
lower wages and higher rates of interest.

Others note that in boom capitalists are full of hope and dream
of selling more and more at ever higher prices, whilst in the slump
they are filled with despair and do not believe that industry will
ever again be profitable. These phenomena inspire the economists
to develop a *psychological* theory of crisis. For psychological reasons,
they say, capitalists over-estimate future demand at one stage and
under-estimate it at another. This leads to decisions by those who
run business which result in boom, then in slump. Undoubtedly

psychological factors may influence the impetus of the boom or the continuance of the slump, but the disproportions between the various elements in the economy which *initiate* expectations or fears at particular times or in particular parts of the economy, are real and not imagined. The psychological factors are secondary and not basic causal factors.

When the slump comes, stocks pile up in the factories and in the shops, business comes to a standstill, no one can afford to buy what is produced. So, say the economists (for example, J. A. Hobson and to some extent Keynes), the crisis must be due to *under-consumption*, if people had more to spend then there would be no crisis.

Others (such as Professor W. G. Mitchell) see the cause of crisis in the *rise in costs* that takes place in a boom. This is sometimes put in the form that it is the increase in wages which accompanies a boom that causes the crisis. These, they say, eat into profits and force expansion to stop and give way to recession.

Others again look for the cause of crisis in the uncertainty of harvests and the effect that reductions in the purchasing power of the agricultural communities have on economic activity as a whole. Thus Jevons evolved the famous *sun-spot theory*, which argued that spots on the sun occurring every ten years tended to cause bad harvests which in turn caused general economic crisis.

The detailed criticism of each capitalist theory of crisis would require a volume on its own. Here it must suffice to point out that each grasps at one fraction of the whole truth and builds this into a theory. The distinctive feature of the Marxist theory of crisis is that it sees crisis as an expression of the contradictions inherent in commodity production for profit, namely private ownership of the means of production under circumstances of widely extended economic interdependence. That is, in the Marxist view, the tendency to crisis is inherent in the capitalist mode of production itself. In practical application none of the various bourgeois theories have proved successful. The up and down swing of the trade cycle has continued, throughout the 15 years following the Second World War, despite the use of "Keynesian techniques" in many of the leading capitalist countries during this period. At the present time, however, Keynesian theory is tending to oust all other bourgeois theories and warrants, therefore, rather greater attention.

Keynesian Theory

The essentially new feature of Keynes' theory as against other bourgeois theories was his contention that the capitalist system, if left to itself, does not necessarily lead to full employment.

Bourgeois economists before Keynes had argued that unemployment, idle capacity, etc., must always be due to artificial interference with the laws of the market (by, for example, trade union action forcing up the price of labour or monopolies forcing up the price of goods). The pre-Keynesians argued that every product that went to market created a purchasing power corresponding to its value, since production costs and other incomes generated in the processes of production and distribution (wages, costs of materials, rent, interest, salaries, profits, etc.) exactly equalled the total value of the product sold. (This doctrine is generally known as "Say's Law".) Unemployment and idle capacity could only be due to friction in the economic system preventing the price of labour power, etc., from finding the proper level at which all labour and all capacity would be employed.

Keynes opposed the view that the capitalist system necessarily generated enough purchasing power, or as he put it, enough *effective demand* (meaning *effectively used* purchasing power) to keep all factors of production employed. He argued that the whole system could finally settle down ("reach equilibrium") at any level of employment even if there were no "frictions" or temporary maladjustments. As a leading American Keynesian puts it, the Keynesian revolution, "was solely the development of a theory of effective demand, i.e., a theory of the determination of the level of output as a whole". (Klein, *The Keynesian Revolution*, Macmillan 1950, p. 56.)

From this Keynes went on to say, however, that appropriate action by the government and central banks could ensure that output and employment were maintained at a high level (without superseding the capitalist form of production).

The orthodox bourgeois theories were not, in Keynes' view, far wrong except in this matter of the level of employment. If full employment were assumed, then they were true. They were true for the special case of full employment, whereas his theory had a wider general application.

"If", he writes (*General Theory*, pp. 378-79), "our central controls succeed in establishing an aggregate volume of output

174

corresponding to full employment as nearly as is practicable, the classical theory [by which he means orthodox bourgeois theory—J.E.] comes into its own again from this point onwards. Then there is no objection to be raised against the classical analysis of the manner in which private self-interest will determine what in particular is produced, in what proportions the factors of production will be combined to produce it, and how the value of the final product will be distributed between them. . . . I see no reason to believe that the existing system seriously misemploys the factors of production which are in use. . . . The result of filling in the gaps in the classical theory is not to dispose of the 'Manchester System' but to indicate the nature of the environment which the free play of economic forces requires if it is to realise the full potentialities of production."

This quotation makes it quite clear that Keynes opposed change in the basic economic relations of capitalism. The special significance of Keynes' theory was that it attacked *laissez-faire* doctrines (which taught that the economic system should be left to run itself) without attacking capitalism, without removing the fig-leaves with which theory hid the nakedness of capitalist exploitation, without conceding anything to Marxism. Keynes spoke of Marx's *Capital* as "an obsolete economic textbook" which was "scientifically erroneous" and "without interest or application for the modern world" (*Essays in Persuasion*). The essence of the Keynesian standpoint was anti-*laissez-faire* while remaining pro-capitalist and anti-Marxist.

The Keynesian theory of employment broadly runs as follows: Expenditure takes two forms—investment expenditure, and consumption expenditure. The latter depends upon (i) incomes received, coupled with (ii) the extent to which these incomes are spent or saved; for example, if incomes totalling, say, £10,000 million are paid out and of these 90 per cent is spent on consumption and 10 per cent is saved, effective demand arising from consumption expenditure is £9,000 million.

But, says Keynes, the mere fact that people aim at saving 10 per cent of their incomes does not mean that this balance of "unspent" or "saved" incomes (£1,000 million in our example) is forthwith and necessarily spent on investment goods.

In fact, the decision not to spend income on consumption is quite separate and distinct from the decision to increase expenditure on capital equipment, etc. This latter decision is taken by the capitalist or capitalist firm ("the entrepreneur"); and it is taken in light of the prospects of making a profit.

The essence of the Keynesian theory of employment is then this: the level of employment is determined by the total, effective demand, which means total purchases of consumer goods *plus* investment expenditure. In so far as income not spent on consumption fails to be matched by expenditure on investment goods, there is a falling off of total demand and therefore of output and employment as a whole, which, of course, brings with it a reduction in incomes. In our example, total income (apart from price changes) will drop well below £10,000 million, if the decisions to save are not matched by decisions on the part of "entrepreneurs" to spend on capital equipment, etc., at least as much as the intended savings (namely, £1,000 million if 10 per cent of incomes were to be saved).

The decision to invest or not to invest depends upon whether or not there is a prospect of making a profit; and this depends, says Keynes, on the relation between the rate of interest and the returns which the capitalist expects from his investment of capital.

For example, by spending £1,000 on installing new machinery a capitalist expects to increase output from which he forecasts that he will collect additional profits (after allowing for depreciation, etc.) amounting to £80 per annum; if he can borrow £1,000 at a rate of interest of 3 per cent (i.e. for £30 per annum) he sees a clear profit of £50 (£80—£30) and will make the investment. If, however, the rate of interest goes up and the expected yield ("the marginal efficiency of capital") goes down, then the margin of profit narrows, or vanishes away, and so the investment is not made.

The orthodox capitalist economists before Keynes did not, broadly speaking, disagree with this line of argument but maintained that if the desire to save increased, the supply of money to be lent would increase and so the charge for lending it (the rate of interest) would fall. The fall of the rate of interest would, they argued, encourage investment and so all would be well—with every increase in the desire to save there would be a corresponding increase in investment.

It is at this point that Keynes comes in and says: No, things do not work out this way because the public's desire to save has precious little effect on the rate of interest. The rate of interest depends rather on (*a*) the financial policy of the government and the central banks, whose actions can force the rate of interest up or down and in some measure determine the amount of money that the banks are in a position to lend and (*b*) the "liquidity preference" of the people who own capital. (By "liquidity preference" Keynes means the desire to hold wealth in money form rather than to have it tied up in investments.)

In all this, however—and Keynes is quite explicit on this point—the profit motive and private ownership and control of industry remain. In short, Keynesian theory rejects *laissez-faire* economics (which advocated leaving everything to the workings of economic laws.) It admits that capitalism left to itself leads to unemployment, but argues that by certain measures of State intervention capitalism can be so adjusted as to eliminate unemployment and crisis. It sets out to explain:

1. Why capitalism in the past suffered from crisis and unemployment.
2. How capitalism can be adjusted so as to do away with crisis and unemployment.
3. Why State interference is called for.

This being so, the capitalist system is not (as the champions of bourgeois economy had always previously maintained) a system which adjusts itself in such a way as to ensure full employment. It is not true, Keynes maintains, that the economic forces, if left to themselves, will automatically generate an effective demand sufficient to absorb the output of industry at the level of full employment.

The fact that people abstain from spending a certain amount of income on consumption does not in itself create a corresponding new demand for investment goods. On the contrary, to save discourages investment. It causes sluggish market conditions under which there is not any incentive for the capitalists to expand investment expenditure. Investment is unlikely to take up the slack left by a reduction of consumption expenditure due to an increased desire to save.

The consequence is, therefore, that effective demand falls off, prices fall and economic activity diminishes; profits fall, and workers are sacked. Incomes all round are reduced and the whole economic system settles down at a lower level, leaving great numbers of workers unemployed.

Thus, according to Keynes, it is not only possible but quite normal that the whole system should settle down and "reach equilibrium" at a point which leaves millions of workers unemployed.

Keynes, indeed, further extends this theory to say that in industrialised countries both the "propensities to consume" and "inducements to invest" decrease. In this way the theory claims to explain not only the reasons for unemployment but also why (in the absence of Keynesian remedies) economic disorganisation increases with advanced industrial development.

Summarising what has been said above, we may say that for Keynes the villain of the piece is investment expenditure. "The theory", writes Keynes, "can be summed up by saying that, given the psychology of the public, the level of output and employment as a whole depends on the amount of investment." (Keynes in *Quarterly Journal of Economics*, quoted in *New Economics*, p. 191.)

It follows from this line of reasoning that to maintain full or high employment and output it is necessary to maintain investment expenditure at the right level. If this is not done, economic activity falls, incomes paid out in the form of profits and the wage bill dwindle. In short, effective demand in the form of consumption expenditure falls short of the level necessary to maintain full employment and output.

Full employment can, however, be maintained—says Keynes—if the State takes special steps to keep investment expenditure at the right level; this, he says, it may do by (*a*) controlling the rate of interest; (*b*) itself undertaking investment or public works expenditure; (*c*) exercising some general control—about which Keynes is nowhere very precise—over all forms of investment.

Keynes and Keynesians also advocate measures designed to increase the "propensity to consume". These measures include (i) increasing purchasing power (e.g. payment of post-war credits) and (ii) taxation designed to redistribute incomes in favour of the lower income groups (who save less). However, the emphasis on this second group of remedies is less marked.

Keynes spoke of the "socialisation of investment" (*General Theory*, p. 378), but although in this he was advocating a certain measure of economic regulation by the State, he was also setting a limit to such State action. "Beyond this," he writes, "no obvious case is made out for a system of State socialism which would embrace most of the economic life of the community." (*ibid.*)

The connection between Keynesian theory and the historical circumstances of its appearance is fairly clear. It was the child of the great slump of 1929, but it was also the capitalist answer to the challenge that socialism was the only way out of the slump. It reflected the coexistence and competition of the two systems. The ambivalence of Keynesian theory, its twosidedness, its use at one time in service of reactionary ends and at another in service of progressive ends, is to be explained, not only by the content of the theory itself but also by this historical context. Already the First World War and its aftermath had compelled extensive economic activity by the capitalist State when the growth of monopoly and the concentration of capital fostered a closer association between the apparatus of the State and the trustified economy; but this also was the period of the co-existence of the socialist and capitalist worlds, a period also in which the challenge of socialist ideas had acquired a much keener political intensity. Keynesian theory is used by capitalist monopolies as a framework for their economic policies; it is used by reformists and revisionists within the socialist movement as a substitute for socialism (for example, Douglas Jay's *Socialist Case* and *Socialism in the New Society* and Strachey's *Contemporary Capitalism*).

But the fact that Keynesian theory has become that of opponents in the Labour movement of socialism and public ownership of the means of production, and the fact that it provides today the main theoretical basis for capitalist economics, does not imply that Marxists should necessarily oppose what are somewhat vaguely called "Keynesian measures" which attempt to affect the general movement of the capitalist economy. As in the case of other reforms, Marxists, consistently with the aim of over-throwing capitalism, will often be found advocating immediate measures similar to those advocated by people who want to make capitalism work better. Marxists, however, fight for limited measures within capitalism only in so far as they see these as helping the advancement of the working-class movement and so helping the struggle of the people for socialism against capitalism.

Keynesian economic programmes, like so many other things in the period of the coexistence of the two systems (for example, parliamentary procedures, nationalisation, social service ex-penditures, etc.) become, as it were, battlegrounds over which capitalism and the defenders of the existing order of society contend with the working class and the champions of a new order of society.

Without here embarking upon a more detailed criticism of Keynesian programmes (for which the reader may be referred to Chapters 2, 3 and 4 of *Socialism in the Nuclear Age* by John Eaton, Lawrence & Wishart, 1961) it is sufficient to note that they attempt to defend the heart of capitalism whilst making concessions at the periphery. In the same way Keynesian theory works within the general framework of bourgeois theory, whilst criticising some aspects of it. For the working-class movement "Keynesian measures" in the economic policy of capitalist governments can, at the best, be of transitory value. State capitalist programmes which advance the general interest of the people are achieved only and carried through only as a result of sustained popular pressure; but when the pressure mounts beyond a certain point, the popular movement will require more than ameliorative measures to patch defects in capitalism. At the same time the popular forces will then have the strength to assume State power and will go to the heart of the trouble by taking the main means of production into public control and ownership. The major criticism of Keynesism, both its theory and its practice, is that it distorts the defects of the market-private-capital system by representing them—falsely—as insignificantly small.

Whilst it is evident that working-class and popular pressure can achieve a certain amount within a capitalist economy, it is also clear that the measures of State policy by which the economy is steered cause at the same time harmful reactions. One amongst these that is easily recognised "with the naked eye" is the trend towards inflation. This socially corroding process, which destroys the worth of monetary savings and fosters speculation, is interrupted periodically by switching to deflation—which in turn involves a different sort of social waste, through stagnation and loss of national wealth. Keynesian measures may cause contradictions within the capitalist economy to assume changed forms but they do not eliminate them. Those who frame the economic policies of capitalist powers repeatedly face an awkward choice between *either* monetary stabilisation plus a strengthened bargaining position for capital vis-a-vis labour but involving stagnation, waste of resources, unemployment, etc., *or* public spending, easy availability of funds for investment, economic expansion but involving a stronger bargaining position for labour, more speculation and often chaotic misdirection of investment.

(The reader is recommended to read Chapter 5, on economic crisis, in *Capitalism Yesterday and Today* by Maurice Dobb— Lawrence & Wishart 1958; also Chapter 3 of *Socialism in the Nuclear Age* by John Eaton, Lawrence & Wishart 1961, in which contemporary theories on the control of capitalism are discussed.)

CHAPTER IX

IMPERIALISM AND FINANCE CAPITAL

"England became a capitalist country before any other and, in the middle of the nineteenth century, having adopted free trade, claimed to be the 'workshop of the world', the great purveyor of manufactured goods to all countries, which in exchange were to keep her supplied with raw materials. But in the last quarter of the nineteenth century *this* monopoly was already undermined. Other countries protecting themselves by tariff walls had developed into independent capitalist States." (Lenin, *Imperialism*, Chapter IV.)

In 1860 England produced over half of the world's coal and pig-iron, and about half of the world's cotton goods. By 1913 her share in world production of each of these commodities had fallen to 22 per cent, 13 per cent, and 23 per cent respectively. Vast new industries had grown up to rival Britain in other countries—in particular Germany and the U.S.A.

Immediately before the great crisis of 1873 output per head in Britain was 20 per cent more than in U.S.A., 40 per cent more than in Canada and 65 per cent more than in Germany. Just before World War One it was 20 per cent *below* U.S.A., level with Canada and 40 per cent more than Germany.

During the first three-quarters of the nineteenth century British capitalism had grown rapidly. Though shaken by economic crises at roughly ten-yearly intervals, it continued, despite the checks that each crisis imposed, to expand fairly fast and constantly to find ever new markets throughout the world. This was the great era of Free Trade, in which British capitalism could rely on the technical superiority of its industrial production to safeguard its position as the "despot of the world market". The great crisis of 1873 gave warning that the days of easy prosperity for British capitalism had come to an end. Britain's exports, which had between 1847 and 1872 increased fourfold—from £59 million to £256 million—fell between 1872· and 1879 by one-quarter and did not again reach the 1872 level until 1890. Tariff reform, the taxing of foreign goods, trade with the colonies, colonial expansion began to be advocated. Britain under the leadership, in particular, of Joseph Chamberlain began to turn from Free Trade to imperialism. Important economic developments had been taking place; capitalism had entered a new stage —the stage of *imperialism*.

The term *imperialism* is used in political economy to describe a particular *stage in the development of capitalism*. It is quite distinct, therefore, from the colonial empires of the sixteenth and seventeenth centuries (from which the merchant classes accumulated their fortunes whilst capitalism was still in its infancy) or the empires of the ancient world built up on the basis of slavery, such as the empire of Athens or that of Alexander the Great or the empire from which Rome exacted her vast tributes by force of arms.

They are all forms of exploitation of weaker nations by stronger nations, or more precisely by the ruling class of stronger nations; they are, however, fundamentally different in so far as the economic basis in each period (namely, ancient slavery, the beginning of capitalism, and latter-day monopoly-capitalism) is completely different.

Lenin, in his *Imperialism: the Highest Stage of Capitalism** defines imperialism as the monopoly stage of capitalism and picks out the following as its five essential features (*Imperialism*, Chapter VII):

(1) The *concentration of production and capital* develops to such a high stage that it creates monopolies which play a decisive role in the economic life.

(2) The *merging of bank capital with industrial capital* and the creation, on the basis of this "finance capital", of a financial oligarchy.

(3) The *export of capital*, which has become extremely important, as distinguished from the export of commodities.

* In this work Lenin makes considerable use of *Imperialism* by the English economist, J. A. Hobson, "who"—to quote Lenin—"adopts the point of view of bourgeois social reformism and pacifism" but none the less "gives an excellent and comprehensive description of the principal economic and political characteristics of imperialism."

(4) The formation of *international capitalist monopolies* which share the world among themselves.

(5) The completion of the *territorial division* of the whole world among the greatest capitalist Powers.

Concentration of Production

Accumulation of capital always leads to concentration of production and capital. The concentration of production in large units makes possible far-reaching division of labour and specialisation to a degree that is not attainable in smaller factories, reduction in the costs of management, sales organisations, etc., and the use of specialised, costly, and massive machinery that is remunerative only when the scale of production is large. As a rule, therefore, technical advance involves the concentration of production.

There is ample factual evidence of increasing concentration of production in capitalist countries. In Germany, for example, in 1882 22 per cent of the industrial population worked in factories employing fifty or more persons; by 1895 this percentage had risen to 30, by 1907 to 37, and by 1925 to 48. In U.S.A. firms with over fifty workers already employed in 1909 three out of every four workers, and 16 per cent were employed in firms with 1,000 or more workers. By 1929 the share of the "over 1,000" firms had risen to 24 per cent. Similar concentration of production took place in Japan, France, and Britain. In Britain in 1935 there were in manufacturing industry approximately 250,000 firms; 200,000 of these were small firms employing each less than ten workers and in all 827,000. There were 50,000 firms employing more than ten workers apiece and in all 7,200,000. Half of these "over ten" firms employed only one-ninth of the workers and each had less than fifty workers in its employ. At the other end of the scale there were 2,000 firms employing 55 per cent of all the workers and each having over 500 workers in its employ. At the very peak of the industrial pyramid there were 52 firms together employing one million workers and individually employing more than 10,000 workers each.

Industrial concentration and centralisation of capital under a single ownership does not take place in a smooth and gradual way, but more often spasmodically by fits and starts. In particular, concentration and centralisation are accelerated at each recurrence of economic crisis, since the weaker and more backward firms either go out of existence or are absorbed by the stronger and more technically advanced firms. On the other hand the crisis is a warning to the firms that survive that they must amass more resources if the next crisis is to be weathered. As capital becomes concentrated into bigger units a greater share of profits tends to be accumulated and as a consequence the rate at which concentration proceeds tends to increase.

Certainly in Britain after the Second World War concentration and centralisation of capital has been very rapid. The measures taken against "restrictive practices" (in particular against "trade associations" which fix prices and make sales agreements— normally including small or medium as well as large firms) have probably speeded the growth of monopolies in the form of larger centrally controlled companies. In 1961-62 many of the mergers taking place are between the "giants" themselves in each industry, the most striking example of the tendency being the attempted merger between I.C.I. (total assets 31.12.60—£695 million) and Courtaulds (total assets 31.3.61 £207 million). On a sales basis, even without the merger, I.C.I. was the largest group in Britain; with Courtaulds it would have become the sixteenth largest in the world and, in Europe, would have been surpassed only by Royal Dutch Shell, and Unilever.

The privately owned concerns dominating American, British, German, French, Italian and Japanese industry today are of staggering size. For example, the annual sales in 1960-61 were, to mention some mainly American companies $12,736 million for General Motors, $8,034 million for Standard Oil, $4,197 million for U.S. General Electric, $3,007 million for U.S. Steel, $5,237 million for Ford Motors; and in the case of companies in which there are large British interests, Royal Dutch Shell had sales of $5,481 million, Unilever $3,883 million, I.C.I. and Courtaulds together $2,044 million. Others in Europe include Nestlé's $1,518 million, Philip's Lamps $1,253 million, Volkswagen $1,096 million and Krupp $982 million.

Between 1954 and 1961 21 per cent of the 2,100 public companies in Britain with assets of more than half a million pounds were absorbed into other companies and everywhere the dominance of the very big firms increased. At the end of 1957 in Britain, the distribution of companies by net size of assets was as follows:

Size		*No. of Companies*	*Total net Assets* ($£$ *million*)
£25 mn. and over	..	70	4,938
£10 mn. to £25 mn.	..	110	1,723
£5 mn. to £10 mn.	..	159	1,119
£2½ mn. to £5 mn.	..	282	985
£1 mn. to £2½ mn.	..	649	1,023
£½ mn. to £1 mn.	..	612	432
Total ..	..	1,882	10,220

The companies covered by this table are mainly those in industry operating in Britain; shipping, insurance, banking and property companies are excluded. The assets of all the smaller industrial companies put together would not substantially increase this total and one may say therefore that some 200 companies control about two-thirds of British industry at the present time.

Concentration of Production Leads to Monopoly

It is easy to see that the largest production units as they develop tend more and more to dominate their competitors in their own branch of industry. In some cases a few firms will have a half or more of the output of a particular type of product. Clearly when this happens the few large firms will, if they get together and pursue a common policy, be able to have things very much their own way. Such co-operation amongst a few giant firms will face the smaller firms with the choice of falling in line with the wishes of the big firms or being forced out of business.

Once the dominance of a few big firms is established in a particular branch of industry, they will be able to fix prices at levels above those that would prevail under conditions of free competition, and thereby reap extra profits. Thus competition gives birth to its opposite—*monopoly*. (The strict meaning of monopoly is "sole seller"; it is rare for the concentration of production to lead to the elimination of all but one supplier of a particular commodity. The expression is therefore used in a relative sense to express the tendency in the direction of sole control of the market. The capitalists who individually or working in with other big capitalists are able to exercise such control and to dominate their several branches of industry, fixing prices and allocating production quotas, are, therefore, given the name of *monopoly capitalists*.)

Types of Monopoly

There are many ways in which a group of capitalists or an individual capitalist may succeed in bringing a decisive part of an industry under sufficient control to make possible the allocation of output quotas, price fixing, etc. Such instruments of monopoly include, for example, Trusts, Combines, Cartels, Trade Associations, etc.; where there are legal or other obstacles to open monopoly organisations, the same purpose may be served by Price Agreements, and informal "understandings" and "gentlemen's agreements".

The most direct and decisive form of monopoly is the domination of a single large firm. The outstanding example is the giant Imperial Chemical Industries Ltd.—I.C.I.—which was formed in 1928 with a capital of £77 million to merge the interests of Brunner Mond, British Dyestuffs, Nobel, and United Alkali. I.C.I. is a compact, solid monopoly running virtually the whole of the British chemical industry, ever expanding its sphere of operations more widely into new branches of industry and new territories overseas. As a matter of convenience, I.C.I. operates through a number of subsidiary companies, which cover particular branches of industry or territories; as a rule these subsidiary companies are wholly owned by I.C.I.

Slightly less compact are *combines* such as Unilever, which controls some hundreds of concerns in the soap and food trade throughout the world. Their interests include, in addition to the manufacturers, the producers of the raw materials at one end and the retailers at the other. The Joint Stock Limited Liability Company which provided capitalism in the days of "free competition" with a means of collecting and concentrating capital, provides in the days of monopoly capitalism an admirable means for the monopoly control of industry. "Ordinary" shareholdings in Limited Liability Companies normally carry voting rights proportionate to the amount of the holding: thus any one holding more than 50 per cent of the shares can exercise absolute control over the policy and administration of a company. In practice a very much smaller shareholding will suffice; small shareholders do not often trouble to attend company meetings and a voting block covering no more than 10 per cent or 15 per cent of the total number of shares may in fact be decisive. The Joint Stock Company provides therefore the means of exercising monopoly control by means of Holding Companies, that is, companies holding shares in a number of other companies.

In this way, an individual or group holding a decisive block of shares in a "parent company" which holds a majority of the shares in a number of subsidiaries—which in turn hold shares in subsidiaries, etc.—may control industrial wealth which many times exceeds their own personal fortune. For example, Messrs. O. P. and M. J. Van Sweringen were able in the U.S.A. with a capital of 20 million dollars to control eight Class I railroads with combined assets of over 2,000 million dollars. In addition to direct control exercised through share-ownership powerful industrialists are able to extend their control over wide ranges of industry by what are known as *interlocking directorships*, that is, they or "their men" secure appointment as directors of a number of associated companies in which they aim to pursue a unified policy.

Another common form of organisation used by the monopoly capitalists is the *cartel* or group of firms which combine to fix prices, allocate production quotas, and so forth. Clearly this form of monopoly is less stable than the trust or holding company. If violent conflicts occur between the members of the group—and in fact they often do—the cartel agreement is liable to break down. Frequently *trade associations* dominated by a few large firms provide the organisational framework for monopoly.

Monopoly Profits and Prices

The monopoly capitalists can use their power to get for themselves extra profits. One way in which they do this is by keeping the prices of their products high. In earlier chapters it has been explained how, as a result of competition, commodities tend to exchange at their values (or, in developed industrial capitalism— see Chapter VI—at "their prices of production"). The law of value operates through competition. What then happens in the period of monopoly capitalism, when out of competition the opposite of competition, namely, monopoly, has arisen? The monopoly capitalist is able, in conditions which make this course the most profitable, to restrict production and, by reason of the relative scarcity that he can create, to get enhanced prices for the goods he produces. The extent to which he can raise his prices is limited by the fact that, if he puts them too high, sales will fall off (people will either go without or use substitutes) and though he makes a big profit on each commodity he sells, his total profits (that is, profit on each commodity sold multiplied by the number sold) will fall. Market conditions still assert themselves, but the monopoly capitalist (because he has a monopoly) is able to sell above the price of production. He is able therefore to appropriate for himself some extra surplus value. As a consequence the surplus value created by capitalist production as a whole is no longer equally distributed in proportion to the capitals engaged and profits are not equalised (see Chapter VI). Instead an extra profit goes to the monopoly capitalist, and the surplus value that remains to be shared out between the other capitalists is correspondingly reduced. Thus the monopoly capitalists get their higher rate of profit *at the expense of the non-monopoly capitalists.*

At the same time the monopoly capitalist also makes extra profit at the expense of the worker, the small shopkeeper, and the producers of raw materials (usually "simple commodity" or peasant producers).

Many commodities entering into the everyday consumption of the working-class household (e.g. Flour—Ranks and Spillers; Chocolate—Cadbury-Fry's group; Tobacco—Imperial Tobacco Company; Meat—Union Cold Storage; Soap and Fats— Unilever, and so on) are supplied by "monopolies". So far as monopolies are able to raise prices of essential consumers' goods the cost of living goes up and *real* wages therefore come down. In this way the share of the working class in the national output may be reduced by the action of the monopolies (and the capitalists' surplus value correspondingly increased).

The shopkeeper can be squeezed by the monopoly cutting down the sales margin allowed to the retailer on the "proprietary" or "branded" goods which the monopoly produces. The monopolists are in a position to penalise the retailer who refuses to observe the conditions they lay down, by cutting off supplies. Clearly a tobacconist, confectioner, or grocer has little chance of making a living if he is debarred from selling the monopolies' products, which are kept in demand by the extensive publicity which the wealthy monopolies undertake.

The monopoly capitalist may enrich himself at the expense of the producers of raw materials (in the main small peasant producers in colonial countries), since he faces them as the sole buyer of their products and forces them to accept the price offered or none at all.

Monopoly and Competition

The emergence of monopoly—the opposite of competition—does not mean the end of competition. On the contrary, competition assumes new and more violent forms, which give rise not only to ruthless trade wars but also to war of arms between the monopoly capitalist powers. "Imperialism", writes Lenin, "complicates and accentuates the contradictions of capitalism, it 'entangles' monopoly with free competition, but *it cannot abolish* exchange, the market, competition, crises, etc. Imperialism is capitalism which is withering but not yet withered, dying but not dead. Not pure monopolies, but monopolies in conjunction with exchange, markets, competition, crises—such is the essential feature of imperialism in general. . . . This combination of antagonistic principles, viz., competition and monopoly, is the essence of imperialism, it is this that is making for the final crash, i.e., the socialist revolution." (Lenin, *Materials on Revision of Party Programme*, 1917.) In contrast, Hilferding and other Social Democrats argued that monopolies lead to "organised capitalism" in which competition and capitalist anarchy are eliminated. Subsequently numerous "right-wing Socialists" have tried—and even today still try—to resurrect the theory of "organised capitalism" in one or another new form. But the reality, the actual history of imperialism in the last fifty years, has again and again disproved these theories and proved that Lenin was correct when he said that "imperialism complicates and accentuates the contradictions of capitalism".

Competition in the period of monopoly capitalism continues in the following forms:

(i) Competitive capitalism continues to exist alongside of monopoly capitalism—the monopolies dominate all aspects of economic life but hundreds of thousands of other capitalists still remain; small capitalists are again and again eliminated but again and again new small capitalists spring to life.

(ii) Few monopolies are complete and there is always some threat of an outsider "breaking the ring" (as Deterding's Royal Dutch broke Standard's world monopoly in oil).

(iii) There is acute rivalry between monopoly capitalists

themselves; (a) between capitalists jockeying for position *within* the same national or international monopoly grouping; (b) between monopoly capitalists in different fields of industry struggling to extend their influence at the expense of others.

(iv) Acute rivalry between international groupings of monopolies, seeking to extend their spheres of operation and using the State machine to this end, striving to bring new territories and their governments under their influence, and ultimately to break their rivals by force of arms.

In the period of monopoly capitalism, competition appears in other forms than price-competition, such as advertising and sales campaigns, contracts tying purchasers to one supplier, boycott and semi-racketeering measures. The "peaceful" competition of the market is largely replaced by price wars, the manœuvrings of industrial diplomacy of cartels and international trade associations, manipulation of State policies and ultimately war of arms.

Banks and Finance Capital

Industrial concentration is accompanied by the concentration of banking and this gives an added impetus to the growth of monopoly. "The principal and primary function of banks," writes Lenin, "is to serve as an intermediary in making payments. In doing so they transform inactive money capital into active capital, that is into capital producing a profit; they collect all kinds of money revenues and place them at the disposal of the capitalist class." (*Imperialism*, Chapter II.) The bigger the bank the less likely is it to succumb to economic disaster; "to him that hath shall it be given". The big banks get bigger and oust the smaller banks. At the same time, as banks get bigger so the revenues they collect (see Chapter VI) reach vast proportions, and the ability to determine how these resources shall be disposed increases their economic power, which in its turn further accelerates the growth of monopoly in banking. In Britain, for example, by 1936 the "Big Five" (Lloyds, Westminster, Midland, Barclays, and National Provincial) controlled three-quarters of all funds deposited in British banks; the domain of these five banks has steadily grown since the beginning of the century when they already held over one-quarter of total deposits. Similarly in U.S.A., Germany, France, and Japan, banking came more and more into the hands of a few big banks.

Once this concentration has taken place the banks acquire a

position of exceptional importance and power. "They can . . . first *ascertain exactly* the position of the various capitalists, then *control them*, influence them by restricting or enlarging, facilitating or hindering their credits, and finally they can *entirely determine* their fate, determine their income, deprive them of capital, or, on the other hand, permit them to increase their capital rapidly and to enormous proportions, etc." (Lenin, *Imperialism*, Chapter II.)

This immense power over industry is not, however, opposed to or separate from the power of the biggest monopolies in industry, since with the growth of huge banking monopolies on the one hand and industrial monopolies on the other, there has taken place a merging or fusing of banking capital with industrial and commercial capital through acquisition of shares and the appointment of industrialists as directors of banks and vice versa. In 1938 there were in Britain 142 directors of the "Big Five" Banks; these 142 directors between them held over 1,000 outside directorships in companies with total capitals exceeding £3,000 million.

The great power of the banks is well illustrated by the case of Richard Thomas & Co. This firm decided to build a giant strip mill of American pattern at Ebbw Vale in South Wales. This decision was taken in face of opposition from the highly mono-polised steel industry which did not like the threat of competition from a new low-cost unit. "Delay was experienced in obtaining the necessary steel for the erection of the plant", says Mr. Ernest Davies ('*National*' *Capitalism*, p. 66), "and in some quarters it is believed that deliveries were deliberately held up."

At all events the venture took longer to complete and cost more than was budgeted for at the outset. In the spring of 1938 the firm's credit was exhausted. As a condition for temporary finance the firm had to agree to an inquiry by representatives of the steel industry and in the end the project was permitted to go ahead only on the condition that the company should be put under the control of a committee over which the Governor of the Bank of England presided. At the same time directors of rival steel companies were added to the Board of Directors of Richard Thomas & Co.

The merging of bank and industrial capital has taken place in all imperialist countries. In Germany, and to a considerable extent in U.S.A. also, the banks played a major part in stimu-lating the growth of large-scale industry and in the building up of monopolies. In Britain, where industrialism had developed earlier and more extensively than elsewhere, the funds for large-scale industry were found to a greater extent from the accumulated profits of the industrial capitalists themselves. However, despite characteristics peculiar to different countries, monopoly capitalism has led in all cases to a similar merging of bank and industrial capital—that is, to *finance capital* described by Lenin as follows: "The concentration of production; the monopoly arising therefrom; the merging or coalescence of banking with industry—this is the history of the rise of finance capital and what gives the term 'finance capital' its content." (*Imperialism*, Chapter III.)

The Finance Oligarchy

This development of finance capital has produced great changes in the structure and character of the capitalist class and indeed in the whole of capitalist society. A comparatively small clique—numbered at the most in hundreds—have concentrated in their hands control over the greater part of the economic system and dominate all other sections of the population, the working masses, the middle classes, and also the lesser capitalists. This small group of people—to which Lenin applied the title "Financial Oligarchy"—appropriates to itself immense profits acquired in a variety of ways. "Financial capital," writes Lenin, "concentrated in a few hands and exercising a virtual monopoly, exacts enormous and ever-increasing profits from the floating of companies, issue of stock, State loans, etc., tightens the grip of the financial oligarchies and levies tribute upon the whole of society for the benefit of the monopolists." (*Imperialism*, Chapter III.) In times of boom these giants of industry and finance reap huge profits; in times of slump they are able to extend their domain at the expense of the lesser capitalists, many of whom fail and are forced to sell up their businesses—often to the big monopolists—at ruinous prices.

A great part of British industry lies, as shown above, within the orbit of a hundred or so banker-industrialist directors of the Big Five Banks. Of particular importance in Britain are those who control the "merchant banks",* banking houses such as Lazards, Schroeders, and Hambros, from whose directors for year after year before the war the governing body ("The Court") of the Bank of England was mainly chosen. The leading figures in these

* So called since they grew up originally on the finance of overseas trade.

banking houses, these "merchant bankers", are men with financial and industrial connections throughout the world, not only in the British Empire, but also in Britain's traditional spheres of influence (now often U.S. spheres of influence) such as South America and the Middle East. Often they are aristocrats or landowners whether of British or foreign descent; always there are close links between the merchant bankers and the leading circles of the Services and the Law; through clubs and family connections they are always closely in touch with the political leaders of the capitalist parties. Such are the dynasties, often inconspicuous and publicly little known, who have concentrated in their hands an immense degree of industrial, financial, and political power, not only in Britain but throughout the British Empire and wherever British money talks.

In Germany the "financial oligarchy", the powerful groups, the Thyssens, Krupps, and I.G. Farbenindustrie, the big bankers and landowners, used the Nazis to give expression to their policies. In the U.S.A.—despite its anti-monopoly legislation—there is an unparalleled concentration of financial and industrial power.

In the 1920's, 200 companies controlled half of all the non-banking corporate wealth of the U.S.A. and these giant corporations were growing twice and three times as fast as the smaller and less powerful corporations. In 1935, 400 men held between them nearly one-third of the 3,544 directorships of the 200 largest non-banking corporations and the fifty largest in banking and insurance. Eight more or less distinct groups controlled two-thirds of the combined assets of these 250 corporations. The foremost of these groups, the Morgan group associated with the First National Bank of New York, controlled forty-one of the 250 largest corporations, including the American Telephone and Telegraph Co. (said to be the largest private industrial corporation in the world), the Central Railroad Co., the United States Steel Corporation (the largest steel undertaking in the world), also coalmining, copper, electricity, etc., etc. The Morgan group controlled about 15 per cent of the corporate wealth of the U.S.A. Three other family groups, Du Pont (chemicals), Mellon (aluminium and electricity), and Rockefeller (oil and the Chase National Bank) had shareholdings of nearly $1,400 million which gave indirect control over fifteen corporations with aggregate assets of over $8,000 million. The Kuhn-Loeb group, with its main interests in railways, controlled some 7 per cent of America's corporate wealth. The war brought further concentration of power in the hands of the finance oligarchy. A report of the U.S. Senate Committee on small businesses states that "wartime business casualties reached alarming proportions. Government figures indicate that there were over one-half million fewer businesses in 1943 than 1941. . . . The war period saw great increases in the concentration of the American economy and startling developments of those monopolistic controls and practices which recent history has shown mean curtailed opportunity for successful independent business". Already before the Second World War the exhaustive survey of *The Modern Corporation and Private Property* by Berle and Means had concluded that "the rise of the modern corporation has brought a concentration of economic power which can compete on equal terms with the modern State".

The Export of Capital

"Under the old capitalism", writes Lenin, "when free competition prevailed, the export of *goods* was the most typical feature. Under modern capitalism, when monopolies prevail, the export of *capital* has become the typical feature." (*Imperialism*, Chapter IV.)

As capitalism developed a greater amount and an ever greater proportion of surplus value tended to be accumulated. At the same time this same development tended to bring about a fall in the rate of profit (see Chapter VIII) and so the fields for *profitable* new investment in the home country became more limited. Thus there was a hesitancy to invest at home that gave rise to an apparent superabundance of capital. "It goes without saying", writes Lenin, "that if capitalism could develop agriculture, which today lags far behind industry everywhere, if it could raise the standard of living of the masses, who are everywhere still poverty-stricken and underfed, in spite of the amazing abundance in technical knowledge, there could be no talk of superabundance of capital. This 'argument' the petty-bourgeois critics of capitalism advance on every occasion. But if capitalism did these things it would not be capitalism; for uneven development and wretched conditions of the masses are fundamental and inevitable conditions and premises of this mode of production." (Lenin, *Imperialism*, Chapter IV.)

In the course of the nineteenth century manufacturing industry had grown apace in Britain. Britain was "the workshop of the world" and flooded overseas markets with her goods, which, produced in the new steam-powered factories, could sell much more cheaply than the products of other countries. Not only were machine-produced cotton goods from the Lancashire mills ousting the products of more primitive industry, but England had built up a great heavy industry largely engaged on the construction of railways and rolling stock, and sought to use it to supply the whole world. Even in the mid-nineteenth century many overseas railways were financed by British capital, of which in all some £200 million was already invested abroad in the 1880's. By the latter half of the century new industries able to challenge Britain had developed in Germany, America, France, and other countries. The new industries presented formidable rivals in the competition for world markets and threatened to bring to a halt the unfettered industrial expansion that Britain had hitherto enjoyed.

It is not hard to see how these developments upset the old market conditions of "competitive capitalism". The great investments of capital that took place in Britain throughout the first three-quarters of the nineteenth century, the investments which built the industries of Manchester, the Black Country, the Tyne and the Clyde, and so forth, were profitable only because new markets were continually being found overseas. If this had not been so the internal contradictions of British capitalism would have found earlier more violent and more prolonged expression in economic crises than in fact was the case. However, towards the end of the nineteenth century Britain had on the one hand lost her "monopoly of industrial technique" and on the other hand her great banker-industrialists had more funds than ever for which they sought profitable investment. Where could these funds be invested? The great crisis of 1873 and the sharp fall in Britain's exports showed clearly that expansion of British industries involved the serious risk that the additional products could neither be sold at home nor abroad. In these circumstances the finance capitalists increasingly exported their capital to colonial and other "undeveloped" countries where capital was scarce, where the native masses were subjected by violent means to the rule of foreign capital and cheap labour was made abundant and where, consequently, the rate of profit was higher than at home. By 1880 British capital invested abroad totalled over £1,000 million against the £200 million in the 1850's, by 1905 it exceeded £2,000 million, and in 1913 it was near on £4,000 million and constituted probably between one-third and one-quarter of the total holdings of the British capitalist class. At that time current foreign investment possibly exceeded the total net investment of capital at home (see M. H. Dobb, *Studies in the Development of Capitalism*, p. 315). Britain in the years before the First World War was drawing an income of some £200 million from overseas investments, at a time when her total imports were between £480 million and £800 million per annum.

Similar forces were at work within other industrial countries, and by 1914 France had overseas investments totalling about £2,500 million, Germany about £1,750 million, and U.S.A. about £400 million.

The British monopoly capitalists were able to adapt to the purposes of capitalist imperialism the colonial empire from which capitalist traders of an earlier age had enriched themselves. In the early years of this century three-quarters of the foreign capital invested in Asia and Africa was British capital. Colonial territories provided a source of extra or "super-profits" in a number of ways. In *trade* the advanced industrial country is able to exchange "more labour for less"—the products of a few hours' labour-time in home industry are exchanged for the products of many hours in the colonial countries; the terms of trade favour the imperial power. In the *exploitation* of labour extra profits can be earned because, backed by the force of arms, the imperialist power keeps the standards of life, and therefore wages, down to the lowest minimum. For example, copper from the mines of Northern Rhodesia sold in 1937 for £12 million, of which £5½ million went in royalties and dividends (mainly to British interests), whilst the 17,000 Africans employed received only £244,000 in wages (less than £15 per annum each). Even without taking into account taxation, distribution charges, etc., the rate of surplus value was over 2,000 per cent!

The imperialist policy of exporting capital accorded, in addition to a high rate of profit, other advantages; in particular, control of sources of raw materials and orders for capital goods. When British capital was invested abroad it was possible to arrange or stipulate that when the capital invested was spent and converted into commodities, the orders for capital goods should in the main be placed in Britain. (Other imperialist countries, of course, played the same game with their overseas investments, and still do in various forms, for example in some of the U.S. foreign aid programmes.)

The export of British capital in addition to providing overseas markets for British goods—and in particular investment goods—supplied Britain with cheap sources of raw materials (such as copper, rubber, jute, cotton, wool, timber, etc.) and foodstuffs. Control of sources of raw materials was in itself an advantage to the British monopolies and at the same time it provided the means by which the colonial and semi-colonial countries in which British capital was invested could pay interest on these investments. This was the basis for Britain's adverse "balance of trade". Regularly Britain imported more than she exported, the balance being accounted for by the interest due to British capitalists on overseas investments, etc. It, therefore, paid the big capitalists to develop overseas supplies of raw materials and foodstuffs. It did not pay them to develop British agriculture which, until the circumstances of the Second World War forced some changes, remained relatively backward and short of capital.

As the export of capital from the several imperialist countries proceeds, so different groups of monopolists concentrate their attentions on particular territories. Naturally this process provokes the sharpest rivalry and rapid reversal of fortunes in favour now of one group, now of another. Since the First World War, and to an even greater extent since the Second, the biggest U.S. monopolists have been able greatly to advance their interests at the expense of the other imperialist powers. Lenin described this process at the time of the First World War as follows: "Finance capital, almost literally, one might say, spreads its net over all countries of the world. Banks founded in the colonies, or their branches, play an important part in these operations. German imperialists look with envy on the 'old' colonising nations which are 'well established' in this respect. In 1904, Great Britain had fifty colonial banks with 2,279 branches (in 1910 there were seventy-two banks with 5,449 branches); France had twenty with 136 branches; Holland sixteen with sixty-eight branches; and Germany had a 'mere' thirteen with seventy branches. The American capitalists, in their turn, are jealous of the English and German; 'In South America', they complained in 1915, 'five German banks have forty branches and five English banks have seventy branches. . . . England and Germany have invested in Argentina, Brazil, and Uruguay, in the last twenty-five years approximately 4,000 million dollars, and as a result enjoy together 46 per cent of the total trade of these three countries.' The capital exporting countries have divided the world among themselves in the figurative sense of the term. But finance capital has also led to the *actual* division of the world." (*Imperialism*, Chapter IV.)

Division of the World Among Capitalist Combines

The characteristic manner in which capitalist monopolies get for themselves extra profits consists in using their monopoly position to restrict production whilst keeping prices at a level that gives an abnormally high margin of profit. It is common practice, therefore, for the big firms in an industry to control and divide out between themselves the home market for their products. As monopoly capitalism further develops it becomes more and more common for the markets of the *world* to be divided in this way between the most powerful groups of monopoly capitalists. Before the First World War the electrical industry was virtually under the control of two huge trusts, the General Electric Co. of America, and the German A.E.G.; oil was similarly dominated by two trusts, rail production was controlled by an International Railmakers' Association, which assigned to the various groups their respective shares in the markets of the world. Explosives were controlled by the International Dynamite Trust (which reappeared after the First World War in the form of the international agreements between giant chemical trusts, I.C.I. in Britain, Du Pont de Nemours in U.S.A., and the German I.G. Farbenindustrie, probably at that time the most powerful international trust in the world). In 1897 there were 40 international cartels, by 1910 the number had increased to 100, and by 1931 to 320.

The capital exported itself creates more capital, seeking profitable new investment, and at the same time narrows the field for such investment. Thus the struggle between the monopoly groupings tends to become more acute as the contradictions of capitalism reproduce themselves on a world scale and the means of even partially and temporarily resolving them become more difficult to find. Under these circumstances the struggle between the capitalist giants becomes keener as each seeks to preserve for himself profitable fields of investment, sources of raw materials, trade, and other economic rights on privileged terms. They make trial of their strength; they bargain over cartel agreements—which are, as it were, economic peace treaties reflecting the relative strengths of the contestants for the time being. But when the relative strengths of these monopoly groupings change, the stronger elements hasten, as opportunity offers, to make new agreements, to divide out spheres of influence on a new basis more advantageous to themselves. International cartels of monopoly capitalists have nowhere proved themselves to be stable organs of economic planning replacing capitalist anarchy; they have rather been the battlefields on which the contesting monopolists manoeuvre their forces one against the other prior to the clash of arms. Imperialism in dividing the world did not overcome its contradictions, but sharpened them.

The Division of the World Among the Great Powers

"The epoch of modern capitalism", writes Lenin, "shows us that certain relations are established between capitalist alliances, *based* on the economic division of the world; while parallel with this fact, and in connection with it, certain relations are established between political alliances, between States, on the basis of the territorial division of the world, of the struggle for colonies, of the 'struggle for economic territory'." In 1876, 10.8 per cent of Africa, 56.8 per cent of Polynesia, and 51.5 per cent of Asia belonged to the European imperialist powers and to the U.S.A.; by 1900 these figures had increased to 90.4 per cent, 98.9 per cent, and 56.6 per cent respectively. By 1900 practically the whole of the world was divided out between the great imperialist powers. There were, of course, a number of countries which in theory were independent, but such countries fell under the dominance of one or other of the imperialist powers (as, for example, Argentine used to be under the dominance of British capitalism). Undoubtedly, however, the monopoly capitalists reaped the most solid advantages from countries which had been subjected to complete political domination. Here State power could ensure the subjection of the exploited people, preference in trade for the metropolitan power, and a number of other material perquisites. The British State paid the expenses and the capitalists drew the profits. It is not surprising, therefore, that the monopoly capitalists in each of the great industrial countries urged on their own governments in the scramble to annex colonial territories. The world was divided *politically*. This division was achieved "by fire and the sword". Redivision can only come about as the result of tremendous clashes between the great powers.

Uneven Development of Capitalism in its Imperialist Stage

It has already been pointed out that development in capitalism as between one firm and another tends to be very uneven. Now one is ahead and prospering, now another. This unevenness marks also the development in the economic fortunes of whole countries. Now one country leaps forward, now another. Moreover, as industry is more and more concentrated in large-scale monopoly undertakings, the unevenness of development becomes more pronounced. How quickly, for example, did the new iron and steel industry of Germany and U.S.A. outstrip Britain, the home of modern industrialism? In 1880 Britain's output of pig-iron was 7.7 million tons against Germany's 2.5 million and U.S.A. 3.8 million; by 1913 Britain's output had risen to 10.3 million tons, but Germany's had risen to 19.3 million and U.S.A. to 31 million. In steel production (then a relatively new industry) the relative differences in the rate of development were even more striking.

As the relative strengths of the great imperialist powers and of the main groupings of monopoly capitalists within the international combines and cartels change, there develops a lack of balance, a lack of correspondence between the political influence of the great powers, as measured, for example, by colonial territories controlled, and their economic strengths. Naturally the economically strong but politically less favoured powers will be under special pressure from their monopoly capitalists to follow an aggressive policy and to turn their economic strength into military strength—a process which is in itself most profitable for the monopoly capitalists who receive large orders for armaments. Ultimately the antagonisms between the imperialists are resolved by war. Indeed, how else could the redivision of the world be settled? "Is there", says Lenin, "*under capitalism,* any means of removing the disparity between the development of productive forces and the accumulation of capital on the one side, and the division of colonies and 'spheres of influence' for finance capital on the other side—other than by resorting to war?" (*Imperialism,* Chapter VII.)

Imperialism Inevitably Tends to War

The imperialist stage of capitalism witnessed within less than 40 years the two most appalling wars in the history of the world; and still the piling up of arms, on a scale unseen before, continues. Arms expenditure is directed now primarily against the socialist section of the world, as it grows in strength and size; but also is an instrument of class rule, at home and overseas, of domination over other peoples. The restless rivalry, the insecurity and the social conflicts generated in private-property economies dominated by huge concentrations of economic power breed the philosophy of militarism. This does not, of course, mean that world war cannot be held in check by the struggle of peace forces within the capitalist sector of the world together with the peace forces of the socialist sector of the world. However, so long as imperialism continues to be able to pile up the instruments of war, the peace of the world cannot be secure.

For the masses of the people throughout the world imperialism has meant starvation, political oppression, and war. The workers in the imperialist countries have seen the cost of living soar; they have experienced continuous mass unemployment, and all the economic chaos to which the "entangling" of monopoly with free competition in the capitalist world must give rise. They have suffered, too, the death, destruction, and chaos of war—war to bring colonial peoples into subjection, war between rival imperialist powers. And to them imperialism has given nothing. The rivalries of the great imperialist powers have forced the monopoly capitalists to seek from the workers an ever greater surplus out of which to arm themselves for their struggle against their rivals, profits out of which to accumulate more and more capital, profits out of which to pay incomes to all the coupon-clippers and other parasitic hangers-on of imperialism, profits out of which to organise their trade wars and battles for markets, profits out of which to maintain their vast organisations for subjecting the workers and undermining the workers' organisations (press campaigns, blacklisting, spying, etc.), profits out of which to build up reserves of wealth that can quickly be mobilised for such purposes as their wars against the workers, the colonial peoples and their rivals may at any time dictate. All these profits they must exact from the toil of the workers they employ. The monopoly capitalists themselves are, of course, anxious to disguise the true consequences of imperialism for the workers.

They spread the illusion that the big monopolies make things better for the workers. It is, in fact, true that the wages paid by the monopolies may be sometimes higher than those paid by the smaller capitalists (who, as we have already seen, are put into difficulties and deprived of surplus value by the monopoly policy pursued by the big capitalists). However, what the monopolies fail to point out is that the output per worker in their undertakings is higher, and their stop-watch methods and highly organised technique for getting the last ounce of effort out of their workers ("scientific management of labour") increase the intensity of the workers' labour and greatly raise the ratio of labour-time to paid labour-time. In short, the exploitation of the workers greatly increases in the period of monopoly capitalism in the metropolitan country as well as in the colonies.

For the colonial peoples imperialism has meant adding to their old exploiters (the semi-feudal landowners or princes, usurers and tax-collectors) the new burden of foreign oppression. It has meant also the ruthless breaking up of their old ways of life; it has meant military occupation and new heavy taxation. It has meant also, for those forced to work for foreign capital, direct exploitation of the most brutal kind; in India, for example, wages in the Assam tea-gardens of 2s. 8d. a week for men, 2s. for women, and 1s. 5½d. for children (in the 1930's); in the Indian jute industry as a whole (in the early 1920's) profits of £100 a year a worker and yearly wages a worker of £12 10s.; in Malaya in 1922 wages for tin miners of 8½d. a day (profits £100 a ton).

Imperialism also means war and preparations for war. This ever-present weight of military expenditure in the epoch of imperialism falls on the backs of the workers and the masses of people. They too bear the havoc and destruction of war.

Imperialism, however, is capitalism "on its deathbed" (dying—but not dead). Imperialism is the highest and the last stage in the development of capitalism. Capital in the advanced countries has outgrown the boundaries of national States and it has established monopoly in place of competition. There have developed throughout the world "all the objective prerequisites for the achievement of socialism" (Lenin). The productive resources that imperialism creates, it is unable to use; the social relations of monopoly capitalism act as fetters on the development of production. The contradictions of capitalism express themselves in the most acute, heightened forms. The whole imperialist world is torn by violent conflicts. To the antagonism between capitalist and worker within each country there are added the antagonism between the imperialist powers themselves, and the antagonism between each imperialist power and the colonial and backward peoples subject to its rule. Out of the conflicts between these antagonistic forces came during the First World War, in 1917, the beginning of the end for capitalism, the first challenge of a new socialist order of society. The victory of socialism in Russia marked the beginning of the death-process of the old capitalist order and the dawn of the epoch of socialism.

CHAPTER X

THE NATIONAL PRODUCT AND ITS DISTRIBUTION

The size of the national product depends upon the number of workers *productively* employed, "the annual labour of the nation" which Adam Smith in the opening words of his *Wealth of Nations* described as "the fund which originally supplies it with all the necessaries and conveniences of life". It depends also on the productivity of labour which, though hampered and fettered by monopoly capitalism, still tends to increase but at a rate far below that which new productive relations could make possible. This liberation of productive forces is the central point of socialism, providing the soil out of which the culture of a democratic community can grow, free from prepossession with material wants.

The "economic superiority" of socialism consists essentially in the ability of the new productive relations to accelerate economic growth or, to say the same thing in other words, to speed the rate at which the "national product" increases. In contrast to capitalism a fuller and more effective use is made of manpower—including, of course, woman-power—in a socialist economy. It is the particular virtue of production planned to meet social and individual needs, that whatever anyone has to offer in terms of energy and talent, anything of social value, is wanted and can be used. Economic planning, increasing production and consumption together, can *maintain* a continuous increase of the national product, whereas slumps and economic stagnation in a "market-economy" cause millions of productive man-hours to be lost over prolonged periods. The cumulative effect of such losses is tremendous. The 5 or 10 year periods during which growth proceeded without serious interruption suggest what the cumulative growth of the economy could be if it were not for the slumps and phases of stagnation. The *average* rates of increase in national products over the whole period of the last century have been much less than the potential indicated by the shorter "uninterrupted" periods. For example, in the U.S.A. 3.8 per cent per year against 7 per cent per year in 1872-80, in Germany 2.5 per cent against 4.6 per cent in 1874-82, and the U.K. 2 per cent against 3.5 per cent in 1867-75. (Estimates based on data in *National Institute Economic Review* No. 16 July 1961.) In this last century the best periods for growth rate in Britain were not spectacular, but if a growth rate of 3½ per cent per annum could have been maintained throughout this period instead of an actual growth rate averaging only 2 per cent per annum, today the national product in Britain would be four times as large as it is. (A 2 per cent growth per annum yields a 7-fold increase over a 100 years whereas a 3½ per cent growth rate yields a 30-fold increase.)

In a socialist society planning on a national scale and removal of obstacles created by private property in means of production, patents and technical know-how, make possible a much fuller application of science to the problems of production and, consequently, a more rapid increase in productivity. It is not unreasonable to hope that productivity could be increased in a socialist economy in Britain—or in other countries with developed industries—at annual rates of between 5 per cent and 10 per cent. (These are fairly cautious estimates by comparison with actual achievements in the U.S.S.R. and other socialist countries.)

The national product of capitalist Britain would clearly provide the starting point for the development of a new socialist economy. It is, as it were, the base line from which one can project in imagination the economic growth from which the higher standards of material wealth available for everyone in a socialist society, would be derived. Study of the national product is also important for the light it throws upon economic relations between classes within the existing capitalist society.

In 1959 the population of the United Kingdom was 52 million. Of these just over 23 million were "occupied". The remainder—the "unoccupied"—included housewives (very much occupied but not engaged in the production of commodities), children and old people, and the "idle rich"; however, the "idle poor"—those who wanted to be occupied but could not find work—are counted by the statisticians amongst the occupied. The tables opposite analyse the various kinds of people described as occupied:

Table A

Distribution of Occupied Population—1951

(Figures in thousands)

	Males	Females	Total	% of Total
Employers, Directors and Managers	1,105	202	1,307	5.7
"Operative Employees"	13,301	6,378	19,679	87.1
Working on own account	902	246	1,148	5.1
Out of Work	340	136	476	2.1
Totals ..	15,648	6,962	22,600	100%

Table B

Percentage Distribution of Employed Manpower 1960
(by Occupation)

Occupation	Percent of Total	
(A) *Productive*		
1. Agriculture	4.3	
2. Mining and Quarrying	3.1	
3. Manufacturing	36.5	
4. Construction	6.5	
5. Gas, Electricity and Water	1.5	
6. Transport and Communication ..	6.8	
Total A ..		59
(B) *Non-Productive (Commercial and Financial)*		
7. Distributive trades	13.6	
8. Insurance, banking and finance ..	2.3	
9. Professional and Scientific Services ..	8.8	
10. Miscellaneous Services (Entertainment, Hotels, Domestic, etc.)	9.3	
Total B ..		34
(C) *Armed Forces and Public Administration*		
11. National Government	2.1	
12. Local Government	3.0	
13. Armed Forces	2.1	
Total C ..		7
Total above		100%

Productive Workers

All these people, including the "unoccupied", of course, consume food, clothing, housing, in short the bare means of living. Many of them also smoke, drink, read books, and so on. Some of them also have luxuries such as motor cars, refrigerators, silks and satins, and so forth. All these goods which provide the bare means of living and the means of luxurious living are the products of human labour, but only a part of the community actually expend their labour on their production. In a developed capitalist country such as Britain the means of life are practically all produced in the form of commodities. Commodity production, however, is but a particular historical form of the general activity of production on which the life of all human societies is founded. "The fact", says Marx, "that the production of use-values, or goods, is carried on under the control of a capitalist and on his behalf, does not alter the general character of that production." (*Capital*, Vol. I, LW p. 177, A p. 156.)

"Productive work" is not identical with socially useful work. Moreover the "social usefulness" of work is highly equivocal. What is socially useful to the capitalists or to their order of things, may be quite the opposite for the masses of the people and the socialist order of things. Furthermore, though rich idlers are neither productive nor socially useful to the workers, there are people such as doctors, teachers, nurses, writers, and the like who are "socially useful" to them but must none the less be classed (as we shall see) as unproductive workers. In short "productive work" is not the same as "socially useful work", nor is "unproductive work" the same as "socially useless work".

The distinction between productive and non-productive work is not the same as that between manual and intellectual work. Brainwork which forms part of the collective harnessing of the goods of nature is also productive work. Productive work is not distinguished from unproductive by the fact that it becomes embodied in material objects; there are kinds of work which do not directly produce objects but which are certainly kinds of productive work and are used in the sphere of material production—for example, transport, communication, signals, etc. The precise definition of "productive work" is not at all easy, since the point of view from which the definition is made makes a difference. For a capitalist that work is productive which produces surplus value. By spending on such workers, as Adam Smith observes

(*Wealth of Nations*, Book Two, Chapter 3), a man grows the richer by employing many, whereas he grows the poorer if those he employs are attendants, servants and other "non-productive" workers.

For many purposes it is useful to draw the distinction between "material" production and services; and certainly the tendency of many capitalist economists to treat all services (even the service of administration supplied by a civil servant or legal advice by a lawyer) as if, economically, no different from, say, the production of machines or coal, causes a considerable confusion in their treatment of the national product. However, not all production is of material goods and this cannot provide a criterion of what is and what is not productive.

In analysing a capitalist economy the social product must necessarily tend to be equated with "production of commodities"; but, to a certain extent, in looking at the national product *as a whole*, we are stepping outside the viewpoint of the commodity producer and trying to look at the economy in the way that it would be viewed by a socialist planning body. It is not therefore to be wondered at, if the analysis may involve some points of ambiguity. However, the outlines of the general picture that we are seeking to draw are clear enough. There need be no doubt about the fact that the bulk of the workers in industry, agriculture, building, transport and communications generally, are productive workers, whereas those employed in the fighting services, the police, the civil and local government services, health services, education, finance, culture, science, etc., are not, in general, productive workers. In distribution there is often an element of production, but in the main distributive workers are not productive workers. In the specific circumstances of a capitalist economy the distinguishing mark of productive work is the production of surplus value or, more generally of exchange value.

Classification of Productive and Non-Productive Occupations in Britain

The population of a capitalist country such as Britain may be grouped broadly as follows:

    I. Productive workers, that is, commodity producers or producers of values, comprising:

        1. Producers of surplus value, namely workers employed in capitalist enterprises who produce values over and above the value of their own labour-power. These and

their families live on the wages they earn, that is, the values they get by selling their labour-power.

2. Independent producers, such as self-employed workers, "workers on own account", producing goods for exchange (commodities), but not employing wageworkers, and not themselves working for wages. These live by exchanging the values they themselves produce (but in practice are often subject to indirect forms of exploitation and must surrender some of the values they produce in taxes, rent, etc.).

II. All others who directly or indirectly live out of the surplus values created by workers in Group I.

Broadly speaking those listed in items 1-6 of Table B on page 207 make up Group I (just under 60 per cent of the total manpower) and the others (just over 40 per cent of the total) are in Group II.

In 1959-60 the number of workers in Groups I and II may be roughly estimated as follows:

	million
Agriculture and Fishing ..	1
Mining and Quarrying ..	¾
Manufacturing	9
Construction	1½
Gas, Water, Electricity Transport and Communications	2
Group I total productive workers about	14
Group II non-productive workers about	10

The Sources of Personal Incomes

So far attention has been directed to the pattern of employment. We now turn to look at the sources of incomes. The worker who produces surplus value, as has been explained already, gets his income by selling labour-power to the capitalist for wages. This he is compelled to do by economic necessity since he does not own the means of production, and, having no commodity to sell but his labour-power, he only has the choice of working for the capitalist or starving. For his labour he gets broadly speaking the value of the means of subsistence, the actual level of wages depending on historical conditions, the current economic situation and the organised strength of the labour movement. In the U.K. before the war (1937) the sum total of wages paid to workers producing values in agriculture and industry was approximately £1,400 million (£1,150 million after taxation) whereas the values produced by these workers were approximately £4,000 million.* From these figures the over-all rate of surplus value in British industry can be estimated. Necessarily, the estimate is only a rough one but it certainly gives a broadly accurate picture. The total value of a commodity, as has been explained in earlier chapters, may be expressed by the formula

$$c+v+s=C$$

where c=constant capital, that is the "dead labour" embodied in the raw materials, machinery, etc., used up in production, v=wages, s=surplus value, and C=total value of the commodity. In estimating the rate of surplus value one need only be concerned with the new values added by the living labour (that is, v+s). Statistics available for net output from which the figure given above at £4,000 million is derived, correspond roughly to v+s for all industry; that is, the net output represents the total new values created in the course of the year and omits the "old values" embodied in raw materials, etc. (constant capital). The total surplus value therefore equalled total new values (£4,000 million) minus wages of the workers who produced these values (£1,400 million.)† Therefore the total of surplus

* A precise estimate of the new values produced annually by capitalist industry and agriculture is not easy, but as a round figure this estimate is certainly not far wrong. It is somewhat less than Dr. Barna's estimate for net national output, that is £4,146 million, which includes values produced by workers "on own account" and similar non-capitalist production which is not extensive in Britain. On the other hand, the net output of transport, mining, agriculture, building, and industry estimated from the *prices received by the producers* is a little over £2,600 million, to which figure it is reasonable to add 50 per cent (making over £3,900 million in all) for commercial costs and profits; whilst commercial costs and profits vary considerably in different branches of industry, it is certainly not unreasonable to estimate final selling prices of most commodities as 50 per cent above "factory-gate" prices. This 50 per cent addition that is suggested above means that two-thirds of the final price goes to the "producers" and one-third to the "traders"; in the case of a bar of milk chocolate, for example, the final price was made up as follows: raw materials 34 per cent, production costs 21 per cent, selling and advertising 8 per cent, transport 4 per cent, wholesaling and retailing charges 33 per cent.

† No good statistics are, however, available for estimating what allowances should be made for maintenance of machinery, etc., but any shortcomings in this respect would not cause an error of more than 5 per cent. For the purpose of this rough estimate we disregard taxation; rate of surplus value would be somewhat higher if we took it into account.

value was £2,600 million and the division of the total social product was thus:

Wages	Surplus
£1,400 million	£2,600 million

And roughly speaking the division of the average working day was this:

Paid	Unpaid
One-Third	Two-Thirds

This "one-third: two-thirds" division probably underestimates the share of surplus value since no account has been taken of the wastefulness of capitalism, for example machines produced and never fully used, components manufactured and then scrapped because they do not find a market, raw materials and food produced and then allowed to deteriorate or destroyed in order to keep up prices. Waste such as this was a common occurrence in pre-war capitalism and though not always as conspicuous as during the 1931 crisis is constantly recurring today. All this waste is waste of values produced by the workers' labour.

Any estimate of the rate of surplus value in the economy as a whole must necessarily be rough. It is possible to establish only a general "order of magnitude". For example, the allocation of occupations as between productive and non-productive workers can never be more than a broad estimate. However, the improved national income figures for the U.K. in the post-war years tend to confirm the general picture given above. In 1959, for example, it appears from Table 16 of the Government's *National Income and Expenditure 1960* that the wages in "productive industry" (items 1 to 6 in Table II above) totalled just under £6,000 million and salaries just under £2,000 million out of a gross domestic product (at factor cost) of just under £21,000 million.

Wage-earners directly engaged in production (that is, industrial workers, transport workers, agricultural workers, etc.) form the bulk of what is normally described as the "working class"; it is these workers who are most highly organised in trade unions and form the backbone of the labour movement. They produce the commodities consumed not only by themselves but by the rest of the community as well. In what way do other groups of the community who buy these commodities receive their incomes?

First, how should the other "income-receivers" be grouped? It takes all kinds to make a world and there will be many people (such as fortune-tellers or tipsters) who do not fit easily into any economic category, and a lot of time might be wasted in arguing about them—to little purpose since they take only a very small fraction of the nation's income. There will also be people who belong to several groups at the same time. However, bearing these points in mind, one may divide the community in Britain today into the following broad groups:

1. Wage-workers who produce values and surplus values (productive workers who produce the annual social product).
2. "Workers on own account."
3. (a) Unemployed, etc.
   (b) Pensioners.
4. Armed Forces, Police, etc.
5. Civil Servants, Local Government Officers, etc.
6. Nurses, Doctors, Teachers, etc.
7. Clerical and distributive workers, etc., engaged in commerce and finance.
8. Capitalists and Landlords.
   (a) "Working" capitalists, company directors, etc.
   (b) Recipients of unearned income, i.e. rent, interest, and profit.
   (c) Recipients of interest on the National Debt.
9. Various professional workers and higher range salary earners.
10. Domestic workers, etc.

No more need be said about Group 1.

"Workers on own account", if they are engaged in production for exchange (for example, cobblers) are, of course, producing values, but they are not subject to direct capitalist exploitation. None the less, squeezed out of business by big capitalist undertakings, their lot is normally one of poverty and uncertainty. In Britain, however, these small men, such as individual craftsmen and working farmers (simple commodity producers) are not numerous. They get their living from the values they produce which, in view of their backward technique, are anyhow low, but are further reduced by the weakness of their economic position, taxes, rates and so forth. (In Britain the proportion of "simple commodity producers" is exceptionally low. In the world as a whole "simple commodity producers" in the form of impoverished and oppressed peasantry constitute the vast majority of those engaged in production. (The position of the peasantry and the indirect forms of exploitation to which they are subjected were dealt with in Chapter VII.)

Every one in Groups 3, 4, 5 and 6 (apart from a comparatively small number of private teachers and private doctors, etc.) gets his or her income from the State or other public body; Local Authorities are for present purposes considered as included in "the State", and rates as a form of taxation. The State, in the main, gets its money by taxation. Taxation may be *direct*, namely, a direct deduction from incomes such as Income Tax, or *indirect*, that is, a tax which is added to the purchase price of commodities, such as the tax on tobacco which is paid indirectly by the consumer in the enhanced price, comprising the customs or excise duty which the importer or manufacturer has to pay to the State. Payments made by the State for unemployment and health benefits, pensions, etc., might be properly regarded as deferred wages since they are largely financed by contributions which come out of wages. Since, however, these contributions are compulsory, for present purposes they may be regarded as a special form of taxation. It must be emphasised that different methods and forms of taxation have important social and economic consequences (for example, indirect taxation falls most heavily on the lower income groups); however, it is not proposed here to go into the details of State finance and the budget, but to point only to the broad fact that the funds raised by the State are by one means or another lopped off wages, salaries, and profits. All this money raised by the State is in effect surplus value, appropriated by the State. In a capitalist society the whole machinery of government and administration is subordinated to the ruling class, i.e. the capitalist class. State expenditure is, therefore, unceasingly the battleground of class interests, the desire of the capitalist class being to use State finance to strengthen their domination, to facilitate means of increasing profits and impose exactions that hit the masses of the people. The working class on the other hand fight for the improvement of social services, against State expenditures to buttress up the capitalist class, and for lightening the burden of taxation falling on the masses of the people. In short, a battle of the classes is unceasingly waged over methods used by the State to "appropriate surplus value" and the use to which the State's revenue is put.

Interest on National Debt (8c), is of course, just as much surplus value as interest paid by one capitalist to another, but it makes its way into the hands of the capitalist by a peculiar route. The State collects this surplus value in the form of taxation on the community and then hands it out to the "owners" of the National Debt as a company hands out interest on loans it has received. There is, however, an important difference between the State and a company engaged in production, in that the latter pays interest out of surplus values created by the workers in the undertakings in which the borrowed capital is used, whereas the State appropriates surplus values created elsewhere with other capital than that borrowed by the State.

It is sometimes thought that the interest on National Debt does not go to the capitalists but to small men owning War Loans, etc. This is not the case. For example, in 1937* only 13½ per cent of the interest went to persons with incomes under £250 a year. Almost half the interest went to holding companies, banks, and other financial institutions.

The total payment in interest on the National Debt is very great. Before the war it was already over £200 million. In 1947 it was approximately £550 million and now that compensation is being paid for the nationalisation of mines, transport, Bank of England, steel, power, etc., its magnitude and economic significance as a means of distributing surplus value is becoming still greater. In 1959 debt interest paid by the Central government totalled £778 million.

Dr. Barna has made some interesting calculations which indicate broadly the distribution of taxes between classes in 1937. In all, £1,157 million was collected in taxation, direct and indirect; £472 million was paid on rent, profits, and interest, representing 34 per cent of the total of incomes received in this form, £309 million on wages (18 per cent of total wages), £234 million on salaries (22 per cent of total salaries). The balance of £142 million cannot be clearly allocated. After the Second World War, in addition to the huge weight of indirect taxation borne by them, a greater number of workers have had to pay direct income taxes and direct contributions to social insurance schemes. In this connection Callaghan in *The British Way to Socialism* says: "The view of the present writer based on such

* Details are given in *Redistribution of Incomes* by T. Barna, Clarendon Press, 1945, pp. 83, 193.

figures as are available, is that in 1947-48 the lower income groups financed the social security schemes through their direct and indirect tax payments. . . . If this is so then the traditional Tory cry that 'the rich are being taxed out of existence' in order to provide social services for the workers is no longer true. . . . The cost is broadly met from within the working class themselves; they are beholden to no one, least of all the rich." (pp. 139-40.)

Those who are engaged in finance and commerce (Group 7) are paid by the capitalists who employ them. They include several different kinds of people such as (i) shop-assistants behind the counter; (ii) clerical workers in commercial houses, insurance companies, banks, etc.; and (iii) professional men such as lawyers, chartered accountants, etc. It is quite clear that the last two types of people play no part in the production of commodities. They are merely "overheads" of the capitalist system, that is, people who are occupied only in enabling the capitalists to realise the values created in the undertakings of the "productive capitalists". The shop-assistants' activities cannot be classified quite so sharply. The shop-assistant's main job is salesmanship and taking the money—activities which have nothing to do with the production of values but merely with the realisation of values. A shop-assistant has, however, also some jobs which are "a continuation of production in the sphere of distribution". A commodity's use-value comprises being in the right place and condition; butter storing, mixing, packing, and delivery are, for example, productive activities carried out to this end by the grocer's assistant. (There are, vice versa, a number of activities in a productive undertaking concerned only with the process of selling.)

Despite exceptions, distributive and clerical workers in a modern *capitalist* society do not, broadly speaking, produce values. They are not "productive workers", do not produce any surplus value; their incomes must therefore come out of the surplus value produced by others. This is not to say they are not of importance to the functioning of the economy as a whole—as they would also be in a socialist economy; but the more efficient and expeditious the distribution machinery is, the more manpower is freed for other purposes. Enlargement of "sales forces"— a tendency to which industrial capitalism becomes more and more prone in the course of years—adds nothing to the size of the national product.

Strictly speaking, the distributive workers are not exploited in the same way as, for example, the factory worker. The difference is—so far as these workers are concerned—theoretical rather than real. They are all paid by capitalists who see their wages as costs eating into profits. The lot of the distributive or clerical worker is the same as (or worse than) that of the industrial worker. The laws which determine the level of the productive worker's wages apply equally to the commercial worker, but the capitalist by cutting the commercial worker's wages and lengthening his hours does not get more values produced, but cuts down commercial and distributive costs and thereby (in the manner explained in Chapter VI) gets bigger profits out of the margin between the selling price and what the industrial capitalist gets.

The incomes of this group (though some of them are "wage-earners") are in the main included in what national statistics describe as salaries.*

In 1959 income from employment in the distributive trades totalled £1,527 million and profits £1,058 million.

Group 8—the capitalists proper—receive surplus value in its well-recognised forms of rent, interest, and profit. However, company directors and "working" capitalists are included here because, particularly in these days of vast limited liability companies, a substantial amount of surplus value is expropriated in the form of inflated salaries and excessive "expenses" paid to men who have placed themselves and their friends in key positions. In so far as these people really contribute to the organisation and carrying out of production, what they receive is not surplus value; but it is common to find in the large-scale organisations of modern capitalism a hierarchy of highly paid people superimposed on the working managers who receive relatively modest incomes. For example, it is not uncommon for a big capitalist to hold several directorships each at about £1,000 a year, for which he does no more than attend a monthly meeting. It should also be pointed out that these big capitalists who play a part in the control of company policy and are "in the know", are exceptionally well placed to collar big extra profits by buying and selling shares and doing other deals in capital—profits made at the expense of the small "dormant" and inactive capitalists.

* The normal distinction between salaries and wages is that the term of engagement is for one week or more in respect of salaried employees, while wages are paid by the hour.

Thus this group may be said to be divided into three sub-groups (which, of course, overlap); the inner ring of big capitalists, the smaller "working" capitalists, and the idle, parasitic recipients of unearned incomes who sit back and wait for their dividends to come in—the *rentiers* and *coupon-clippers*.

We have here lumped rent and profits together. As explained in Chapter VII, there is economically an important difference between rent and other forms of surplus value. A hundred years and more ago there were also clear divisions and distinctions between the landlord class and the industrial capitalist class; however, in Britain today (though in many other countries the distinction remains) the two classes have very largely merged and no significant distinction can be drawn.

Group 9 comprises a miscellaneous set of people who are not easily fitted into hard and fast economic categories. To some extent this group merges with the professional people in Group 7; however, almost all will be non-productive workers.

This miscellaneous group also includes activities which might be classed as small-scale commodity production, activities which could be said to be "wage-labour" used by a productive capitalist, and activities which are concerned only with the realisation of surplus values. Sometimes all three types of activity will be carried out by one and the same person, such as an architect, who builds a house for a client, gives an industrialist advice on the building, maintenance, etc., of his factories in return for an annual fee or "wage", and advises a capitalist about the structural soundness of property he proposes to buy as an investment.

As a rough generalisation it is fair to assume that in the main this miscellaneous group receives incomes out of surplus value and does not produce values; but in all the members of this group constitute less than 1 per cent of those who receive incomes and the way in which they are classified will not alter the broad picture of Britain's economic structure with which we are primarily concerned.

Privately employed domestic workers, etc. (Group 10), are primarily employed by the capitalist class and people with salaries in the higher ranges. Their wages are simply incomes transferred to them in order that work, not to produce commodities but directly to satisfy the wants or whims of the well-to-do, may be carried out. Obviously domestic employment is necessary;

but equally it is certain that a vast amount of manpower has been wasted on domestic drudgery or pandering to the wants of the wealthy. In 1931 there were in Britain 1½ million indoor domestic workers (though by 1960 the number was certainly much lower—probably about 250,000). The worker's wife or family who do domestic work looking after the worker and his household, of course, consume a part of what the worker receives as wages, but they do not themselves produce commodities and do not therefore add to the *social* product, that is, the sum total of values that make up the "National Income".

The National Turnover

It may help the reader to grasp this important idea of the national product, if we depict in a simplified, schematic way (by using orders of magnitude roughly corresponding to the contemporary reality) the process by which the national product is generated, what happens to it and how the means are provided for continuing the generation of new national products in successive periods.

The new values which constitute the national income are created in the first instance in the form of commodities produced by manufacturing, mining, construction, etc., concerns. The bulk of this production is accounted for by about 2,000 large firms with capital totalling about £10,000 million (of which about two-thirds are in fixed assets and the rest stocks, "work-in-progress" and funds at the bank for payment of wages, new purchases etc.). The prices received by the manufacturers will be less, of course, than the final selling prices, a part of the values being surrendered to the capitalists engaged in distribution and out of this difference, distributive costs and profits will be met.

The total receipts of the capitalist will then be disposed of in the following ways:

(A) Replacement of stocks and plant (this part of the price does not represent any new value created but merely maintains the resources of industry as they were originally).

(B) Payment of wages and salaries (some part of which is paid in income tax creating income for the government).

(C) What remains is the gross income of the capitalist concerns. (To simplify the picture public corporations are omitted.) This in 1960, for example, was disposed of as follows:

1. Taxation—23.2 per cent
2. Dividend and interest payments—31.3 per cent
3. Depreciation and Other provisions—21.4 per cent
4. Retained in Reserves—24 per cent

1. *Taxation:* The direct taxation of companies is not, of course, the only source of revenue for the central and local governments. Other sources are (a) personal income tax, e.g. on incomes paid out as wages, salaries, interest or dividends, (b) taxes on sales, e.g. purchase tax or custom duties on imports and (c) taxes on property, in particular, rates.

2. Dividends and interest payments in part become personal income but also represent income for other capitalist concerns in finance, insurance, etc. and so become also sources of accumulation.

3. Depreciation allowances strictly represent the value of existing plant used up; but in practice these allowances represent more and merge into

4. Funds *accumulated* to provide increasing financial strength to the capitalist concerns and the wherewithal for enlarging and improving the means of production.

The incomes arising in these various ways give rise to the total of "Final Expenditure" for the nation as a whole (i.e. expenditure excluding intermediary expenditure on goods passing from hand to hand for further manufacture or re-sale and excluding expenditure that merely replaces used-up capital). In 1961 "Final Expenditure" in the U.K. was officially estimated as follows:

	£ million
Consumers Expenditure	17,302
Public Authorities Current Expenditure ..	4,596
Gross Fixed Capital Formation at home ..	4,530
Value of Physical Increases in Stock and Work in Progress	264
Exports of Goods and Services	5,351
Total "Final Expenditure"	32,043

This total for "Final Expenditure" is considerably in excess of the total national product because it includes exports, without setting against them imports, and in the market prices of the goods bought there is also an element of indirect taxes. The official estimate for the "Gross National Product at Factor Cost" is, therefore, derived from the above figures by deducting:

			£ million
Taxes on Expenditure	..	..	3,635
Less Subsidies	..	..	598
			3,037
Imports of Goods and Services		..	5,569
			8,606

to give "Gross Domestic Product" = £23,437 million

But this figure is still too high from our point of view, because within "Consumers' Expenditure" are included items such as rent, insurance, and miscellaneous services which are payments from one income-receiver to another and not payments for commodities produced and sold. These items probably total over £2,000 million. Allowing for this the division of the national product can be broadly depicted as follows:

Disposal of the National Product

Consumers' Expenditure		70 per cent
of which:		
Wages paid in Productive Establishments	27½ per cent	
Salaries paid in Productive Establishments	10 per cent	
Wages and Salaries paid in Distribution, Finance, and Professional services	15 per cent	
Wages and Salaries paid by Central and Local Governments (including education, health services, etc.)	10 per cent	
Consumption Expenditure out of profits, etc. ..	7½ per cent	
Public Authorities' Expenditure on Goods		7½ per cent
Additions to Fixed Capital (and stocks) ..		22½ per cent

National Income: Marxist and Bourgeois Views

Adam Smith (1723-1790), whose work laid the basis for a truly scientific study of political economy, set himself the task of inquiring into the "Nature and Causes of the Wealth of Nations", or, as one might say, using modern terms, he sought to explain what the national income is and what determines its amount. Adam Smith approached this question armed with a labour theory of value, the significance of which for his inquiry is clear from the very first sentence of his book (which is quoted at the start of this chapter). Marxist economic theory, taking the labour theory of value as its foundation, has elaborated a full and scientific picture of capitalism and the laws of its development which makes possible a clearer understanding of the "nature and causes" of the national income.

The national income in a capitalist economy is the sum of newly produced commodities, the total net social product, the new values created in a given period of time, say, a year.

A nation's income, leaving aside payments from abroad, such as surplus value from capital invested abroad, can only be what it produces. The meaning of production has been discussed above (pp. 208-9). A nation's annual income must be taken as equal to the net product within a year. Factories and other productive undertakings buy raw materials, semi-finished goods, etc.—all the components of *constant capital*—to which new value is added by the productive process, that is, the expenditure of labour in production. The finished products of some undertakings will become the materials of others (as bricks from the brick company become the materials of the builder). The national income is, therefore, not the total of gross products of each productive undertaking but the total of the *new* values added, the *net* products of each undertaking. The gross product of each undertaking equals, in Marxist terminology, its constant capital plus variable capital plus surplus value, $c+v+s$. The new value added equals the variable capital plus the surplus value, $v+s$. Values produced to *replace* constant capital (to replace stocks of materials, for example, or the wear and tear of plant) do not create new income; they simply replace the old, previously produced values, the "dead labour" embodied in means of production produced in previous years. In so far, however, as capital is accumulated and additional constant capital is produced as a basis for extended reproduction, the new values produced in the form of means of production are a part of the national income. The national income therefore equals the sum total of new values produced, which equals the sum total of wages plus the sum total of surplus value, $v+s$, and includes accumulation which comes out of the surplus value. The rate of accumulation, as shown in Chapter VIII, has far-reaching consequences for the development of capitalist economy.

The national income will normally be expressed in terms of money; for example, it may be said that Britain's national income was in the years before the Second World War in the region of £4,000 million and today is somewhat over £20,000 million—which, however, is less than double the pre-war level allowing for the three-fold increase in prices. Here money is used as a measure of value; each £ represents let us say, five hours* of "abstract, average, socially necessary labour-time". A national income of £4,000 million therefore represents new values produced by 20,000 million hours of abstract labour-time. This figure of £4,000 million reflects the total volume of productive labour effectively engaged. If the volume of commodities produced is to be measured from year to year, the money measure may have to be adjusted. Measurement needs to be in *constant prices*, if the money measure is not to be a misleading measure when values of money and goods alter relatively to one another. If productivity of labour increases the *mass* of commodities will increase; but the sum total of *values* will not increase unless there is also more labour used on production.

Bourgeois theory, when it comes to deal with national income gets involved in the greatest difficulties. For example, Professor A. L. Bowley, who was one of the first to tackle the statistics of the national income, wrote: "By *total national income* is generally meant the aggregate of the incomes (including earnings) of the persons composing a nation; income is taken as meaning the money, or money value of goods, coming into a person's possession during a year for his own use (subject to rates and taxes), after all expenses connected with it are substracted. . . . It is doubtful whether a perfectly definite meaning can be attached to National Income. The sum of money nominally representing it, of course, does not actually exist. . . . The utility of £1 to a person is in

---

* Very roughly correct for the years before the Second World War; in 1948 two-and-a-half hours would be nearer the mark, and in 1962 under one-and-a-half.

general the less the greater his income and the total utility of all incomes depends on how they are distributed among persons. On the other side, the value of services and commodities depends upon the demand for them. In fact the hundreds of millions of pounds which make the aggregate are not a homogeneous total." (*An Elementary Manual of Statistics*, Chapter IX, p. 119.) Professor Bowley has put his finger right on the "sore spot" of bourgeois theory; on a subjective utility theory of value, £1 measures nothing but subjective valuations of relative utilities and therefore adding up national income in money terms has "no definite meaning". Professor Bowley points out that national income would only have meaning if it could be aggregated in terms of a homogeneous total. This is so. Recognition of the common element entering into the multiplicity of commodities produced is necessary to the analysis of national income. This common element is the fact that they are all produced by human labour employed within the capitalist system. (As such, commodities have exchange-value proportionate to the homogeneous abstract labour-time that they embody—see p. 24 ff.) At the same time they are designed to satisfy a multiplicity of diverse human wants. As such, they have use value and embody concrete labour. The error and confusion of bourgeois economics derives from its attempt to explain matters as if commodities were *nothing but* use-values. The aspect of homogeneity in commodities is completely disregarded. Bourgeois theory comes, therefore, to the conclusion that it is meaningless to add and average subjective utilities—which is indeed so.

If the logic of the utility theory of value were adhered to, national income analysis would be impossible. Here, however, as on many other current issues (for example, economic growth), bourgeois theory is compelled to discard—or disregard—its value theory. Even so elements of confusion persist. So in national income analysis, there persists the tendency to regard all income as payment to "factors of production", e.g. interest for the "service" of lending capital, forces pay for "producing" the service of defence, etc., etc. Here one sees the influence of bourgeois theory which argues that income is the reward of the various "factors of production", such as labour, capital, managerial ability, salesmanship etc., and that each "economic factor" is brought to a market on which it gets what it is worth as a result of each man measuring the deal subjectively in terms of utility to himself.

To sum up, national income is the total of new values produced and embodied in the commodities sold or for sale for the community's use. These new values equal the sum of total wages of productive workers plus total surplus value (v+s in the Marxist formula). The surplus after payment for wages is the sum total available for rent, interest, profit, for accumulation, for commercial services and other "overheads" of the capitalist mode of production, for the armed forces and other non-productive expenditures by the State.

Company Finance

One can also see from the study of company finance how the values produced in the factory (the point of production where the values are created) flow out to the various classes and sections of the community. Today almost all Joint Stock Companies take the form of Limited Liability Companies—Ltd. for short. Suppose that the capital structure of a company (here an imaginary one) is as follows:

£1,000,000 in £1 Ordinary Shares.
£400,000 in 7 per cent Preference Shares.
£1,000,000 in 4 per cent Debentures.

What are the peculiarities of these three main types of share? First, *Debentures*: these are loans plain and simple on which a specified interest (in this case 4 per cent) has to be paid every year until the Debentures are repaid (conditions for which will be laid down). The company must pay interest on Debentures whether it makes a profit or not; if it does not, it is liable to be made bankrupt and forced to go into liquidation (that is, all its assets must be sold to repay its debt). *Preference shares* are, as the name implies, shares which take preference over other shares— when the company divides out its profits (pays a *dividend*), the prescribed dividend, in this case 7 per cent, must be paid on the Preference shares before any other dividends are paid out. Last of all, the *Ordinary share*-holders come in for payment. If profits have been small, no dividend at all may be paid to the Ordinary shareholders; on the other hand if profits have been large, 20 per cent, 30 per cent, or 40 per cent or even more may be paid out to them, while the Preference shareholders are still getting only 7 per cent. Ordinary shares are therefore more of a gamble; they may get high dividends or none at all. These speculative shares that gain and lose most from the fortunes of business are often described as *equity* shares.

Control of company policy is in theory generally exercised by the Ordinary shareholders, each shareholder having as many votes as he has shares; but in practice a few large shareholders control policy and see that the directors they want (often themselves) are elected. In this way the whole of the capital is in effect controlled by only a part of the shareholders. Sometimes in order to safeguard control, there are special classes of shares which carry preferential voting rights which give complete control of company policy.

The working capital of a company by no means necessarily corresponds to the issued capital. In some cases, the issued capital may have been expanded by issuing free shares (*bonus shares*) to shareholders and sometimes the money value of the assets belonging to the company is considerably less than the issued capital. If this is so, the capital is said to be "watered". After the First World War the money figure for the capital of many textile companies was inflated far beyond the real value of the assets they owned. Again, the railways maintained an excessive money figure for their capitals. On the other hand, a company may have accumulated each year profits which instead of being paid out in dividends, have been put to reserves, and thus reserve funds as great as the issued capital may have been built up. In this event, the actual working capital will have been greatly increased and, other things being equal, the profits will be correspondingly bigger, and large dividends are likely to be regularly paid. The reasonably certain prospect of getting large dividends will lead to the value of such a company's shares on the Stock Exchange going up. A share of nominal value of £1 may then cost £5, £10, or £20 to buy. The rise and fall of the prices of individual shares on the Stock Exchange may, however, be due to nothing but gambling and financial manipulation.

Consider now some figures in the accounts of our imaginary company. The Company's income will come mainly from receipts for the sale of its products, for which it will get not the full price paid by the consumer but "the factory gate" price. Let us say also that it receives income from a *subsidiary* company which we will suppose markets the products of the parent company and is engaged solely in trading. The profits of this company may be taken to represent that portion of the surplus value which (though produced, of course, in the factory) is realised only in the sphere of distribution. (See section on Commercial Capital in Chapter VI.) From this source let us say that the parent company receives £200,000. Its receipts will therefore be:

Receipts from Sale of Products	£1,300,000
Income from dividends on shares in subsidiary company	£200,000
Total receipts ..	£1,500,000

Against the receipts must be set expenses. The main expenses will be purchases of fuel, raw materials, etc., out of which the capitalists selling these products make their profits. The other large item on the expense side will be wages of the productive workers, incomes which will be spent by the workers on the means of living. Then something will be set aside for the depreciation of plant, etc. This money will periodically be spent on new machines or component parts, repairs to buildings, etc., and will eventually pass into the hands of the capitalists owning the factories which produce these things. There will also be a number of "expenses" which are really (in the main) payments out of surplus value, such as directors' fees, rates (which then pass into the hands of companies or individuals employed by Local Authorities), rent (which is unearned income going to landlords), insurance, etc. (income for financial concerns), legal expenses (incomes for lawyers, lawyers' clerks, etc.), and so on. The *expenses* side of our company's accounts might therefore be as follows:

	£
Purchases of raw material, fuel, etc. ..	800,000
Wages, etc.	200,000
Directors' fees	30,000
Rent and Rates	20,000
Depreciation of Plant, etc.	40,000
Legal Expenses, Insurance, etc. ..	10,000
Total Expenses	£1,100,000

Receipts exceed expenses by £400,000. What happens to all this? The 4 per cent will have to be paid on the 4 per cent Debentures; this will take £40,000. There will be certain taxes to be paid direct by the company (which we assume in all to total £100,000). After payment of debenture interest and taxes £260,000 will be left. Next the 7 per cent will be paid on the Preference shares, taking £28,000. Having handed over to the State in taxes such part of the surplus value as the law compels and having handed out those unearned incomes which fall as a first charge on the surplus value produced, the directors will decide how they want to see the remainder of £232,000 divided between the Ordinary shareholders and "profits put to reserve", that is, profits accumulated so that they can function as new capital in the next turnover of capital. It is now usual for capitalists, in their anxiety to expand their future profits and economic power, to put bigger and bigger sums to reserve. Suppose that they decide that 10 per cent is an ample dividend for the Ordinary shareholders and accordingly pay out £100,000 in this way, leaving £132,000 to put to reserves. In order to disguise the true size of total profits, the payment into reserves will probably not be made in a straightforward way. They may, for example, make excessive allowances for depreciation of stock and plant, £80,000 say instead of £40,000, thus hiding away £40,000 as a secret reserve; of the balance they may put £20,000 openly to ordinary reserves and £70,000 to a special contingency reserve, spinning an appropriate story about the contingency they have in mind. And what will they do with the remaining £2,000? Perhaps one of the directors will have a brain-wave; he will say, "Our workers are not such fools. They will see, despite all our 'secret' and 'contingency' reserves that we have made handsome profits this year. Would it not be a good idea to forestall their demands for increased wages and keep them quiet and sweet, at a great saving to ourselves in the long run, by paying them the remaining £2,000 as a special bonus? Then who can say that the workers don't share in the profits?" The proposition will be carried unanimously with Colonel Blimp, the Vice-Chairman, muttering that all the same the workers get more than they are worth. One further device for making the profit look small and keeping the workers quiet may be adopted; with much self-righteousness it will be announced that dividends are only 8½ per cent of total receipts. But those who know what to look for will note that the rate of surplus value is 230 per cent! (Surplus value = £400,000 plus £60,000 for Directors' fees, rent and legal expenses against £200,000 for wages.)

The capitalist owner of the productive undertakings is the first appropriator of surplus value; but through his hands and those of the merchant, capitalist surplus value passes into innumerable other hands. It goes far outside the factory in which it is produced. Only the part that is accumulated and turned into new capital, returns to industry; the rest goes to build the vast pyramid of capitalist exploitation, the incomes of the millionaires, of the rentiers and landlords, the many hundreds of thousands operating the costly business of capitalist distribution and commerce, the bankers and lawyers, the commission agents and brokers, the vast apparatus of the State machine by which the capitalist class maintains its power, all the "overheads" of the capitalist mode of production. The weight of this huge superstructure may be told in figures. In 1959 in Britain profits, rent and interest—the general category of "unearned income"—were, before tax, approximately £7,000 million. Wages and salaries of those engaged in distribution, commerce, administration, the armed forces, and other "non-productive" occupations, totalled £5,700 million; and wages and salaries of those in "productive" occupations totalled £8,300 million. From these figures the share of surplus value in the national product can be roughly assessed as about 60 per cent. The share of the total passing into the hands of the State (central and local government) was approximately 30 per cent, and in considering the figures given above it should be borne in mind that State taxes on expenditure (falling mainly on workers and lower incomes) plus insurance and health contributions, totalled £3,400 million, and taxes on income and capital (falling mainly on middle and higher incomes) totalled £3,000 million.

These figures show the magnitude of the surplus produced. From the standpoint of capitalism this is the measure of national wealth, but from the standpoint of the nation, that is, the people as a whole, it is not a measure of national wellbeing. Apart from capitalist consumption the surplus is used largely to keep the system of capitalism in being. This system does not make a good life for the people and has outlived the day of its usefulness in the historical development of human society. Today it remains as a breeding ground for crises and wars. But if, with all the waste that capitalism entails, a comparatively small proportion of the national manpower could produce so great a surplus to maintain the edifice of capitalist society, how much better and how much richer in interest and enjoyment could the conditions, both of work and of leisure, be in Britain if the resources that we use socially, were owned and controlled socially! If all those who worked in production, if all scientists, technicians, etc., were free to use and develop all the forces of production latent in modern society—in short if production were for use and not for profit, poverty could be abolished altogether and work itself could become a matter of enjoyment. For this to become possible it is necessary that the working class should take State power and change Britain's mode of production from capitalism to socialism.

CHAPTER XI

SOCIALISM AND MAN'S FUTURE

The General Crisis of Capitalism

The vast political, economic and cultural crises by which capitalist society has been torn, now in one way, now another, throughout the last five decades—the clash of imperialist arms, the breakthrough of the Russian Revolution in 1917, i.e., the first successful proletarian revolution, the successful struggle of oppressed nationalities for their independence in country after country, the surging movements of the workers in the imperialist countries, the defeat of fascism and the determined struggles of the peoples against it, socialism in Eastern Europe, the Chinese Revolution, and the revolution in Cuba—all these are symptoms of a world in transition to socialism and of the deepening crisis of capitalist society. The problems of British monopoly capitalism are paralleled by problems that are different but no less great in each of the monopoly capitalist powers.

At root, social crises have their origins in underlying economic circumstances. This, however, is not to say that they are explicable in economic terms only. That would be an absurdity. The context in which social struggle develops is the cultural, political and, in general, historical tradition of each country and its working-class movement. But disturbance of the social *status quo* is constantly and repeatedly occurring, because the economic foundations of society keep changing; and it is these changes rooted in the economic foundations of society—rather than contemporary history in general—with which we here need to concern ourselves.

Capitalism—for reasons which we sought to show in earlier chapters—is always restless, forced by competition to be on the move, seeking expansion; expansion in the magnitude of capital owned or controlled, and expansion of the markets in which to sell commodities. This leads to concentration and centralisation of capital, the emergence of *monopoly* capital and imperialism and the subordination of the whole world to the most powerful trusts. But with the world once seized by the trusts, further change implies not division of the world but redivision. Hence also the increase in militarism as the political instrument of redivision and the occurrence of wars—the First and Second World Wars—unparalleled in scale throughout human history hitherto. At the same time the policies of imperialism comprised attempts by the capitalist class to relieve the pressure against itself from its own working class by making some concessions at home out of the surplus value which expanded capital turnover, coupled with a widened field for exploitation and markets overseas, brought to them. But the relief afforded by such imperialist policies could be no more than transitory; for oppression of subject nations, as the sphere of capitalism expanded, provoked in turn more unified and determined national resistance. Also the concessions made to industrial workers were petty compared to the potential of modern industry and science. The emergence of socialist powers strengthened the working-class and national opponents of imperialism within the imperialist world; and armed with new knowledge, understanding and experience, the pressure of the masses for social advance increased in scope and intensity. Today the masses of ordinary people no longer look upon poverty and subordination to a privileged ruling minority as inevitable or historically necessary circumstances of life to which they must just resign themselves.

Such factors as these, constantly at work, expressing in fact an incompatibility between the economic and political relationships of capitalism on the one hand and the potentialities of modern science and technical power on the other, underlie the accentuation of all the struggles that are today tearing monopoly capitalism apart. The period since the First World War—described by Marxists as "the period of the general crisis of capitalism"—has been one of wave after wave of social and political upheaval with only brief intervals of relative stability. The power of the old order is repeatedly undermined by conflicts of interest between its own protagonists, and these are exacerbated by the continuing conditions of political and economic crises in one form or another. The conflict between British and American imperialism on the one side and German on the other, and the internal conflicts between feudal and bourgeois interests within Russia, gave Russian workers under Bolshevik leadership the opportunity, which they seized, of breaking through, winning power and setting out to construct a socialist society.

That the first socialist revolution occurred in a country in which modern capitalist industry accounted for only a small percentage of the working population, and in which the vast mass of the people were peasantry living under semi-feudal conditions, is not—as critics of Marxism argue—in contradiction to the Marxist theories of historical development. Marxism recognises the complexity of historical processes and sees the need for carefully examining its theoretical generalisations in the light of actual historical developments in their concrete particularity. Marx and Engels themselves changed their ideas about where and how a socialist society might first emerge. Marxists can only determine the possible forms and the possible lines of advance towards socialism by the most thorough study of the world in which they live. It was already clear, however, in the last quarter of the nineteenth century, when Marx and Engels were still alive, that capitalism was embracing the whole world, that imperialist powers—led then by Britain—were subordinating to themselves, politically and economically, all the other peoples of the world, and that successful struggles by these peoples against the metropolitan imperialist powers might well need to precede the victory of the workers' movements within the imperialist powers. The industrial organisation of the workers in the economically advanced countries with large industrial concentration certainly became formidable (in Britain, U.S.A., Germany, for example); but it was also clear that the ruling classes of the great industrial powers were most firmly entrenched in the metropolitan countries themselves. The weakest spots in the world-wide arena over which capitalist domination stretched were in the countries where modern capitalism was still but shakily established and restricted in scope (such as Russia) or where, as in the colonial territories, foreign domination stunted the growth of indigenous national capitalism. To argue under such circumstances that socialism ought necessarily to have emerged first in the industrially advanced countries would be sheer pedantry—certainly not Marxism, science or even common sense.

Marxist analysis led Lenin to believe, already at the turn of the century, that the Russian workers might be the first to break through and win power; and Marx, too, thought this a serious possibility. At the time of the Russo-Turkish War he spoke of the revolution beginning in the East, "hitherto the unbroken bulwark and reserve army of counter-revolution". (Letter to Sorge 27.9.1877; see also letter to Sorge dated 19.10.1877 in which he speaks of the need for studying forms of historical evolution separately to arrive at an understanding of events, and adds: "one will never arrive there by using as one's master key a general historic philosophical theory".)

That the movement to socialism must be international in character is perhaps too obvious to require stressing. Every country is economically tied to every other country in the world, and each ruling class draws strength from or is weakened by its foreign relations. At the same time the socialist movements of the workers must draw strength from brother movements abroad and moral support from a community of views that spreads throughout the world. The successes and failures of the workers' movement in one country tend, inevitably, to help or hurt movements in other countries. Also the struggle of nationalities oppressed by imperialist powers is a struggle against the imperialist ruling class that opposes the workers' movement at home. So, inevitably, a conflict between capital and labour has a multitude of connections with the political relations of progressive and reactionary forces on the world arena. Obviously—certainly and inevitably, one might say—the winning of political power in one country by a working-class movement dedicated to the construction of socialism was an event of striking and persisting importance for every other socialist movement, for every other progressive movement, for every force struggling against imperialism and equally, of course, for every force struggling against socialism or to maintain the *status quo* of imperialist power.

Marxists are often accused of "always bringing up Russia". But, of course, "not to bring up Russia" is simply to run away from reality. The emergence of a socialist State power has coloured every major issue since. Socialist movements everywhere have been compelled to declare their attitude to the Soviet Union; opportunists in the working-class movement have tried to avoid conflict with their own ruling class by dissociating themselves from Soviet Socialism and presenting themselves as protagonists against it. Naturally such opportunist attitudes are combated within the movement, and preoccupation with this issue is in fact inescapable, because the reasons for it reach down to the roots of the historical process. Within ruling circles there is also preoccupation with this issue, degenerating repeatedly into monomaniac obsession. The all-pervading impact of this issue can only be attributed to the very facts that Marx's analysis of the laws of social development brought to light, namely the rivalry of the old and new economic systems, reflected in the battle between the old and new social systems. Capitalism breaks down because it cannot provide scope for human progress, cannot make proper use of the power of modern science or apply it adequately to production and man's mastery over his natural surroundings generally. Because of these contradictions between capitalist relationships and the developing productive forces, capitalist society is bound to be surpassed by a new social system (new because the economic basis is new) just as capitalism itself surpassed and replaced feudalism. Once a socialist State is established over a considerable part of the world this issue must tend to dominate all other issues—as contemporary history establishes for all to see without any dubiety.

In the years 1917, 1918, 1919 it was not only in Russia that the flames of revolution burned. In Germany, Hungary, Italy, France, and in Britain too, great tides of protest and struggle swept through the masses. In Germany and elsewhere certainly the possibility of overthrowing capitalism existed, but in the great struggles of those years the movement of the masses was thrown back—leaving its mark on all subsequent developments, but not leaving in power representatives of the workers and the people able to harness the productive forces of any developed capitalist power to the construction of an economic base for socialism. The first economic base of socialism—the "economic prototype"—came to be built in a country hitherto employing only one or two million workers in industrially developed enterprises, whose population was preponderantly composed of peasants knowing nothing of modern industry and largely illiterate. In the succeeding period the issue overshadowing all others was that of the survival of the first socialist State and the establishment in it of the foundations of a modern industry.

In the capitalist world the attempted redivision of spheres of interest in World War I had solved none of the contradictions by which the war had been provoked. Now the world for the capitalists was narrowed by being broken up into a socialist and capitalist sector; nor within the territories still dominated by big capital were new fields for investment or markets opened up.

World agriculture in the 1920's and 1930's was in a situation of chronic, persisting crisis, with the peasant masses throughout Asia, South America and Africa at or near starvation levels. Now imperialism began to face a more determined and a politically more formidable opposition from the anti-imperialist movements in the colonies. At the same time, the economies of the capitalist powers themselves were in a far from healthy state. The First World War had cost the belligerent nations, it is estimated, £75,000 million and caused their wealth to be reduced by one third. The U.S.A. and other countries of the Western hemisphere alone profited economically from the war; and the U S.A. emerged as the predominant capitalist power.

When the war was ended, a short boom in which prices and profits rocketed still higher than they had in the war was followed by slump and mass unemployment in 1921. The unemployed in Britain increased from half a million at the end of 1920 to two million at the end of 1921 (not to fall thereafter below one million until a Second World War again created a labour shortage). In the decade 1900 to 1910 unemployment ranged between 2.5 per cent and 7.8 per cent and averaged 4.7 per cent. In 1916, 1917, and 1918 less than 1 per cent of the workers were unemployed. In 1920, 2.4 per cent were unemployed, in 1921 16.6 per cent. In no subsequent year, save 1927 (9.6 per cent), did unemployment fall below 10 per cent until the world was again plunged into war in 1939.

The crisis of 1921, which was a world crisis with its storm centre in U.S.A., occurred before production had returned even to pre-war level. It was a crisis of a peculiar kind precipitated by unbridled speculation and profiteering by the capitalist class. In Britain the price of producers' goods (taking 1913 as a 100) rose from 261 in 1919 to 355 in 1920. Export prices stood at 359. Since import prices at 298 had advanced less rapidly, the British capitalists were clearly enriching themselves at the expense of the raw material producing countries overseas (particularly Empire and colonial countries). Wages barely kept pace with the rise in prices, and although money wages were in 1920 more than 2¼ times pre-war, real wages were only about 5 per cent above pre-war (and about the same as in 1900). At the height of the boom in 1920 the *value* of exports was 2¼ times pre-war, but the *volume* was less than three quarters—only 70 per cent of 1913. The purchasing power of the masses was, of course, too restricted both abroad and at home to sustain production geared to such fantastic price levels.

To the problems of economic transition were added artificial shortages of raw materials due to speculation. National output, in terms of money, reached record heights (about £4,500 million); but in volume even at the height of the boom in 1920 it was barely 90 per cent of pre-war. In 1921 it fell to 61 per cent and exports to 50 per cent of pre-war. The prices of producers goods came down to 178 per cent of pre-war, roughly half what they were in 1920. The boom had turned to slump before economic activity had returned even to pre-war levels.

The war and the post-war boom transformed the whole structure of British capitalism. The most important changes being the inflation of capital and accelerated growth of monopoly.

The extreme difficulties of the capitalists in the immediate post-war period receded in the course of the 20's. This phase of improvement resurrected all sorts of illusions. Calvin Coolidge, as president of the greatest capitalist power in the world, in December, 1928, on the brink of the greatest crisis ever experienced by the capitalist world, said: "Enlarging production is consumed by an increasing demand at home and an expanding commerce abroad. The country can regard the present with satisfaction and anticipate the future with optimism."

Many Labour leaders made the same mistake. Philip Snowden, for example, said that "he did not agree with the statement of some of their socialist friends that the capitalist system was breaking down". (*Daily Herald*, 17.4.1926). Hilferding, the German social democrat, declared in 1927 that a period of capitalism had begun "which in the main has overcome . . . the sway of the blind laws of the market"; we were, he said, entering a period of *organised capitalism* which "signifies the suppressing, in principle, of the capitalist principle of free competition by the socialist principle of planned production". The trade union right wing in Britain openly advocated collaboration between big business and the trade unions—the doctrine of Mondism—so called after Sir Alfred Mond (later Lord Melchett) of Imperial Chemical Industries Ltd. The theory of Mondism was typically expounded by Lord (then Mr. Walter) Citrine in the *Labour Magazine* (October 1927), when he wrote of collaboration between the capitalists and trade unions as "eliminating unnecessary friction and avoidable conflict in order to increase the wealth produced and provide a steady rising standard of social life and continuously improving conditions of employment for the workers". Other Labour leaders found their new prophet in Henry Ford. "If this is capitalism," wrote H. N. Brailsford in the *New Leader* (1st October, 1926, in an article entitled "Ford versus Marx"), "it is a variety which has discarded the fundamental principle on which Marx based his prediction." The *Daily Herald*, (9th September, 1926) said that Mr. Ford reminded them of "a thoughtful Labour leader". (Such mistakes might have been avoided by paying less attention to what Ford said and more to his industrial organisations, which provide a copy book illustration of so many of the developments that Marx discerned in capitalist production, such as the growing concentration of production, mechanisation and division of labour, intensification of labour, and increase in relative surplus value.)

The theoreticians of socialism most influential in the leading councils of British Labour mostly rejected Marxist economic theory in favour of economic analysis derived from the mainstream of bourgeois economic theory; and it is an ironical fact that Sidney and Beatrice Webb—the father and mother of Fabianism, who rejected Marx for Alfred Marshall and did more than anyone else to foster bourgeois economic theory in the Labour movement—came at the end of their lives to recognise the superiority of Marx's understanding of capitalism. "Where we went hopelessly wrong," wrote Beatrice Webb in 1938, "was in ignoring Karl Marx's forecast of the eventual breakdown of the capitalist system. . . . Karl Marx foresaw that the exploitation of land and labour by the private owners of the means of production, distribution and exchange would lead inevitably and universally to a corruption and perversion of the economic system . . . that it would concentrate power in the hands of the wealthy and keep the wage earners and peasants in a state of poverty and dependence; that it would produce a disastrous alternation of booms and slumps, with a permanent army of unemployed persons . . . [that] the profit-making motive would lead surely and inevitably, not to peaceful emulation between individual capitalists to lower prices and improve quality . . . but to a trustified and imperialist capitalism." (*Our Partnership*, page 488.)

Many of the illusions which the 20's nurtured crashed in the great crisis of 1929. The severity of this crisis was attributable to the fact that it took place against the background of—and intertwined with—the general crisis of capitalism. Industrial crisis was linked with agrarian. Between 1929 and 1932 the industrial production of the capitalist world fell by almost 45 per cent. In America, industrial production dropped to below half the pre-crisis level; in Germany by 45 per cent, in England by almost 25 per cent. The relatively lighter effect of the crisis in Britain must be seen against the fact that Britain's economy never fully recovered from the consequences of the First World War and per head production even in 1929 had only just regained the pre-war level. Britain's recovery was made the more difficult by her precipitate return to the Gold Standard in 1925—a move which, though damaging to British economy at home, was an attempt by the monopoly capitalists to safeguard their imperial and world-wide financial and commercial interests.

Every branch of industry and every country, apart from the Soviet Union, was affected by the crisis. The crisis lasted longer than any previous crisis. Prices fell by almost a third in each of the major industrial countries. In 1931 England went off the Gold Standard. By the middle of 1934 only France, Switzerland, Holland and Belgium remained on a Gold Standard; the old framework of international credit, currency and finance had been destroyed for all time. Reparations and war debts ceased to be paid. Almost every government of central Europe and Southern America ceased payments against loans from abroad. When the debtor nations ceased to pay, the creditor nations naturally hesitated to throw good money after bad. The export of capital was no longer profitable, had become a heavy risk and so ceased. U.S.A., which in 1928 had exported $1,325 million in 1933 only exported $1.6 million. Britain's export of capital to the colonies dropped from £219 million in 1928 to £30 million in 1933 and to foreign countries from £86 million to £8 million. Foreign trade collapsed throughout the capitalist world; the total volume of world exports (expressed in pre-crisis gold dollars) fell from $33 billion in 1928 to $12 billion in 1933. Industrial capacity which capitalism failed in this period of general crisis to use fully, even in boom years (for example, 67 per cent utilisation in Germany in 1929), stood idle everywhere (36 per cent utilisation in Germany in 1932). At the same time millions were added to the armies of unemployed. Industrial unemployment throughout the world tripled between 1929 and 1932. In Germany 44 per cent of the workers were unemployed in 1932; in England 25 per cent, in U.S.A. 32 per cent (figures available only for trade unionists), in Denmark 32 per cent, in Norway 31 per cent.

Meanwhile in the Soviet Union socialist construction was advancing. Between 1929 and 1933 industrial output in the U.S.S.R. more than doubled. In the main capitalist countries there was on average a *fall* of over 25 per cent in the same period. In 1933 industrial output in the U.S.S.R. was almost four times pre-war; in Britain it barely attained the pre-war level even in the boom year of 1929 and in 1932 it was 20 per cent below pre-war. Whilst in U.S.A. production expanded in 1929 to 70 per cent above pre-war, it dropped back in 1932 to 10 per cent below pre-war.

The world crisis of 1929 to 1932 greatly increased the tensions between and within capitalist countries. Japan made war on China and occupied Manchuria. Fascism came to power in Germany. An arms race began. Italy seized Abyssinia. The first steps were being taken along the road that led to the crushing of democracy in Spain and to the Second World War. All the antagonisms of the capitalist world were sharpened by the crisis; the conditions of the workers were attacked, the struggle between the imperialist powers and the colonial peoples was intensified, the rivalry between the great imperialist powers was sharpened. The danger of imperialist attacks on the Soviet Union increased.

In 1933 capitalist economy began to emerge from four years of economic crisis. The next crisis, 1937-38, was most marked in U.S.A. and Great Britain. In Germany feverish preparations for war sustained economic activity and the volume of industrial production showed an increase in 1938 over 1937. The economic crisis of 1937 became, however, submerged in the Second World War in which the antagonisms of the capitalist world again burst into flame.

The resuscitation of German militarism in the form of Nazi fascism was, in a certain sense, the consequence of the 1929 crisis. Capitalist democracy hampered the unrestricted dominance of the monopoly capitalists; they therefore fought against it. "The political superstructure of the new economy of monopoly capitalism," wrote Lenin, "is the turn from democracy to political reaction. Democracy corresponds to free competition. Political reaction corresponds to monopoly." (*A Caricature of Marxism*,

1916.) Reaction triumphed most completely where the roots of bourgeois democracy were less deep—in Germany and Japan, where the tradition of feudal reaction and autocracy was still fresh and where the popular movements against reaction were less well established. Monopoly capitalism used fascism for a "struggle on two fronts", against the people at home and against capitalist rivals abroad. In Germany monopoly capitalism had become unstable in the extreme. The volume of output, which in 1929 had been restored to 13 per cent above pre-war, dropped in 1932 to less than 60 per cent of the 1929 level. Two in every five workers were unemployed. The petty bourgeoisie, already ruined by the post-war inflation, were again plunged into poverty and despair. In this precarious position monopoly capitalism unreservedly put its money and its influence behind the Nazis, a divided working class failed to stop them and Hitler came to power.

The Nazis at once began their preparations for war. War expenditure, which in 1932 accounted for 2 per cent of the national income, reached 10 per cent in 1934, exceeded 20 per cent in 1937, and 40 per cent in 1939. This militarisation of the economy reduced unemployment. (Of this Hitler boasted as an economic achievement, but militarisation in all countries led to this "achievement".) Long hours were worked and the incomes of the working class as a whole rose by comparison with the years of crisis and unemployment, but real wages per hour fell.

The vaunted economy of Nazi Germany with its high level of economic activity (industrial output in 1938 was 25 per cent above 1929 as against 12 per cent in Britain and 28 per cent below in the U.S.A.) was nothing but a war economy. It fulfilled a double purpose: it equipped Germany for aggression and it gave huge profits to the monopoly capitalists whose stronghold lay in heavy industry. From the start the control of Germany's "planned economy" was in the hands of the millionaires. The Supreme Economic Council appointed in 1934 included Krupp von Bohlen (armament manufacturer, capital of £15 million), Fritz Thyssen (steel, £540 million), von Siemens (electrical industry, £12½ million), Karl Bosch (Die Trust, £55 million), A. Vogler (steel, £40 million), A. Diehn (potash, £10 million), von Schroeder (banker). The same story was repeated in all the organs of Germany's "State-controlled" economy. For example, Krupp, von Schroeder and other big businessmen of this type formed the executive board of the National Railways. State-controlled German economy certainly was, but the monopoly capitalists might well have said: "The State, it is us!" They, together with a handful of Nazi adventurers such as Goering, Goebbels and Hitler, who had acquired vast personal fortunes, owned and ruled Nazi Germany.

The indictment made before the Nuremberg Court strikingly illustrated the association of monopoly capitalism and fascism. "In the early days," to quote *The Times* (May, 1947), "Farben saw in Hitler and his movement the possibility of extending its empire . . . with the unleashing of war, Farben, it is alleged, entered upon a systematic programme of spoliation by seizing the chemical industries of the overrun countries. By the time France was defeated Farben's dream of world conquest under its own New Order, a document of several thousand pages setting forth detailed schemes for the whole of Europe's chemical production, were rivalled only by Hitler's . . . .Finally . . . I. G. Farben . . . is charged not only with a share of responsibility for the slave labour programme in drawing upon foreign workers for its factories, but by the construction on its own recommendation of a buna plant at Auschwitz, of direct complicity in the human sufferings and murder of the concentration camps."

With the ending of the war, the death sentence of I. G. Farben Industrie was, it seemed, pronounced in the Potsdam Agreement; but the sentence was not executed. The same people who had been in charge of industry when fascism ruled were back in the saddle. New international connections were established; the German industrialists, smashed by the military defeat of Nazism, were to be resuscitated once again to stand guard for reaction in Europe. However, the reactionary forces were, following the Second World War, in a far weaker position. The defeat of fascism had been in large measure effected by the vast military effort of the Soviet people and by the struggles of anti-fascist mass movements throughout Europe. It demonstrated the vitality of socialist society in the Soviet Union and the strength of the democratic forces opposed to fascism. The reactionaries throughout the capitalist world who had shown sympathy for fascism were to some extent weakened and constrained; and the political demands and expectations of the popular forces were advanced.

The general crisis of capitalism was further deepened by the fact that the colonial movements surged forward towards national independence with a force that could no longer be resisted. This is a period in which the problems of capitalism keep mounting, in which capitalism as a system shows itself to be less and less adapted to the problems it confronts. At the same time it is a period in which social contradictions become more acute and the general crisis of capitalism deepens, in the sense that it is a period in which socialism is advancing. This is so in two respects; the socialist countries have become more numerous and economically stronger and, also, socialist ideas implant themselves in the thinking of the people everywhere and impress their stamp on the political demands with which the ruling circles of capitalist society are confronted.

The General Characteristics of a Socialist System

Socialism must be seen as an historical development. In the Preface to the *Critique of Political Economy*, describing how (in about 1844), he was led to the study of political economy, Marx says he felt that legal relations and forms of State could not be understood by themselves nor explained "by the so-called general progress of the human mind". He came instead to believe they were rooted in the material conditions of life. The anatomy of the "civic society" in which these material conditions found their expression, was, he concluded, to be sought in political economy. From the study of political economy he reached the general conclusion, which "served as a leading thread" in his studies. This was that the relations of men in production constituted the foundation "on which rise legal and political superstructures and to which correspond definite forms of social consciousness". In the study of the underlying economic structures Marx sought the main explanation of the changing phases through which human history had passed, and concluded: "Bourgeois relations of production are the last antagonistic form of the social process of production—antagonistic not in the sense of individual antagonism, but of one arising from conditions surrounding the life of individuals in society; at the same time the productive forces developing in the womb of bourgeois society create the material conditions for the solution of that antagonism. This social formation constitutes, therefore, the closing chapter of the pre-historic stage of human society."

The view that the main determining factor in human history is economic has widely permeated modern thought, but the revolutionary implications of this idea are not so generally drawn, nor is it so generally accepted that the capitalist mode of production, predominant in human society through some three centuries, is now likely itself to be overtaken by the socialist mode of production.

It is, however, a peculiarity of the socialist mode of production that it cannot develop gradually and within the framework of capitalist society but requires first the winning of political power— that is, State power—by the working class and the masses of the people. The reason for this is not hard to find. The basis of a socialist economy is publicly owned means of production, which are used according to a social plan to meet the needs of the community. Political power must pass into the hands of the socialist forces, that is the workers' movement, in order to effect the necessary transfer of the largest, key concerns to public ownership and in order to carry through effectively the necessary measures of social planning. The overthrow of capitalist class rule and of capitalist property relations is a *political* act, the success of which depends on the relative strength of the class forces within a particular country (and in the world outside) at the time. Socialism can never develop as an economic formation within capitalism in the way that capitalism developed as an economic formation within feudalism. The reason for this is that capitalist production is governed and regulated by the market, which already existed, despite limitations, within feudalism; and so could develop wherever it could establish capitalist production and sustain itself, initially at all events, by entering the already existing market. Socialist production is governed by a plan, consciously conceived and co-ordinated to meet the needs of the community, that is, a plan that must be framed and implemented by a political entity—be it large or small—a politically independent State. Socialist relations cannot be effectively or genuinely socialist except on a *national* basis. This is necessitated by the two basic ingredients of socialism as a mode of production— namely, planning and public ownership of the means of production. (The converse of this proposition is not true, for capitalist relations can exist within socialism; for example, lesser capitalists and numerous small-scale commodity producers can exist within the framework of a socialist economy, provided the main means of production are publicly owned and the main ends toward which production is directed are determined by the plan.)

However, although socialism as a social formation implies that the State power has been taken out of capitalist hands, the pressure of socialist demands from the workers and the masses of the people generally plays an important part in preparing the way to socialism and is an expression of capitalism's general crisis, of the sharpening contradiction between the possibilities for social progress and the failure to realise them within the social relationships of capitalism.

Processes within capitalism that prepare the way to socialism include also the formation of the working-class movement itself, which feels the pressure of capitalist exploitation and understands in its conditions of work the potentialities of modern industry. The constant development of productive forces coupled with concentration and increasingly large scale production points to the need for public ownership and planning in production.

The "preparations for socialism within capitalism" may, in summary, be said to consist of (a) material changes in the structure of the economy and in productive techniques, (b) political changes, in particular the emergence of the working-class movement as a political force, and (c) ideological changes, that is, a new understanding amongst the democratic forces and industrial workers in particular of the economic and social possibilities to which the economic and social relations of capitalism create a barrier.

Socialism as an economic system can best be defined by noting the respects in which socialism as a mode of production is the "opposite" of capitalism. Socialism is *planned production for use on the basis of public ownership of the means of production*. Capitalism is *commodity production for private profit on the basis of private ownership of the means of production*. The essential respects in which capitalism is the "opposite" of socialism can be contrasted as follows:

	Capitalism	*Socialism*
Regulating principle	"the market" (commodity exchange)	"the social plan"
Motivating force	profit	satisfaction of needs
Property basis	private ownership of capital	public ownership of the means of production
Political basis	dominance of the wealthy—viz. the owners of capital	The rule of the working people, with their mass organisations playing a major role in government and administration

245

In time economic science, as applied to socialism, "the political economy of socialism", will no doubt be developed in considerable detail, as a political economy of capitalism (which is the main topic of this book) developed in the past. However, more than a century went by from the time of the Cromwellian revolution which established State power in Britain in capitalist hands before the economic science of capitalism passed beyond its rudimentary stages. The detailed political economy of socialism is developing more rapidly, but necessarily this requires time and practical experience in the construction of a socialist economy, e.g. the experience of the Soviet Union since 1917 plus the experience of Eastern Europe since 1945 and China since 1949.

The first economic policies of the Soviet Government were dictated largely by the exigencies of the war that the "White Guards" with the help of the capitalist powers were waging against the Soviet Government. This was the period of "War Communism" when requisitioning and centralised allocation of supplies replaced the market. These were desperate measures dictated by a desperate situation—not, as some Leftist dreamers at the time thought, a leap towards socialism. "War Communism," said Lenin, "was thrust upon us by war and ruin. It was not, nor could be, a policy that corresponded to the economic tasks of the proletariat. It was a temporary measure." "Some things we were compelled to do by necessity . . . we did much that was simply wrong. We went further than was necessary theoretically and politically." (Quoted by Maurice Dobb, *Soviet Economic Development since 1917*, p. 123, 1948 edition. For an appreciation of the economic problems that confronted the first socialist country from the October Revolution up to the end of the Second World War Maurice Dobb's book is unsurpassed.)

When in October 1920 an armistice had been signed with Poland it was possible to begin to tackle the vast problem of reviving and transforming the economy. A transition to the "New Economic Policy" began. "Only by coming to an agreement with the peasants," wrote Lenin, "can we save the socialist revolution. We must either satisfy the middle peasants economically and restore the free market, or else we shall be unable to maintain the power of the working class." The economic system of the period which then began—the period of the New Economic Policy—was a mixed one, difficult to define with precision. Most of the large scale and modern industry was nationalised.

246

The land was worked mainly by small peasant proprietors. It remained a market system in so far as it was the market that linked industry and agriculture; but this market was subject to taxation and control measures exercised by the State, State power being in the hands of the working class. This mixed economy of the N.E.P. was a preparatory stage to socialism, in which collective forms of production predominated, but in which private ownership of the means of production persisted and public ownership of the means of production in agriculture was very limited in extent.

In 1925-26, when industry and agriculture had been restored after the extreme disorganisation of the war and the civil war, the Soviet Government faced the gigantic task of embarking upon a programme of industrialisation. In 1926 work started on the drafting of the first Five-Year Plan; and its implementation, began in 1928-29, in face of great difficulties, falling prices for exports, resistance to collectivisation in the countryside, threats of war in the Far East, and consequent cuts in the targets for the consumption goods industries.

In 1933 the Soviet Union embarked upon its second Five-Year Plan, of which the fundamental purpose was to complete the "technical reconstruction of the whole national economy". By 1940 (when the Soviet Union was half way through her third Five-Year plan), production of the following basic products had increased as follows:

			1940	1928	1913
Steel	..	million tons ..	18.3	4.3	4.2
Coal	..	million tons ..	166	35.6	29.1
Electricity		milliard KWT	48	5	2
Aluminium		thousand tons	55	–	–
Tractors..		thousands ..	80 (1937)	1.2	–
Grain	..	million tons ..	119	73	81

(source: Dobb *op. cit.* p. 311)

The Second World War tested and proved before the eyes of the world the reality of the U.S.S.R.'s industrial progress and achievements; but it dealt desperately heavy blows to the development of the economy. The loss of human life had been appalling and with the ending of the war the new production targets for 1950 in most cases fell short of those originally planned for 1942. However, with the war ended, again the industrial base of the Soviet economy began to be developed with sustained rapidity. A steady annual increase of between 9 and 10 per cent has been maintained in industrial production—which by 1962 had risen to about two-thirds of the U.S.A. compared with less than half in 1957. Steel production in 1962 was 76 million tons and electricity generated 369 milliard kwh. Progress in agriculture was less rapid but none the less, without favourable weather conditions, a grain crop of 145 million tons was harvested in 1962.

The figures above indicate something of the strength of the economic forces liberated by the new economic relationships that socialism brought into being—the essentials of which are public ownership of the means of production and production geared to a national plan. The workers' and peasants' revolution of 1917 had opened the way to the construction of a socialist economy and the creation of a new society which liberated gigantic, irrepressible social and economic forces. These forces, despite the major crimes and mistakes on which recent discussions in the Soviet Union have focused attention, asserted themselves and left their mark in major achievements in every aspect of social life. They have generated also forces capable of combating abuses and distortions in the practice and in the theory of socialism, and opening up a vast perspective of new achievement. The economically advanced industrial base that has been established firmly in the capital goods industries is now being turned to a far more diversified range of products that will make possible great advances in the consumers' goods industries. With this the way to a communist society comes into sight—a society, that is, that presupposes so plentiful a supply of the means of living as to make possible the communist principle of distribution: "From each according to his ability, to each according to his needs."

Speaking at the Twenty-Second Congress of the Communist Party of the Soviet Union, Khrushchov said, with reference to the 20-year national economic development plan then being initiated, "that by 1980 output of plants producing means of production for industries producing means of production will have increased six-fold and plant producing means of production for industries producing consumers' goods will have increased thirteen-fold".

Great advances are also being made in the techniques of planning, and discussion of the theoretical problems underlying the administration of a socialist economy is developing with great vigour. These discussions involve many fundamental questions of economic theory that it is now becoming more pressing to solve in the interest of practical advance. For example, discussions on the theory of value and prices in a socialist economy, on the principles by which to evaluate choice between alternative investment expenditures and on many other basic questions are still far from finality, and much exploratory research and debate is being devoted to problems of improving and refining planning techniques and to discover how to use more effectively modern computers and mathematical techniques in economic planning.

In short, new potentialities of socialism as an economic system are constantly showing themselves and it will take time for the full scope of the socialist mode of production to become apparent. However, the initial achievements of socialism have in themselves been striking enough and have ensured certain fundamentals of inestimable significance—namely rapid industrial growth and a vast extension of educational opportunities. These—and the great educational advance in particular—provide strong foundations for future social development.

Despite the cost of the Cold War to the Soviet Union, in terms of defence expenditure, its sustained growth of industrial production is sufficient to provide year by year more resources for investment and more resources for consumption. The special advantages of a socialist system include the fact that the surplus social product available for developing social services and increasing investment are under the direct control of the State. Available capacity never need be left idle awaiting a shift in market trends. Foreign trade in the hands of public authority obviates paralysis, such as that by which the British economy is periodically reduced to stagnation for fear that expansive market forces may precipitate a balance of payments crisis. The advance of wage incomes in step with the advance of social production can be assured. The basic economic relationships of socialism do not come into conflict with the requirements of technical progress. The economies of the countries added to the world of socialism in the period following the Second World War, were, generally speaking, ones in which industrial development was small and restricted to a few undertakings or a few places. In every case, however, socialism resulted in sustained and rapid economic advances and these have been further facilitated by the existence of other socialist countries and, in particular, the now advanced economy of the Soviet Union.

The existence of this socialist sector of the world also profoundly influences economic developments throughout the capitalist sector of the world. It becomes more and more clear that the great issue of our times is the struggle between socialism and capitalism, the economic competition between the systems and also the battle between socialist ideas inspiring the worker's movements in all parts of the world and the ideas of capitalism looking back always to the past. The struggle coincides with the world-wide breakdown of the domination of the imperialist powers over the colonial and other oppressed nationalities within their spheres of influence. Clearly these struggles are closely connected. The contradictions within the system of capitalism as it developed led to greater and greater concentration of capital coupled with expansion of the spheres of influence of the most powerful groupings of capital more and more widely over the world, an expansion, that is, of exploitation, provoking in its turn the resistance of the exploited. With the victory of socialism over a large part of the world, the exploited peoples gained both encouragement in their own struggles and also new allies to whom to turn from the imperialist powers to which their economies had hitherto been made appendages.

The epoch in which we live is that of transition from capitalism to socialism, an epoch which opened with the October Revolution in Russia in 1917, and in which each phase sees a widening of the world-wide alliance of popular forces, comprising also a growing sector of socialist States in the world. The most ruthless representatives of imperialism hoped to see the socialist world destroyed by fascism. The defeat of fascism in World War Two was a stunning blow, but not a death blow to reaction. Rabid anti-communism has reappeared in the U.S.A. and exerted a powerful influence also on the State policy of that country. Collaborating with the most reactionary forces in the U.S.A. there are reactionary forces in Japan and Western Europe. These extremists of reaction are prepared to stake the very life of humanity on the gamble of a nuclear war.

In this context the problem of peace and war becomes the most burning problem of our times. The danger of a nuclear holocaust hangs over the heads of mankind, but against the reactionary forces that are making for war the world-wide alliance of popular forces dedicated to struggle for peace is extending and growing more powerful and determined. These forces are now strong enough to curb the forces of reaction and aggression. In the struggle for peace, the conflict between the old world and the new, between the past and the future of mankind, finds its focus. Through 5,000 years war has been the concomitant of class society. Once the force of the people grips and stays the hands of the warmongers and the dismantling of the apparatus of aggression begins, the face of the world will change and the march of mankind towards the future that socialism and communism offers will begin to gather a new momentum. Already, in further building up productive forces in the Soviet Union, the conscious aim becomes the creation of a material and technical basis for a new stage of socialist society, the stage, that is, of communism.

The economic future of Britain is inextricably intertwined with the world-wide forces struggling for progress, peace and socialism. For Britain to make progress it is necessary to break free from the costly entanglements of the Cold War and imperialist exploitation, and to stimulate, on the basis of public ownership of the greatest industrial and financial organisations, a full use of our considerable productive capacity. Once this course is embarked upon, Britain will soon be able to set her sights upon what Marx called "the second stage of socialism" or "communism". Advance in scientific and technical knowledge and better understanding of the economic and organisational means required for its fullest application will ensure ample supplies of basic material requirements without excessive expenditure of time or effort. Automation and nuclear energy provide an adequate material and technical basis for achieving this, given suitable economic organisation.

We live in the period of a second industrial revolution but are not yet grasping the opportunities that it offers. It is hard to imagine how life will be if means are found of ending insecurity, anxiety, wasted exertion and drudgery, unceasing rivalry and continued preoccupation about getting the bare means of existence. If the necessities of life flow as water today flows in economically developed countries, man will no longer need to sell himself in order to "keep himself". The possibility will at last exist to end the "alienation of labour" which the capitalist market for labour compels. Work will become less and less a drudgery, less a means to the end of living outside of the hours of work, less alienation of man from himself by selling his labour power to another. But to end the denuding of life which the sale of labour power involves, implies ending the capital-labour relation. Whatever improvements in real wages, etc., may or may not be achieved within the conditions of capitalism, dreary and life-destroying conditions of work must remain as these are inherent in the capital-labour relationship.

"Machinery", writes Marx, "is put to a wrong use, with the object of transforming the workman, from his very childhood, into a part of a detail machine. In this way, not only are the expenses of his reproduction considerably lessened, but at the same time his helpless dependence upon the factory as a whole, and therefore upon the capitalist, is rendered complete. Here as everywhere else, we must distinguish between the increased productiveness due to the development of the social process of production, and that due to the capitalist exploitation of that process. In handicrafts and manufacture, the workman makes use of a tool, in the factory the machine makes use of him. There the movements of the instrument of labour proceed from him, here it is the movements of the machine that he must follow. In manufacture the workmen are parts of a living mechanism. In the factory we have a lifeless mechanism independent of the workman, who becomes its mere living appendage. . . . At the same time that factory work exhausts the nervous system to the uttermost, it does away with the many-sided play of the muscles, and confiscates every atom of freedom, both in bodily and intellectual activity. The lightening of the labour, even, becomes a sort of torture, since the machine does not free the labourer from work, but deprives the work of all interest. Every kind of capitalist production, in so far as it is not only a labour process, but also a process of creating surplus value, has this in common, that it is not the workman that employs the instruments of labour, but the instruments of labour that employ the workman. But it is only in the factory system that this inversion for the first time acquires technical and palpable reality. By means of its conversion into an automaton, the instrument of labour confronts the labourer, during the labour process, in the shape of capital, of dead labour, that dominates, and pumps dry living labour power. The separation of the intellectual powers of production from the manual labour, and the conversion of those powers into the might of capital over labour, is, as we have already shown, finally completed by modern industry erected on the foundation of machinery. The special skill of each individual insignificant factory operative vanishes as an infinitesimal quantity before the science, the gigantic physical forces, and the mass of labour that are embodied in the factory mechanism and, together with that mechanism, constitute the power of the 'master'." (*Capital*, Vol. I, LW pp. 422–3, A pp. 421–2.)

A changed material basis and a new economic structure of society makes possible man's escape from the spiritual and material wasteland of capitalism. About what life will be like when this new material basis has been fully built it is not as yet possible to say much. But the germ of this new world was already seen by Marx. Nearly a hundred years ago he wrote: "In a higher phase of Communist society, after the enslaving subordination of individuals under division of labour, and therefore also the antithesis between mental and physical labour, has vanished; after labour, from a mere means of life, has itself become the prime necessity of life; after the productive resources have also increased with the all round development of the individual and all the springs of co-operative wealth flow more abundantly—only then can the narrow horizon of bourgeois law be fully left behind and society inscribe on its banner: 'From each according to his ability, to each according to his needs!' " (*Critique of the Gotha Programme*, 1875.)

INDEX

Bold type indicates the pages on which can be found a brief definition of technical terms (shown in CAPITALS)